FEMINISTS RETHINK THE NEOLIBERAL STATE

Feminists Rethink the Neoliberal State

Inequality, Exclusion, and Change

Edited by Leela Fernandes

NEW YORK UNIVERSITY PRESS
New York

NEW YORK UNIVERSITY PRESS
New York
www.nyupress.org

References to Internet websites (URLs) were accurate at the time of writing. Neither the author nor New York University Press is responsible for URLs that may have expired or changed since the manuscript was prepared.

Library of Congress Cataloging-in-Publication Data
Names: Fernandes, Leela, editor.
Title: Feminists rethink the neoliberal state : inequality, exclusion, and change / edited by Leela Fernandes.
Description: New York : New York University Press, [2017] |
Includes bibliographical references and index.
Identifiers: LCCN 2017012918| ISBN 9781479800155 (cl : alk. paper) |
ISBN 9781479895304 (pb : alk. paper)
Subjects: LCSH: Women's rights—History—21st century. | Women—Legal status, laws, etc. |
Women—Social conditions—21st century.
Classification: LCC HQ1155 .F467 2017 | DDC 305.42009/05—dc23
LC record available at https://lccn.loc.gov/2017012918

New York University Press books are printed on acid-free paper, and their binding materials are chosen for strength and durability. We strive to use environmentally responsible suppliers and materials to the greatest extent possible in publishing our books.

Manufactured in the United States of America

10 9 8 7 6 5 4 3 2 1

Also available as an ebook

CONTENTS

PREFACE

There is no issue that is more central in the twenty-first century than the growing forms of socioeconomic inequality and exclusion that have become entrenched across the world. Debates on globalization, free trade, and economic development have been shaping political dynamics within and across nations. These debates often have been linked either implicitly or explicitly to particular sets of economic policies (often identified with market liberalization, financial restructuring, and privatization) that have come to be encapsulated by the term "neoliberalism." The idea of neoliberalism indeed captures very real processes—and sets of policies—that have become a dominant model for national and transnational economic arrangements. However, neoliberalism has also too easily become a self-evident catch-all phrase that serves as an explanatory device for the inequalities, exclusions, and forms of social change that have been unfolding in comparative contexts. I have been struck over the years by the ways in which the term "neoliberalism" increasingly has become a rhetorical device—particularly in intellectual (and often but not exclusively interdisciplinary) arenas in the United States. Such rhetoric is often couched in universal, ahistorical, and transnational claims that do not account for differences between nations or the interrelationship between the effects of recent policies of liberalization and earlier political economic models of development. Narratives centered on privatization and market rationalities, for instance, are often depicted as key drivers of socioeconomic, political, and cultural change. This volume is an effort to deepen interdisciplinary understandings of how policies of economic liberalization shape and produce various forms of inequality in comparative contexts.

The book brings together feminist scholars who have been working on such questions in a range of contexts in order to delineate what is distinctive about the "neoliberal" state (and the production of inequality) and what is linked to longer, complex processes that have produced long-standing forms of inequalities within and between nations. The feminist lens of the volume, in particular, seeks to bring a textured understanding of inequality to the fore (through a focus on the linkages between interrelated forms of inequality such as gender, race, sexuality, and class). Such a layered analysis is still too often missing from dominant social scientific understandings of structures of political economy. However, this comparative, textured approach does not adopt a checklist model that reduces the relations between inequalities to a presumed static list of identities and geographical locations that must be covered. Rather, the volume brings a theoretical lens that seeks to deepen our understanding of the role of the state in shaping policies and processes that reproduce inequality. Such an understanding of the state is critical, as the volume seeks to show, for the development of adequate responses that can redress inequality and produce meaningful social and economic change.

At the time this volume goes to publication, the United States has undergone a significant political shift with the election of Donald Trump. Many of the issues that played out in the campaign—debates over trade and protectionism, the rise of populist anger and the continued politicization of race—are key themes that essays in this volume take up. However, the framework of this volume also cautions against reading broad global political and economic trends through a singular event or through a purely U.S.-centric lens. What seems initially like significant potential shifts in the new administration's approach to global trade are also accompanied by strong indications of pro-corporate policies on regulation and taxation. The brand of racialized populist nationalism evident in the 2016 U.S. election did not begin with the U.S. election. It was evident in the 2014 religious nationalist and populist election that brought Prime Minister Narendra Modi to power in India. Modi's campaign promised state action for social groups left out of growth even as it sought to continue India's policies of economic liberalization. Similar trends are evident in Europe. Such parallels and divergences are fundamentally connected to the approach of this volume, which seeks to unpack a unitary model of "neoliberalism" and pays sustained attention to the ways in which transnational political economic processes shape and are shaped by the situated dynamics and contexts of nation-states. This includes unsettling easy invocations of transnationalism that fail to grasp both the sustained historical power of nationalism and the importance of state actions.

The volume was initially framed by a productive set of intellectual conversations at a symposium that I organized at the University of Michigan in 2014. I am grateful for generous funding from the Institute for Research on Women and Gender as well as numerous departments and centers that co-sponsored the event. Heidi Bennett provided tremendous administrative support for the event that was crucial to its success. Thanks also go to Saisha Nanduri for her thorough research assistance. A distinctive feature of the initial symposium and this volume is that they both sought to bring together scholars working in "Western" and "non-Western" contexts. In particular, the symposium brought together scholars from a wide range of disciplines who have been actively engaged with interdisciplinary work in both international area studies as well as American studies. What emerged was a productive set of discussions that sought to open up intellectual arenas of inquiry and sparked productive conversations and comparative connections. This volume is produced with the hope of continuing such conversations with scholars working in comparative contexts.

—Leela Fernandes

1

Conceptualizing the Post-Liberalization State

Intervention, Restructuring, and the Nature of State Power

LEELA FERNANDES

"The gap between the haves and the have-nots globally is now at the same level as in the 1820s, the OECD said Thursday, October 2, warning it was one of the most 'worrying' developments over the past 200 years. In a major report on global well-being over the past two centuries, the Organization for Economic Cooperation and Development (OECD) noted inequality shot up after globalization took root in the 1980s."[1]

Introduction

The 2014 report from the Organization for Economic Cooperation and Development (OECD) provided a stark warning about the rise in inequality.[2] The growing concentration of wealth and the intensification of inequality has in fact become one of the distinguishing features of the twenty-first century. Public and academic debates on questions of economic inequality and exclusion have centered on the paradigm of "neoliberalism." Popular usage of the term has broadly centered on key features that have dominated contemporary global economic practices. These features include the restriction of state controls of economic activities (and the corresponding dismantling of the welfare state), a belief in the self-regulating power of the market in economic, social, and cultural spheres (and corresponding trends of privatization), and a range of policies of economic liberalization that have been designed to spur economic growth in comparative contexts. Proponents of the model of neoliberalism argue that restricting the state to a market-enabling force is necessary to spur economic growth (Bhagwati 2004).

Indeed, policies of economic liberalization over successive decades have been implemented in varying forms and with varying paces in comparative contexts in the late twentieth and early twenty-first century. Such policies have constituted a new developmental model that presumes that inequality and poverty can only be addressed through economic growth and an expansion of upward mobility and middle-class membership. Meanwhile, critics of neoliberalism have pointed to both the negative economic effects of such policies (Harvey 2005; Piketty 2014) as well as the deleterious political and sociocultural implications as logics of privatization have transformed the texture of both civil society and subjectivity in the twenty-first century (Brown 2005; Gambetti and Godoy-Anativia 2013; Greenhouse 2009; Hall and Lamont 2013).

The ideological paradigm of neoliberalism is invested in models of economic growth that both restrain and retrain the state. The state, in this hegemonic conception, must be restrained from its past regulatory and interventionist impulses and retrained to serve a limited market-enabling role. Critics of this paradigm have analyzed the effects of the ideological paradigm of neoliberalism and its material effects (such as cutbacks on welfare states) as well as the broader normative effects on societies that are structured through the logics of market behavior. There is, for instance, a vast scholarship on various dimensions of neoliberalism and its impact on inequality and identity. Interdisciplinary studies of neoliberalism have primarily focused either on declining state sovereignty in the face of corporate power and institutional forms of national and global governance that enhance the power of political and economic elites (Ong 2006) or on the ways neoliberalism has seeped into civil society, producing new forms of neoliberal subjectivity and disciplinary regimes of power (Laurie and Bondi 2005). Peter Hall and Michéle Lamont describe these trends as a constitution of the "neoliberal imaginary" that marks "a period that has authorized self-interested market behavior in settings where it might not once have been legitimate" (2013, 4). They illustrate the ways in which this imaginary has reconfigured social relationships and transformed the terms of social recognition in comparative contexts. Such changes, as some scholars have argued, have produced new forms of subjectivity that have been shaped in complex ways by the market-oriented logics of rationality, entrepreneurship, and selfhood (Brown 2005; Greenhouse 2009).

While such scholarship has produced critical insights into new modes of power and subjectivity, the primary emphasis of such work has been on the curtailment or displacement of the state by neoliberal modes of governance and identity. An effect of these very real processes of restructuring is a danger of presuming that the state has retreated or vanished in the post-liberalization period or that the neoliberal state is marked by a clear historical break from earlier forms of modern state power.[3] In this context, neoliberalism risks taking on a deterministic and ghostly character—acting as a primary agent that reshapes socio-economic and cultural practices and permeates all forms of cultural, social, and political life. Critics of the paradigm of neoliberalism in effect may run the danger of reproducing the all-pervasive power of the neoliberal imaginary that they seek to contest by reproducing recursive narratives of a vanishing state in the face of the all-encompassing force of neoliberalism.

Although the "neoliberal imaginary" is commonly associated with privatization and market-led growth, the varying perspectives that exist on this paradigm are, in fact, paradoxically, implicitly, or explicitly grappling with the role of the state. The "state" often lurks at the edges of both popular and academic discourses on the neoliberal economic order of the twenty-first century. For instance, consider the strongest case for theories that presume a state in retreat. Policies of economic restructuring have led, rightly, to a great deal of research and analysis of state cutbacks in social spending (such as welfare benefits), of processes of privatization that have led to the decline of public sector employment, and of the naturalization of the ideological tenets of neoliberalism. Yet as recent research has shown, the state has, in fact, not retreated in the post-liberalization period. Gambetti and Godoy-Anativia, for instance, provide an important cautionary reminder that "state power is the paradoxical instrument of the dismantling of the welfare state" (2013, 5).

Processes of privatization are indeed a key dimension both of policies of economic liberalization that have been implemented in comparative contexts and of certain forms of political subjectivity that emerge in particular contexts. However, the premise that the logic of markets (usually coded as "privatization") is the driving impetus of neoliberalism also risks skewing knowledge production in ways that may inadvertently reproduce the logic of neoliberal ideology that such work seeks to disrupt. An adequate understanding of the post-liberalization period in the twenty-first century requires more sustained analyses that also foreground questions of how conceptions of "publicness" are reconstituted and deployed (in relation to privatized conceptions of self and subjectivity), how states shape economic policy and contribute to the reproduction of inequality, and how political and social consent to structures of exclusion are produced and disrupted.[4] Dag MacLeod, for instance, has shown that Mexico's sweeping program of privatization from 1983 to 2000 cannot be understood adequately without addressing the role of the state in carrying this program forward (2004). As MacLeod notes, in the Mexican case, "the real challenge of implementing reform had to do with gaining control over the unwieldy apparatus of the state in order to transfer public assets to private actors" (2004, 26). Thus, for MacLeod, the question of the autonomy of the state can only be understood *relationally* where "the state's ability to act 'autonomously' from one social group simply means that it is acting in the interest of some other social group" (26).

Feminists Rethink the Neoliberal State seeks to understand the post-liberalization period through a redefinition of conceptions of "public" and "private" interests rather than an easy shift from public interests to the interests of private capital. This analysis disrupts the analytical drive to understand neoliberalism through a self-evident market-led logic of privatization. On the contrary, such an approach points to a need to think more deeply about how the state is implicated in and actively shapes policies and processes of economic liberalization. An analytical lens that mirrors a neoliberal logic of a market-dominated world misses the ways in which the restructuring of the state sets in motion a set of state practices and interventions that are not reducible to market actors. The state in effect does not retreat but both redeploys in complex ways (Brenner 2004; Collier 2011; Sassen, 1996) *and* continues to exercise power through long-standing practices, institutions and ideologies that have been historically salient features of the modern state. In this vein, the theoretical framework of the volume disrupts naturalized market-centered conceptions of the post-liberalization period.

The essays in this volume provide an in-depth analysis of the boundaries, practices, and nature of the post-liberalization state. The volume examines the nature of the restructuring of the state and argues for an understanding of the state that moves beyond conceptions of a state in retreat on the one hand and a state that simply mirrors the needs of capital on the other. The book intervenes in this body of knowledge through a distinctive emphasis on the state from both a comparative and transnational perspective. Transnational processes (whether in terms of movements of capital, people, or ideational forms across national borders) are critical to understanding the post-liberalization period. However, transnationalism too often becomes an abstract or overdetermined frame of analysis (Fernandes 2013) when it is dislocated from situated understandings of such processes. Narrow conceptions of transnationalism can also severely underestimate both the sustained power of nationalism (such as the nationalist framings of certain modes of populism) and the significance of state power. This volume seeks to understand how such transnational processes shape and are shaped by the economic, political, and historical contexts of specific nation-states. Drawing on original field research in comparative contexts both globally and within the United States, the essays present a rich set of perspectives on the varied and often contradictory nature of state practices, structures, and ideologies in the post-liberalization era. The essays address four central questions: (1) How has the state been restructured? (2) How is state power exercised? (3) How is the state shaped by the needs of capital? (4) How does the state interact with institutions and organizational forms within the realm of civil society in the post-liberalization era of the twenty-first century?

As the essays in *Feminists Rethink the Neoliberal State* illustrate, the nature of state formation affects processes of economic restructuring in complex ways. New state spaces and new state activities that emerge as the state seeks to direct economic liberalization or manage the political and social conflicts that arise from economic crisis and inequality intersect with and are shaped by historically specific trajectories of state formation in particular places. For instance, as recent research has shown, postcolonial state practices in the post-liberalization period often reflect a continuation of older regimes of state-led development (Fernandes 2006; Gupta 2012; Sharma 2008). Consider, for instance, one of the quintessential hegemonic discursive signifiers of liberalization—the growth of the middle classes in contemporary India. The potential for expanding upward mobility and access to middle-class status has become the embodiment of the benefits of economic liberalization (Fernandes 2006). Public discourses and postcolonial scholarship have tended to emphasize the "newness" of these middle classes—often linking claims about a new middle-class identity to middle-class consumption and India's policies of liberalization (Mazzarella 2003; Rajagopal 2001). What is missing in such analyses are both the ways in which these "new" middle classes are able to access upper-tier, new economy jobs because of historical state developmental patterns that support urban middle-class formation (by focusing, for instance, on higher education rather than primary education) and the ways in which these new middle classes continue to seek and receive substantial state resources (Fernandes 2006, 2015). Middle-class formation is thus still primarily a product of state developmental policies rather than of market liberalization. Such dynamics highlight the need to untangle the ways in which the neoliberal state coexists with older models of the developmental state and more closely investigate the interaction between these two sets of state activities.

Meanwhile, in specific national contexts, the retreat of the state is often due to state failures rather than to conscious policies of privatization. Thus, an analysis of the neoliberal model needs to guard against a conflation between processes of privatization and state regulatory failure. The failure of the state to provide services and to develop effective regulatory frameworks of governance—or what Stuart Corbridge calls "the scarcity of the state" (2005)—has often provided a space that has subsequently been occupied by private actors and privatized practices. This "scarcity of the state" often paradoxically coexists with an intensified set of state practices of policing, surveillance, and containment that marks expanding capacities of state power as exercised within civil society and the public sphere. *Feminists Rethink the Neoliberal State* unpacks such contradictions and examines when and how the modern state contracts, expands, and is reconstituted in the historically specific conditions of late capitalism that are now associated with the ideology and policies of neoliberal economics.

Feminists Rethink the Neoliberal State addresses the systemic and transnational effects of economic liberalization but does not presume a single model of neoliberalism with uniform effects. Research in comparative contexts provides a complex picture of the nature and causes of inequality. States, although restructured in varying ways, continue to play a central role in shaping the causes and responses to inequality (Ewig 2010; Lind 2005; MacLeod 2004). Social movements that respond to various forms of inequality are immersed in complicated political dynamics with both the state and transnational and national capitalist actors. The political dynamics and economic effects of such processes also vary greatly depending on the specific national context being discussed. This volume delves into these questions with the objective of providing an in-depth comparative understanding of the nature and practices of the post-liberalization state. For instance, comparative social science research on economic liberalization shows that policies of economic liberalization are one of the biggest sources of new state activities (Levy 2006). Such research points to the importance of unpacking the normative model of neoliberalism and distinguishing this singular model from the varied economic policies that states have implemented in historically specific contexts.[5]

What Is Neoliberal about the Contemporary State? Historical Continuities and Discontinuities and the Question of State Power

The task of understanding the nature of the state in the twenty-first century requires a careful examination of the term "neoliberal." The term itself is overladen with ideological and discursive meanings in both academic and public discourses. "Neoliberalism" in its overdetermined form often becomes a "master" concept that serves as an explanatory device for economic inequality, poverty, political quietism, alienation, and social exclusion. Complex questions regarding economic policy and ideology are conflated with broad processes of globalization as well as with long-standing historical processes that have shaped capitalist development and political and theoretical conceptions of liberalism. The risk in deploying the term "neoliberal" lies in the ways these overladen meanings that are invested in the term render it devoid of any analytical use. If "neoliberalism" becomes an ahistorical concept that is read back into time even as it becomes a default explanation for the plight of the present, the term itself becomes a symptom of its own conditions. In other words, if the drive of policies and ideologies of neoliberalism is to absorb political, economic, and sociocultural life into an all-encompassing logic of market rationality, taking this all-encompassing logic as an unquestioned analytical assumption inadvertently mirrors the very rationality that critics seek to contest. As Gambetti and Godoy-Anativia note, the challenge is to "avoid constructing neoliberalism as a kind of 'empty signifier' that explains everything and anything" (2013, 4). Any analysis that seeks to demarcate the theoretical usefulness of the concept thus needs to delineate the specificity of the term and to consider where "neoliberalism" is simply an extension of long-standing historical processes and where it serves as a useful analytical marker of discontinuity.

The most well-known understanding of neoliberalism is linked to what is popularly known as the "Washington consensus," which emerged in the late 1980s around a specific set of economic policies designed to restructure economies in comparative contexts. Such policies have broadly included a set of prescriptions that include programs of privatization (and the systematic dismantling of public sector industries), the promotion of free trade through regional and global agreements, and financial deregulation. Such policy frameworks, that have come to be known as structural adjustment, have also been linked to the power of global institutions such as the International Monetary Fund and the World Bank to recommend and enforce such changes through various forms of aid conditionalities. The political implications of these policies have led to conceptions of the neoliberal state as a state in retreat—one that has either lost its power to intervene or regulate or that has been recast as an entity designed to serve the needs of transnational capital. For instance, interdisciplinary feminist scholarship that emerged contemporaneously with the spread of structural adjustment policies in the 1980s focused on particular sites, such as export processing zones, that embodied these trends (Fernandez-Kelly 1984; Ong 1987). The intensity and scale of implementation (and the corresponding ideological support) of this particular set of policies indeed constitute a distinctive moment that requires specific empirical and theoretical attention.

However, the prescriptive and ideological dimension of such policies must be contextualized both in relation to long-standing historical precedents that they build on and the significant variations in the implementation of such policies (including the varying forms of political consent and opposition that accompany these policies). Peter Evans and William

Sewell caution against a conflation of ideas and policies of neoliberalism on the one hand and deep-rooted historical formations of classical liberalism and capitalism on the other. As they argue, "Hence, political and intellectual movements making prominent use of terms such as 'individualism,' 'freedom,' 'human rights,' and 'democracy,' should not automatically be tarred with the brush of neoliberalism because they are at least as likely to be derived from a broad liberal heritage as from neoliberalism per se. Second, we must resist attributing all the distinctive socio-economic trends of contemporary global capitalism to neoliberalism" (2013, 38). This conceptual reminder is of particular significance in understanding the causes and reproduction of inequality. Contemporary political and socioeconomic phenomena, such as the proliferation of public discourses, that center on norms of individualism, patterns of state violence against marginalized communities, and the systematic reproduction of socioeconomic exclusion are *reconstituted* through but not wholly invented by policies of neoliberalism.

The significance of historical continuities also provides an important caution against the temptation to treat the contemporary state as an after-effect of the logic of neoliberalism. While significant dimensions of state power may be restructured through the implementation of policies of structural adjustment, state structures also endure and adapt in ways that disrupt strong claims about declining state power in the context of such policies. The question of what is neoliberal about the neoliberal state is thus more than a rhetorical question—it marks the need to identify more precisely the ways in which contemporary states have been changed in distinctive ways in light of changing state-capital relations and the ways in which the modern state has not changed. Such a shift allows us to move away from the presumption of a retreating state and the corresponding question of *whether* state power is exercised to the question of *how* state power is exercised. This kind of analytical shift moves us away from polarizing debates that reinscribe binary oppositions of the strong/weak state or the interventionist/retreating state.[6]

Let us consider first the distinctive dimensions of state power that are currently associated with the neoliberal state. Contemporary research has focused on three central aspects that distinguish neoliberal state power: (1) transformations associated with changes in the role of global capital (and finance capital in particular), (2) the significance of the security state in the post-liberalization period, and (3) changes in the boundaries between "state" and "civil society." Scholars writing about neoliberalism have focused on the complex and changing relationship between the state and capital. The distinctiveness of the neoliberal state in this context lies in its shift to a set of practices and structures that are specifically focused on producing ideal conditions for capital investment and mobility. While the complex connections between the state and capital are not new (Aronowitz and Bratsis 2002; Jessop 1982, 2002), what distinguishes the neoliberal state from older forms of the modern state is both an intensification of this relationship and the specific characteristics of contemporary capitalism. As Evans and Sewell note, one of the significant differences between theorists of classical liberalism and neoliberalism is that in contrast to classical liberalism's concerns about cartels and monopolies, "neoliberalism was not concerned about great concentrations of private wealth and power" (2013, 43). State power plays out in a paradoxical fashion in the context of neoliberalism. The state actively promotes the conditions that enable the concentration of wealth and the growth of massive corporations and monopolies. This concentration of economic power in turn increases the dependent nature of the state within the state-capital relationship of the twenty-first century. The particular features of finance capitalism underline the specificities of this relationship. As David Harvey argues, state policy now relies on monetarism. This intensifies the paradoxical nature of contemporary state power where "neoliberal states typically facilitate the diffusion of influence of financial institutions through deregulation, but then they also all too often guarantee the integrity and solvency of financial institutions at no matter what cost. . . . The state has to step in and replace 'bad' money with 'good' money—which explains the pressure on central bankers to maintain confidence in the soundness of state money" (Harvey 2005, 73). While Harvey notes that states rely on monetarism, his analysis also implicitly illustrates the point that the financial dimensions of neoliberalism rest on the soundness and strength of the state. Thus, although the state in effect actively promotes policies that may weaken its own autonomy vis-à-vis capital, it is in fact an active interventionist partner within the distinctive state-capital relationship of contemporary neoliberalism.

The paradoxical nature of the role of the state in the twenty-first century is played out through a second feature—the reworking of security and risk. One of the most self-evident arenas for the expansion of state power has been in the realm of security. The security state has expanded through a multitude of activities and institutions that have ranged from policing to surveillance to militarization. Any analysis of the state in the twenty-first century thus has to disentangle and analyze the points of connection, interaction, and divergence between the security state on the one hand and the post-liberalization state on the other. Contemporary scholarship tends to yoke these dimensions of state power together. For instance, Gambetti and Godoy-Anativia argue, "security is a neoliberal technique of power" (2013, 9) that has transformed both state-civil society relations and discourses of "security." Languages of "terrorism," they note, often provide useful tools that allow for an expansion of state power and can consequently strengthen the ability of states to implement policies associated with neoliberalism (15). Meanwhile, even as discourses of security proliferate in both national and global contexts, states increasingly promote policies and ideologies that require their citizens to bear responsibility for their own socioeconomic security. As Lisa Brush illustrates through her analysis of the U.S. state, discourses of personal responsibility (that obscure the structural causes of poverty) cut across both the penal security state and the social security state in the United States (2013). In the twenty-first century, the exercise of state power within civil society is expressed through the rhetoric of security even as it seeks to privatize risk (Lamont, Welburn, and Fleming 2013; Sharone 2013). This privatization of risk displaces state and public accountability for the structural forms of socioeconomic inequality and exclusion that have been intensified through neoliberal policies even as state regulation of poor and socioeconomically marginalized communities expands. As Soss, Fording, and Schram argue, while the state drains resources away from welfare programs in the United States, poverty governance has expanded; processes of "privatization and sanctioning" of the poor complement each other. As they argue, low wage work for welfare recipients is promoted "through affirmative uses of welfare programs as sites where state power is deployed to service markets" (2011, 7). This includes the use of long-standing tools of labor regulation in labor markets that are shaped or produced by welfare policies. The expanding insecurity of marginalized communities and individuals is accompanied by expanding forms of state discipline and control. State power is thus exercised within civil society through both long-standing means of surveillance and control as well as through new regimes of power associated with neoliberal practices.

This body of scholarship provides important insights into the ways in which the economic and security agendas of states intertwine and reinforce each other. While essays in this volume will illustrate this enmeshing of these forms of state power, they also seek to delineate ways in which state security agendas are not reducible to the neoliberal economic agendas that are adopted by the state. Such agendas—whether they pertain to the carceral state within the United States or the historical legacies of the military regimes in Bangladesh—predate the economic agendas associated with neoliberalism. The volume contributes to a deeper understanding of where and when security and neoliberal frameworks intersect without reducing them to a singular monolithic framework of state power. Instead, the volume also seeks to ask the deeper question of how state power is exercised in complex, varied, and often contradictory ways within the realm of civil society.

Rethinking the Boundaries between State and Civil Society in the Era of Neoliberalism

The question of how the economic policies and ideologies of neoliberalism have transformed the boundaries and relationship between the state and civil society represents one of the most analyzed realms in existing scholarly work. A significant approach in this scholarship lies in the analysis of various modes of neoliberal governmentality. From such perspectives, the political technologies of neoliberalism do not require a demarcated state that operates above or in opposition to civil society. Rather, individual subjectivities and modes of being are, in effect, in a mutually constitutive relationship with market-oriented rationalities (Brown 2014; Greenhouse 2009; Ong 2006). The distinctive marker here lies in the fuzziness of the state; the state/civil society nexus is conceptualized through a Foucaultian conception of biopower. Technologies of governance cut across varied spaces and practices that range from nongovernmental organizations (Bernal and Grewal 2014) to communities of experts (Laurie and Bondi 2005) to complex sets of cultural practices that cut across the realms of media, cultural production, and consumption (Chen 2013; Gill and Scharff 2011).

It is at this analytical juncture where the power of the neoliberal project appears close to achieving omnipotence in its ability to soak through and refashion every facet of social and cultural life that the historical distinctiveness of neoliberalism risks overstatement. Hall and Lamont note that such perspectives often underestimate both the social resilience of marginalized communities and the persistence of cultural and institutional frameworks that are not defined by market rationalities (2013). However, the problem of reverting to an overdetermined master narrative of neoliberalism extends far beyond the persistence of alternative frameworks for subjectivity and social and cultural activity. Such a master narrative risks distorting our understandings of how inequality is reproduced and how state power operates. In this process, the distinctive features of neoliberal policies and ideologies are over-read as a sharp form of historical discontinuity from the past so that a murky form of neoliberalism becomes a generalized explanation of inequality, hierarchy, and violence in the twenty-first century.

Consider two examples that would appear to mark the distinctive ascendancy of the neoliberal project—the question of professional expertise and the corresponding proliferation of nongovernmental organizations (NGOs) in non-Western contexts and the retrenchment of state welfare support. In the first case, professional expertise circulates through complex webs of organizational and institutional networks that range from dominant institutions such as the World Bank and the International Monetary Fund to a plethora of nongovernmental organizations in comparative contexts (Bernal and Grewal 2014). Such networks indeed often comprise the everyday practices through which entrepreneurial models socioeconomic mobility and inclusion are dispersed (Karim 2011), sometimes in conjunction with and sometimes in lieu of the explicit exercise of state power. However, such modes of power stem from much longer historical processes that have unfolded through legacies of colonialism and the consolidation of capitalist development in the postcolonial world. Timothy Mitchell, for instance, demonstrates the way the idea of "economy" as an autonomous ontological entity is an outcome of such historical processes; expertise in this context was abstracted from messy, contradictory processes that often belied the sanitized maps and models that were read back onto emerging forms of "capitalist development" in colonial contexts (2002). The circuits of expertise that are now commonly associated with the neoliberal moment (and the complex relationship between the state and capital that they embody or manage) in fact emerged out of the historical legacies of colonial and postcolonial capitalist economic development. In fact, in comparative non-Western contexts, paradigms of the developmental state either coexist with or are aligned with newer objectives of contemporary models of neoliberalism. What are termed "neoliberal policies" are often various configurations of policies of reform and liberalization that are carried out by interventionist developmentalist states (Harvey 2005; MacLeod 2004). Meanwhile, the implementation of policies of liberalization does not necessarily mark a shift from away from the modes of power associated with the interventionist developmental state (Gupta 2012).

The continued power of this form of interventionist state points to a second example of how a presumption of the newness of the neoliberal project can shortchange our understandings of both the state and the intensification of socioeconomic inequality and exclusion. One of the most vivid public markers of the neoliberal project is in the political imperative of dismantling the welfare state. This has unfolded in Western contexts that have had a specific model of the welfare state and that have recently witnessed acute versions of such cutbacks through austerity-based agendas (see Nancy A. Naples's essay in this volume). Non-Western contexts have had different conceptions of such welfare programs. As Akhil Gupta notes, drawing on his research on a welfare program for children in India, "What a welfare program means in a Third World context has to be qualified by the knowledge that the state that runs such a program is not a welfare state. The logic of the program was never one of providing a security blanket for the poorest segments of the population. Rather, the justification for the program arose from the need to invest in human capital for the development of the nation-state" (2012, 248). This is an important reminder that developmental states continue to operate with a distinctive logic that is not reducible to the neoliberal moment of the present. This has led some cultural critics to postulate that neoliberalism has foreclosed on the possible emergence of welfare policies in non-Western contexts. For instance, Gayatri Spivak posits, "In the South, welfare structures cannot emerge as a result of the priorities of the transnational agencies" (1996, 249). Yet this popular assumption regarding the turn away from welfare is riddled with empirical inaccuracies that permeate critical popular and academic discourses. In fact, non-Western states that have pursued policies of economic liberalization have varied in their policies regarding state supports of subsidies or welfare. This variation exists across nations as well as across different historical periods within particular nations.

A reconsideration of the question of state welfare provisions and the persistence of the logic of the developmental state has more at stake than a criticism of the presentist or empirically distorted nature of critical conceptions of neoliberalism that circulate within the academy. What is at stake are the ways in which states in non-Western contexts often strategically deploy welfare provisions and, in effect, depart from the ideal, typical model of the neoliberal project in order to persist with the very economic policies of liberalization that intensify inequality and exclusion. Consider, for instance, the case of Chile, one of the earliest countries to implement extensive policies associated with neoliberalism. Ashley Davis-Hamal demonstrates that Chile shifted from a model of orthodox neoliberalism (implemented by Pinochet from 1973 to 1982) to a form of "pragmatic neoliberalism" that advocated a project of "growth with equity" (2012). Davis-Hamal illustrates that successive Chilean governments have continued with neoliberal policies but have increased targeted spending through social programs. Evans and Sewell further note that countries such as France, Sweden, and Germany have in the past maintained welfare states while adopting many policies that were associated with neoliberalism (2013, 37). For Singapore, Youyenn Teo shows how the state has combined a highly interventionist mode of developmentalism in both the economic and social realms while incorporating ideologies and policies associated with neoliberalism (2011). Meanwhile, in India, one of the latecomers to this model (with the systematic implementation of economic policies of liberalization taking root in the 1990s), successive governments have embraced such policies but have also sought to temper some of the deleterious impacts (Kohli 2012) of such policies through state-run social programs and subsidies. If one assumes that the project of neoliberalism is marked by simple signifiers of welfare cutbacks, one misses the way in which states may in fact strategically deploy welfare provisions or state subsidies either to ameliorate some aspects of socioeconomic inequality or to manage political resistance while in fact continuing to implement economic policies that intensify or produce inequality and exclusion.[7]

The challenge at hand for scholars concerned with the deleterious effects of policies associated with neoliberalism is to keep in tension the normative ideal model of neoliberalism, which has had significant power in both global and comparative contexts, on the one hand, with the complex, varied sets of policies and practices that have unfolded in historically and politically contextual ways, on the other. With this tension in mind, I distinguish the notion of neoliberalism and the ideal-typical understanding of the neoliberal state from the post-liberalization state. My conception of the post-liberalization state signals the array of policies of economic reform and paths of liberalization and also provides the space for an understanding of alternative trajectories that are emerging in the aftermath of the neoliberal turn. The essays in this volume, both individually and as a collective enterprise, seek to deepen our understanding of such varied complexities of the state in the post-liberalization period. Through situated research they examine the spaces where the logic of neoliberalism has sharply transformed state practices and the boundaries between the "state" and "civil society." They also seek to disrupt a mimetic understanding of neoliberalism in which inequality, exclusion, and violence are self-evident reflections of present-day neoliberalism. This conceptual understanding of the state is in line with scholarship that has focused on the shifting line between state and civil society (Gramsci 1971; Migdal, 2001). Joel Migdal's "state in society approach" is particularly effective in grasping the Janus-faced nature of the state. As Migdal argues, "the state is a field of power marked by the use and threat of violence and shaped by (1) the image of a coherent, controlling organization in a territory, which is a representation of the people bounded by that territory, and (2) the actual practices of its multiple parts" (2001, 16–17). The contradictory nature of the modern state allows it to act as a coherent, interventionist, and often seemingly autonomous actor even as it simultaneously permeates and builds on networks and institutions within the realm of "civil society."

Drawing on such an approach, this volume contributes to contemporary understandings of the paradigm of neoliberalism and the nature of the post-liberalization state through a focus on four central themes: First, the volume engages with the conceptualization of the state as a series of boundary projects that reconstitute conceptions of the "public" and "civil society."[8] Understanding the post-liberalization state in this context necessitates a shift from a sole preoccupation with processes of privatization to a deeper examination of shifting conceptions of the "public." Second, the volume uses the state as an entry point into deepening our understanding of various forms of inequality and exclusion that have become almost naturalized markers of social, political, and economic life in the contemporary world. Essays in the volume provide analyses of the complex ways in which the realm of the "economic" is structured by social relations such as those marked by race, gender, and caste. Third, the volume delineates the new state structures, modes of governance, and forms of power that have specifically emerged with the implementation of policies of economic liberalization. The volume thus examines both what is distinctive about the post-liberalization state and what must be contextualized as long-standing features of modern state power. Finally, this volume engages with both the possibilities and limits of political and social change. Individual essays examine the ways in which collective responses seek to combat inequality and are often disciplined by the very terms of the cultural and ideological dimensions of the logic of neoliberalism that such responses seek to contest.

Feminist Conceptions of State Power and Structural Inequality

The essays in this volume develop analyses of the post-liberalization state that build on interdisciplinary scholarship that has interrogated the boundaries of the "state" and "economic" inequality (Bakker and Silvey 2008; Newman, 2013; Runyan and Peterson 2013). Interdisciplinary scholarship in fields such as feminist, queer, postcolonial, and critical race studies has called attention to the ways in which the state represents a gendered, racialized, and sexualized field of power, practices, and institutions (Canaday 2009; Cooper 1995; Omi and Winant 2014; Reddy, 2011; Tripp, Ferree, and Ewig 2013). Meanwhile, a vast field of scholarship has also sought to pry open the category of the "economic" in order to illustrate the ways in which both the nature and reproduction of economic inequality can only adequately be addressed when inequalities such as race and gender in the United States and inequalities such as caste, ethnicity, gender, and religion in comparative contexts are conceptualized as constitutive of economic inequality. As this scholarship has illustrated in both interdisciplinary and cross-disciplinary fields, such inequalities are historically produced structural forces and are not simply epiphenomenal consequences of economic processes. In other words, the terrain of the "economic" is made up of such inequalities even as such inequalities are intensified by specific economic policies.

Despite the existence of this now vast scholarship, major scholarly analyses of the neoliberal state often neglect the critical insights of feminist scholarship and rest on conceptions of both the state and the economy as race- and gender-neutral entities. Much of the existing scholarship that has sought to map the relationship between the state and neoliberalism (Gambetti and Godoy-Anativia 2013; Hall and Lamont 2013; Harvey 2005) through broad and comparative frames has missed the ways in which this relationship is in fact constituted by historically specific relationships between inequalities such as gender, race, caste, sexuality, and class. An adequate understanding of the post-liberalization state requires a framework that treats an understanding of these forms of inequality as integral to rather than as (after-) effects of the policies and ideologies associated with the neoliberal project.

Consider, for instance, one of the significant attempts at understanding the relationship between the U.S. carceral state and the project of neoliberalism. Loic Wacquant makes a powerful case for linking social welfare policies and penal policies in the United States in order to show how "the obsessive focus on crime, backed by ordinary and scholarly commonsense, has served well to hide from view the new politics and policy of poverty that is a core component in the forging of the neoliberal state" (2009, 287). Yet Wacquant is unable to fully grapple with the structural and political dimensions of race either in the organization of the U.S. economy or in terms of the nature of state power. For Wacquant, the mass incarceration of African Americans is an effect of the "remaking of the state" through "the retooling of public authority suited to fostering the advance of neoliberalism" (xviii). Neoliberalism in this context is the driving force for the expansion of the carceral state; incarceration becomes the political tool for the management of dislocations produced by this set of economic policies. Neoliberalism becomes the de facto explanation for the expansion of the carceral state. Wacquant argues that the "penal categories, practices, and policies of the United States find their root and reason in the neoliberal revolution of which this country is the historical crucible and the planetary spearhead" (xv). On one level, race becomes a largely epiphenomenal element in this analysis (rather than an analytical category of analysis necessary for an understanding of the state and political economy in the United States). While Wacquant does address the use of prisons as a racialized response both to the challenge of social movements as well as to socioeconomic forms of segregation (206), the state remains a unitary, neutral entity that deploys such strategies. The deeper problem with such an approach lies in the way in which neoliberalism becomes a de facto ahistorical, functionalist explanation for changes in the state. Such an explanation begs the question as to why the United States has disproportionate rates of incarceration when compared to other states that have pursued neo-liberal agendas? Or if incarceration remains a tool of neoliberalism, why have state prisons (as opposed to privatized prisons) remained the central mode of incarceration (Gilmore 2007)?

The example of the U.S. carceral state illustrates the analytical import of the feminist perspectives of the post-liberalization state presented in this volume. Feminist analyses that take the state (or the terrain of political economy) as fields that are structured by race, sexuality, and gender are not simply calling for a shift to "identity-based" dimensions (Fraser 2014) or to mechanistic intersectional effects of state policies or practices. Rather, such perspectives, by locating the paradigm of neoliberalism in relation to historically situated conceptions of race and gender, deepen our understanding of contemporary political and economic processes without reverting to an understanding of the "neoliberal project" as a totalizing explanation of contemporary inequality and state power. The "racial state" (Omi and Winant 2014) may indeed, as Wacquant (2009) argues, provide the political management necessary for the neoliberal revolution; but the racial state also operates as a distinctive historical and political formation. In other words, the racial state (much like the developmental state of many postcolonial contexts) may align with the objectives of neoliberal policies, but it is not produced by or reducible to the paradigm of neoliberalism.

Feminist theoretical perspectives are well situated to disentangle these formations in ways that address both the complexities of contemporary socioeconomic inequality and the conceptual intricacies of state power. While feminist (and related interdisciplinary) scholarship has engaged in extensive theorizations of neoliberalism (mostly centered around conceptions of neoliberal subjectivity and modes of governmentality), the body of scholarship that has engaged in systematic research on the state is much smaller. *Feminists Rethink the Neoliberal State* builds on and contributes to this small but rich scholarship that has sought to situate understandings of the post-liberalization state through in-depth and grounded research on specific places and nations. Such scholarship has developed analyses of key dimensions of the state in the neoliberal era. First, it has shown how both state-led policies and national languages of development intersect with policies of liberalization through an expanding terrain of "women's empowerment" programs (Sharma 2008). The category of "women" has in effect become a specific kind of technology of governance that must be understood as central to the operation of the post-liberalization state. Second, feminist scholarship has disaggregated the state through careful analyses of how economic restructuring unfolds in specific policy sectors (Ewig 2011). Such state-led processes of restructuring entrench and intensify inequalities of gender, class, and race in ways that are shaped by the political, economic, and historical context in question (Ewig 2011; Lind 2005; Sahle 2006). Finally, such research has also complicated our understandings of women's movements and the ways in which feminism becomes enmeshed in the ideological and institutional investments of the neoliberal project (Prügl 2015; Rottenberg 2014). While, on the one hand, languages of women's empowerment are integrated within state-led policies of liberalization in non-Western contexts, languages of feminism in the United States are also often integrated within state agendas in distinctive ways. Kristin Bumiller, for instance, argues that feminist agendas to combat sexual violence in the United States have become enmeshed in the neoliberal state regulatory practices that have expanded social control through both the welfare and the carceral dimensions of the state (2008).

If such research points to the significance of feminist perspectives for an adequate understanding of the nature of state power and the effects of policies of liberalization, it also dispels any presumed political innocence of either the category of "woman" or of the project of feminism. Particular models of feminism can certainly be compatible with the ideologies of neoliberalism, and the effects of policies of neoliberalism may vary greatly for women from elite and marginalized socioeconomic groups. The theoretical understanding of feminism that shapes this volume is thus one that is not rooted in an identity-based perspective on women's lives. What the essays cohere around are a set of feminist analytical concerns with explaining and understanding state power, inequality, and resistance in the wake of the "neoliberal project" (see chapter 8, this volume). The essays thus do not seek to define themselves either purely through the analytical categories of "gender" or "woman" or through a formulaic implementation of a model of intersectionality. Instead, the analytical frames of each essay draw on the specific historically situated contexts of the countries in question and deploy, combine, and move between three central frames of analysis: (1) an analysis of context-specific intersecting and often mutually constitutive forms of socioeconomic inequality; (2) an analysis of the significance of the category of "women" in understanding the post-liberalization state; and (3) an analysis of policies, politics, and practices that are not specifically focused on women or gender but are critical to any feminist project concerned with the reproduction of inequalities and exclusions that disproportionately affect socioeconomically marginalized women in comparative contexts. In this endeavor, these essays seek to present a set of interdisciplinary, empirically grounded studies, all shaped by feminist theoretical work that seeks to pry open and understand categories such as the "state," "civil society," and "the economy" in the post-liberalization world.

Comparative Perspectives on the Practices, Spaces, and Trajectories of the Post-Liberalization State

Feminists Rethink the Neoliberal State provides a comparative perspective on the nature of the post-liberalization state and the limits and possibilities of challenges to both the state and the neoliberal project in Western and non-Western contexts. Throughout this essay, I have presented an analysis of the project of neoliberalism while framing the approach of the volume through this conceptual lens of the post-liberalization state. I have deployed these two conceptual tools to highlight two significant dimensions that make up the contradictory nature of the project of neo-liberalism. On the one hand, the dominant ideologies associated with neoliberal policies explicitly delineated by the "Washington consensus" have played a central role in shaping economic, social, and political life in the twenty-first century. Dominant ideologies and discourses matter—they shape policies, institutions, and everyday life in material ways. However, neoliberalism does not exist as a totalizing approach to organizing societies or economies (Peck and Tickell 2002) Policies of economic liberalization vary across national contexts and coexist and interact with historically specific political practices, institutions, and policies that long predate the current era of neoliberalism; they also face challenges from movements and nation-states seeking alternative paths. My framing of this volume in terms of the post-liberalization state thus seeks to simultaneously capture the hegemonic power of the project of neoliberalism and unsettle the singular language of neoliberalism. In this endeavor, *Feminists Rethink the Neoliberal State* brings together essays that show how states structure and are reconstituted by complex and varying amalgams of the ideologies, economic compulsions, institutional norms, and political interests that constitute the paradigm of neoliberalism.

Essays in the volume each draw on a range of disciplinary and interdisciplinary perspectives and present original research and theoretical perspectives on various aspects of the state in comparative contexts. The essays draw on original field research in a range of countries and deploy analytical approaches that move between and connect the local, national, and transnational realms. They are shaped by a commitment to the development of analytical and theoretical frames that emerge from the careful study of places, contexts, and nations. In this endeavor, the volume does not rest on area-based claims of geographic coverage of the world. Rather, these essays seek to spark intellectual debates and open up both research agendas and theoretical conceptions that deepen our understanding of the shifting nature of the state and the implications for both the reproduction of inequality and the possibilities of change.

Nancy A. Naples's essay, "What's in a Word?," opens the volume with a comparative materialist feminist examination of the public and political discourses associated with neoliberal ideologies and policies. The development of such a feminist materialistic understanding of the post-liberalization state is central to the feminist analytic that undergirds the volume (see chapter 8). Naples's essay specifically analyzes how government policies of "austerity" seem to circulate as autonomous discourses in a "post-neoliberal epoch" in ways that conceal their deeper links to longstanding policies of economic neoliberalism. Discourses of austerity in Naples's analysis "render invisible the larger scaffolding of neoliberalism." Naples approaches the state as a set of "relations of ruling" (Smith 1999) that shapes the everyday lives of diverse individuals, families, communities, and nations during and following the Great Recession of 2008–9. She specifically focuses on the intersection of the media, state actors, and economic analysts in post-liberal state governance in producing austerity discourses. This construction of "austerity" redraws the conception of "the public" in distinctive ways. The complex relationship between the economic and discursive realms produces differential effects for different social groups and nations and intensifies the precarity of economically vulnerable populations made disposable by late capitalism in the twenty-first century. Naples's essay provides a rich and systematic analysis of the effects of austerity discourses on socioeconomic inequalities of class, gender, and race through a comparative focus on the United States and the European Union.

Ujju Aggarwal's essay, "After Rights," elaborates on the complex connections between public and political discourses, institutional practices, social and economic exclusion, and inequality through an analysis of the relationship between narratives of choice, racial inequality, and state-produced segregation in the United States. The essay draws on extended ethnographic research in New York City and on a fine-grained historical analysis of the judicial dimensions of the state. Aggarwal argues that while *Brown v. Board of Education* (1954) signified a moment when universal rights to education were won (thus indicating a different structure of citizenship than Jim Crow segregation), *how* universal rights were structured becomes critical to understanding why public education is the most universally accessible yet also most unequal institution in the United States. The essay provides an analysis of policies and legislation in the post-*Brown* period that examines how choice becomes an amendment to (rather than a break from) Jim Crow–style segregation. She uses her genealogy of the framework of "choice" to track the realignment that took place in the post–civil rights social structure and shows that the result was a continued production of a tiered citizenship. This tiered citizenship, organized through race and embedded within the public, was assured when universal rights were organized as individual private choices. Narratives of choice, as Aggarwal illustrates, have reinvigorated the story of American exceptionalism and been central to the creation of the "achievement gap." Such narratives have formed a core part of an ideological infrastructure that has become central to the rationalization of the inequality that stems from the socioeconomic exclusion of marginalized African American communities from access to education.

If the rhetoric of choice operates in tandem with specific state policies and legal regimes in the United States, postcolonial contexts reveal new and complex configurations between narratives of microcredit-based entrepreneurship, NGOs within civil society, and the state. Lamia Karim's essay, "The Production of Silence," examines the distinctive nature of neoliberalism in Bangladesh that began under military rule, and she analyzes the discursive silences that neoliberal development policies have produced within the NGO sector. Her essay shows how policies of market liberalization were historically promoted by successive military and democratic governments since independence—prior to the Washington consensus commonly associated with neoliberalism. Her essay specifically examines the impact of market liberalization on the state, NGOs, and the framing of feminist/women's agendas. As she illustrates, policies and ideologies of neoliberalism discursively shape public discourses about NGOs, women, and development. She argues that feminist and women's agendas are themselves often shaped by liberal ideas of empowerment that have been reworked through neoliberal models of economic empowerment and that have silenced more critical discourses questioning free-market policies and their deleterious effects on women's labor and lives. As with Aggarwal's analysis, Karim illustrates that such policies must be contextualized within long-standing, historically specific legacies of state policies that become imbricated in agendas associated with neoliberal economic policies and ideologies.

Dolly Daftary's essay, "An Improvising State," takes up the question of the state-NGO nexus in the context of postcolonial nations through an in-depth examination of the restructuring of rural bureaucracies in India. In contrast to Karim's analysis, Daftary examines the micro-credit model through an analysis of NGOs that are funded by the state. The essay draws on ethnographic research on watershed development, India's largest development intervention for its drylands, and its delivery of state-sponsored micro-credit in Gujarat (a state that has been publicly depicted as an idealized national embodiment of the success of India's economic reforms). Daftary examines the state's devolution of policy implementation to local political actors and argues that the deployment of ideologies and practices of self-governance have transformed the state into an improvising formation—constantly departing from precedent and certainty, and provisionally administering social life. Various forms of socioeconomic vulnerability produced by policies of liberalization are intensified by a state in transition—one that has distinctive gendered implications for women from marginalized castes who are employed at the lower rungs of rural bureaucracies.

The question of vulnerability is foregrounded in Christina Heatherton's essay, "The Broken Windows of Rosa Ramos." Heatherton's analysis takes us to the heart of precarious communities of color in the urban United States and expands the focus on vulnerability to include the political and physical dimensions of life for such communities. Heatherton provides a careful analysis of the intersections and divergences of dimensions of state power that are concerned with security on the one hand and with neoliberal models of urban development on the other. As she illustrates, "broken windows" policing as both philosophy and practice emerged alongside and also facilitated major transformations of the neoliberal political economy. Drawing on an analysis of patterns of policing in Skidmore, Los Angeles, and Ferguson, Missouri, Heatherton argues that the "securitized urbanism" of the model of broken windows policing has become a central form of political expression of neoliberalism in urban U.S. communities. The broken windows philosophy has provided the underpinning for an expansion of police capacities directed primarily at small-scale "crimes of poverty." In the process, deindustrialized cities are constructed as places of disease and disorder so that racialized poverty appears to have no origin in ways that echo Naples' feminist materialist analysis of public and political discourses. However, as Heatherton notes, such processes are not invented by the Washington consensus—they extend and rework historical formations of the racial state (Omi and Winant 2014) and intensify racialized and class-based inequalities produced by processes of deindustrialization that preceded the ascendancy of neoliberal policies. Heatherton argues that the vulnerability of communities of color within these racial and gendered spatial dimensions of neoliberalism must be understood through a feminist analytic of *imminent violability*.

The essays by Karim and Aggarwal point to ways in which liberal feminist ideals of empowerment and choice become complicit with neoliberal ideologies. Their perspectives point to ways in which the rhetoric of neoliberalism can discipline political responses to inequality. The question of the limits of political opposition within the constraints of neoliberal contexts raises the question of alternative trajectories that try to break from the project of neoliberalism. Amy Lind's essay, "After Neoliberalism?," makes a critical shift to an analysis of the apparent move away from neoliberalism in Latin America. Drawing on an in-depth study of Ecuador, Lind analyzes both the possibilities opened up by regional challenges to the global hegemony of the neoliberal model as well as the contradictions that continue to exist within the Ecuadorian nation and within the state apparatus. The essay analyzes post-neoliberal Ecuador's Citizen Revolution and asks whether and how it has fostered more just, "postcapitalist" forms of political, economic, and social life? Lind's research provides a complex set of answers to this question. The chapter highlights the centrality of heteronormativity in understanding post-neoliberal states, including governance and development frameworks that privilege the patriarchal heterosexual family above all others and view it as the foundation of the country's modernization goals. It argues that Ecuador's shift away from neoliberalism is fraught with contradictions and is best understood as signifying only a partial rupture with the neoliberal legacy. Despite progressive legal changes to the definition of family, nation, and economy in Ecuador's 2008 Constitution, a symbol of the country's move away from neoliberalism, it argues that the state nonetheless maintains a heteronormative, colonialist understanding of governance and development, thereby rendering the potentially radical project of reimagining life "after" neoliberalism incomplete and paradoxical at best.

Conclusion

Feminists Rethink the Neoliberal State provides a distinctive comparative perspective on the post-liberalization state through a series of theoretically informed essays on a range of national contexts and transnational processes. The final chapter of the volume, "Toward a Feminist Analytic of the Post-Liberalization State," outlines the theoretical terrain of the feminist materialist approach of the volume. Taken together the essays seek to enlarge, rethink, and challenge some of the conventional assumptions about the project of neoliberalism that are rooted in interdisciplinary scholarship. Such an approach provides a distinctive understanding of the nature of inequality, exclusion, and disenfranchisement in the twenty-first century. The goal of this volume is to open up an intellectual conversation about the nature of inequality, exclusion, and change. Such a conversation is premised as much on what is not changing (how inequality and exclusion are reproduced over time) as it is on what is new and distinctive about contemporary neoliberalism. With this undertaking in mind, the authors of this volume hope to foreground the role of the post-liberalization state.

NOTES

1   Agence France-Presse, "Global Income Inequality Now Back at 1820s Levels: OECD," *Rappler.com*, October 3, 2014, www.rappler.com.

2   The report also produced an immediate critical backlash from mainstream business media outlets. See, for example, Tim Worstall, "OECD: Global Inequality Is Now as Bad as in 1820," October 31, 2014, Forbes.com.

3   My focus here is on dominant trends. Such approaches generally focus on how the state must now be understood through conceptions of governmentality. See, e.g., Brown 2015. For work that has sought to address the restructuring of the state in nuanced ways, see Brenner 2004 and Collier 2011.

4   The theoretical framework of this volume draws in large part on work that I have been conducting on the post-liberalization state in India for my current book, *India's Liberalizing State: Urbanization, Inequality, and the Politics of Water in India*.

5   Such historical processes, of course, have always been encompassed by transnational processes. Structures of political economy in the global south, for instance, have been fundamentally shaped by histories of colonialism. For a critical discussion of more abstract conceptions of transnationalism, see Fernandes 2013.

6   For an example of work that argues that globalization has been accompanied by a decline in state sovereignty, see Brown 2014.

7   As Chandan Reddy argues, such simplified views of neoliberalism also miss the ways in which welfare provisions are reconstituted through exclusionary conceptions of citizenship (2011).

8   There has already been a rich body of scholarship that has sought to unsettle the boundaries between the state and civil society and illustrate how the state

is always enmeshed in the terrain of civil society. Such work has explicitly or implicitly drawn on Foucaultian and Gramscian conceptions of how state power permeates civil society, See, e.g., Migdal 2001; Mitchell 1991.

REFERENCES

Aronowitz, Stanley, and Peter Bratsis, eds. 2002. *Paradigm Lost: State Theory Reconsidered*. Minneapolis: University of Minnesota Press.

Bakker, Isabella, and Rachel Silvey, eds. 2008. *Beyond States and Markets: The Challenges of Social Reproduction*. New York: Routledge.

Bernal, Victoria, and Inderpal Grewal. 2014. *Theorizing NGOS: States, Feminisms and Neoliberalism*. Durham, NC: Duke University Press.

Bhagwati, Jagdish N. 2004 *In Defense of Globalization*. New York: Oxford University Press.

Brenner, Neil. 2004. *New State Spaces: Urban Governance and the Rescaling of Statehood*. New York: Oxford University Press.

Brown, Wendy. 2005. *Edgework: Critical Essays on Knowledge and Politics*. Princeton, NJ: Princeton University Press.

———. 2014. *Walled States, Waning Sovereignty*. New York: Zone Books.

———. 2015. *Undoing the Demos: Neoliberalism's Stealth Revolution*. Cambridge: Zone Books.

Brush, Lisa. 2013. "Work and Love in the Gendered Insecurity State." In Tripp et al., *Gender Violence and Human Security*, 109–31.

Bumiller, Kristin. 2008. *In an Abusive State: How Neoliberalism Appropriated the Feminist Movement against Sexual Violence*. Durham, NC: Duke University Press.

Canaday, Margot. 2009. *The Straight State: Sexuality and Citizenship in Twentieth-Century America*. Princeton, NJ: Princeton University Press.

Chen, Eva. 2013. "Neoliberalism and Popular Women's Culture: Rethinking Choice, Freedom and Agency." *European Journal of Cultural Studies* 16, no. 4: 440–52.

Collier, Stephen J. 2011. *Post-Soviet Social: Neoliberalism, Social Modernity, BioPolitics*. Princeton, NJ: Princeton University Press.

Cooper, Davina. 1995. *Power in Struggle: Feminism, Sexuality and the State*. New York: New York University Press.

Corbridge, Stuart. 2005. *Seeing the State: Governance and Governmentality in India*. Cambridge: Cambridge University Press.

Davis-Hamel, Ashley. 2012. "Successful Neoliberalism? State Policy, Poverty, and Income Inequality in Chile." *International Social Science Review* 87, no. 3–4: 79–101.

Evans, Peter, and William Sewell. 2013."Neoliberalism." In Hall and Lamont, *Social Resilience*, 35–68.

Ewig, Christina. 2011. *Second-Wave Neoliberalism: Gender, Race, and Health Sector Reform in Peru*. University Park: Pennsylvania State University Press.

Fernandes, Leela. 2006. *India's New Middle Class: Democratic Politics in an Era of Economic Reform*. Minneapolis: University of Minnesota Press.

———. 2013. *Transnational Feminism in the United States: Knowledge, Ethics, Power*. New York: New York University Press.

————. 2015. "The Paradox of India's Middle Class." In *Routledge Handbook of Contemporary India*, ed. Knut Axel Jacobsen, 232–42. London: Routledge.

Fernandez-Kelly, Maria Patricia. 1984. *For We Are Sold, I and My People: Women and Industry in Mexico's Frontier*. Albany: State University of New York Press.

Fraser, Nancy. 2014. *Fortunes of Feminism: From State-Managed Capitalism to Neoliberal Crisis*. New York: Routledge, Taylor and Francis.

Gambetti, Zeynep, and Marcial Godoy-Anativia. 2013. *Rhetorics of Insecurity: Belonging and Violence in the Neoliberal Era*. New York: New York University Press.

Gill, Rosalind, and Christina Scharff. 2011. *New Femininities: Postfeminism, Neoliberalism and Subjectivity*. Houndmills, Basingstoke, Hampshire: Palgrave Macmillan.

Gilmore, Ruth Wilson. 2007. *Golden Gulag: Prisons, Surplus, Crisis and Opposition in Globalizing California*. Berkeley: University of California Press.

Gramsci, Antonio. 1971. *Selections from the Prison Notebooks*. Translated and edited by Quintin Hoare and G. N. Smith. New York: International Publishers.

Greenhouse, Carole J. 2009. *Ethnographies of Neoliberalism*. Philadelphia: University of Pennsylvania Press.

Gupta, Akhil. 2012. *Red Tape: Bureaucracy, Structural Violence, and Poverty in India*. Durham, NC: Duke University Press.

Hall, Peter A., and Michéle Lamont. 2013. *Social Resilience in the Neoliberal Era*. New York: Cambridge University Press.

Harvey, David. 2005. *A Brief History of Neoliberalism*. Oxford: Oxford University Press.

Jessop, Bob. 1982. *The Capitalist State: Marxist Theories and Methods*. New York: New York University Press.

————. 2002. "Liberalism, Neoliberalism, and Urban Governance: A State-Theoretical Perspective." *Antipode* 34, no. 3: 452–72.

Karim, Lamia. 2011. *Microfinance and Its Discontents: Women in Debt in Bangladesh*. Minneapolis: University of Minnesota Press.

Kohli, Atul. 2012. *Poverty Amid Plenty in the New India*. Cambridge: Cambridge University Press.

Lamont, Michéle, Jessica Welburn, and Crystal Fleming. 2013. "Responses to Discrimination and Social Resilience under Neoliberalism." In Hall and Lamont, *Social Resilience*, 129–57.

Laurie, Nina, and Liz Bondi. 2005. *Working the Spaces of Neoliberalism: Activism, Professionalisation and Incorporation*. Malden, MA: Blackwell.

Levy, Jonah D. 2006. *The State after Statism: New State Activities in the Age of Liberalization*. Cambridge, MA: Harvard University Press.

Lind, Amy. 2005. *Gendered Paradoxes: Women's Movements, State Restructuring, and Global Development in Ecuador*. University Park: Pennsylvania State University Press.

MacLeod, Dag. 2004. *Downsizing the State: Privatization and the Limits of Neoliberal Reform in Mexico*. University Park: Pennsylvania State University Press.

Mazzarella, William. 2003. *Shovelling Smoke: Advertising and Globalization in Contemporary India*. Durham, NC: Duke University Press.

Migdal, Joel. 2001. *State in Society: Studying How States and Societies Transform and Constitute One Another.* Cambridge: Cambridge University Press.

Mitchell, Timothy. 1991. "The Limits of the State: Beyond Statist Approaches and Their Critics." *American Political Science Review* 85, no. 1 (March 1991): 77–96.

———. 2002. *Rule of Experts: Egypt, Techno-Politics, Modernity.* Berkeley: University of California Press.

Newman, Janet. 2013. "Spaces of Power: Feminism, Neoliberalism and Gendered Labor." *Social Politics: International Studies in Gender, State and Society* 20, no. 2: 200–221.

Omi, Michael, and Howard Winant. 2014. *Racial Formation in the United States.* 3rd ed. New York: Routledge.

Ong, Aihwa. 1987. *Spirits of Resistance and Capitalist Discipline: Factory Women in Malaysia.* Albany: State University of New York Press.

———. 2006. *Neoliberalism as Exception: Mutations in Citizenship and Sovereignty.* Durham, NC: Duke University Press.

Peck, Jamie, and Adam Tickell. 2002. "Neoliberalising Space." *Antipode* 34, no. 3: 380–404.

Piketty, Thomas. 2014. *Capital in the Twenty-First Century.* Trans. Arthur Goldhammer. Cambridge, MA: Belknap Press of Harvard University Press.

Prügl, Elisabeth. 2015. "Neoliberalising Feminism." *New Political Economy* 20, no. 4: 614–31.

Rajagopal, Arvind. 2001. "Thinking about the New Middle Class: Gender, Advertising and Politics in an Age of Globalisation." In *Signposts: Gender Issues in Post-Independence India,* ed. Rajeswari Sunder Rajan, 57–99. New Brunswick, NJ: Rutgers University Press.

Reddy, Chandan. 2011. *Freedom with Violence: Race, Sexuality, and the U.S. State.* Durham, NC: Duke University Press.

Rottenberg, Catherine. 2014. "The Rise of Neoliberal Feminism." *Cultural Studies* 28, no. 3: 418–37.

Runyon, Anne Sisson, and Spike V. Peterson. 2013. *Global Gender Issues in the New Millennium.* Boulder, CO: Westview Press.

Sahle, Eunice. 2006. "Gender, States and Markets in Africa." *Studies in Political Economy* 77: 9–32.

Sassen, Saskia. 1996. *Losing Control?: Sovereignty in an Age of Globalization.* New York: Columbia University Press.

Sharma, Aradhana. 2008. *Logics of Empowerment: Development, Gender, and Governance in Neoliberal India.* Minneapolis: University of Minnesota Press.

Sharone, Ofer. 2013. *Unemployment Experiences: Job Searching, Interpersonal Chemistry and Self-Blame.* Chicago: University of Chicago Press.

Soss, Joe, Richard C. Fording, and Sanford Schram. 2011. *Disciplining the Poor: Neoliberal Paternalism and the Persistent Power of Race.* Chicago: University of Chicago Press.

Smith, Dorothy E. 1999. *Writing the Social: Critique, Theory and Investigations.* Toronto: University of Toronto Press.

Spivak, Gayatri Chakravorty. 1996. "Diasporas Old and New: Women in the Transnational World." *Textual Practice* 10, no. 2: 245–69.

Teo, Youyenn. 2010. "Shaping the Singapore Family: Producing the State and Society." *Economy and Society* 39, no. 3: 337–59.

———. 2011. *Neoliberal Morality in Singapore: How Family Policies Make State and Society.* London: Routledge Press.

Tripp, Aili Mari, Myra Marx Ferree, and Christina Ewig, eds. 2013. *Gender, Violence, and Human Security: Critical Feminist Perspectives.* New York: New York University Press.

Wacquant, Loic. 2009. *Punishing the Poor: The Neoliberal Government of Social Insecurity.* Durham, NC: Duke University Press.

2

What's in a Word?

Austerity, Precarity, and Neoliberalism

NANCY A. NAPLES

Following a crash in the U.S. housing market in 2008 and a failure in the financial sector, due in large part to market speculation and unregulated investments, a period of economic decline occurred in the United States that spread to Europe and had further reverberations around the world.[1] In response, local and national governments, either voluntarily or in response to national or international pressure, instituted austerity measures that included cutbacks in social welfare programs, reduction of public employment, and privatization of public lands and services. Some countries voluntarily adopted austerity measures to counter the effects, while other European nations were forced to do so by extra-local institutional pressures. In both cases, implementation of austerity measures was met with strong opposition and protests (see, e.g., Flesher Fominava and Cox 2013). Beginning in Greece and surfacing in Italy and Spain, the public demanded that large banks and other corporate entities should be held accountable for their part in deepening the economic crisis. Questions also arose about the viability of the European banking system and the euro that continue to be debated.

Austerity policies implemented in Europe and the United States mirrored measures imposed by the International Monetary Fund (IMF) and the World Bank under the terms of structural adjustment to address debt and other economic problems encountered in Latin America and Africa. While structural adjustment was defined as necessary to bring the countries in these regions into the global capitalist economy, austerity measures instituted in Europe and many cities in the United States were constructed as a short-term solution to an "abnormal" economic crisis. In effect, austerity policies masked how the "crisis" was a result of the discourse and practices of neoliberal economic policies. Neoliberalism as an economic ideology and practice rose to prominence in the late twentieth century and displaced Keynesian economics that, among other principals, called for a role of the state in supporting workers during difficult economic times. Instead, neoliberalism, as a form of laissez-faire economics, promoted policies of free trade, privatization, deregulation, and cutbacks in the welfare state and government services more generally.

In both the north and the south, structural adjustment and austerity policies furthered the precarity of those already living on the economic edges of advanced global capitalism and deepened economic inequality. The growing poverty of the middle classes in economically wealthy countries, the eviction of small farmers in poorer countries, and the destruction of the environment through mining and other environmental practices of capitalism lead further to the economic and social dispossession and "expulsion" of vulnerable populations (Sassen 2014, 3).

Austerity discourse simultaneously undergirds and further justifies policies that lead to the expulsion and precarity of a growing number of people who have become disposable in contemporary capitalism. Sanford Schram (2015) explains that "the resultant manufactured austerity did nothing but accelerate the trend whereby growing numbers of people who suffered diminished economic prospects were made all the more subject to disciplinary practices of the state that punished them for their failure to succeed in a transformed economy" (4). Nowhere is this more apparent than in the criminalization of homelessness in cities like Denver, Colorado. Christina Heatherton (2014 and this volume) details the role of police action and warrants that further hastened the dispossession of residents in poor urban areas that deepen the "cleavages of the neoliberal city" which "are built upon existing and heavily entrenched race and class divisions" (5). Schram further argues that, "in fact, neoliberalism begets precarity, where the push to marketize everything and market volatility become pervasive problems people must constantly confront. Increasingly, people are expected to absorb more of the shocks of market volatility in a neoliberal society where everything more and more operates according to market logic" (71).

Focusing on a comparative analysis of Europe and the United States, I highlight when and how localized austerity discourse renders invisible the larger discursive scaffolding of neoliberalism[2] as well as the material effects that austerity measures have on different groups within nations and differences across nations. In this way austerity discourse both depends on and serves to reproduce inequalities. I also examine evidence of resistance to the marketized logic of austerity. Resistance has developed contradictory paths that include populist movements on the left and the right as seen, for example, in the contrasts between Occupy Wall Street and the Tea Party in the United States and the rise of leftist parties such as Podemos in Spain as well as right-wing parties like the Freedom Party in Austria (see, for example, Judis 2016). It has also led to the ouster of diverse political parties in Portugal and Greece as well as a successful mobilization in the United Kingdom that has led to a vote to withdraw from the European Union (see, for example, Sims 2016) and, to a certain extent, Donald Trump's successful campaign for president of the United States (Judis 2016).[3]

Toward a Materialist Feminist Analysis of Austerity Discourse

This chapter considers the following questions: What are the material effects of austerity discourse as it shapes government policies, increasing inequality, and gendered experiences? How are different people affected by austerity measures and which people might, in fact, benefit from it? What forms of resistance are evident and how effective have they been in calling attention to the limits of austerity and related neoliberal economic policies? Sources of data include a review of economic debates on austerity in academic journals and popular press during the years 2005–15, public official statements related to austerity, and select economic data for different countries for the years spanning the economic crisis, 2005–15.

Drawing on a materialist feminist analysis of austerity discourse, I foreground the dynamics of gender, race, nation, and class to put into sharp relief the "relations of ruling" (Smith 1999)[4] that contour the everyday lives of diverse individuals, families, communities, and nations during and following the Great Recession of 2008–9. This approach allows for a comparison of the role of the state in the United States and Europe as well as considers the intersection of the media, state actors, and economic analysts in constructing and reproducing post-liberal discourse.[5]

My argument focuses on three central areas of analysis. First, I begin with a discussion of structural adjustment—how these policies landed in the lives of women in Latin America and Africa and how lessons from these experiences went unheeded as states implemented austerity discourse and policies. I then flesh out the different ways structural adjustment was conceptualized and implemented in different parts of the world, as well as the similarities and differences between the discourse on austerity in the United States and different countries in Europe. Second, I analyze the "relations of ruling" that shape austerity discourses through an analysis of media narratives, policy debates, and academic research. I examine how these discourses produce and mask inequalities in austerity and in state approaches to economic "recovery." Finally, I examine the forms of resistance evident from 2010 to 2015 in both the United States and Europe in response to these relations of ruling and the inequalities they produce.

Shift from Structural Adjustment to Austerity Discourse

Austerity policies are part and parcel of neoliberal structural adjustment policies (SAPs) that have effectively changed the economies of many non-Western countries. Structural adjustment of countries in the southern regions included, among other things, shifting agricultural production from diverse crops for local consumption to mass production of crops for export. The policies have devastated local communities by displacing residents from their homes and removing access to lands needed for feeding families (Bello 1994; Gladwin 1991). They have ended or interrupted the development of government support for the poor and propelled the outmigration of many to service wealthier folks or to work in other types of low-waged labor in different parts of the world.

What is the significance of the shift from structural adjustment as a framing of policies designed to support capitalism at the expense of the broader population in one set of countries to austerity as a government policy in another set of countries that is designed to achieve similar goals? To begin with, attention is now paid to nation-states in the global north that were defined as "developed" or at least existing closer to the center than postcolonial or "developing" nations that were defined as peripheral to the capitalist economy (to borrow from world systems terminology). But the discursive shift also seems tied to the assertion that economies in the so-called third world countries are structurally unsound and therefore need structural adjustments to help refocus their economies in order to better fit into the global capitalist market. Suggesting that the structures of the United States and other developed capitalist economies were systematically unsound would challenge the entire discursive scaffolding for neoliberalism. Policy approaches for austerity are presented as short-term ones that are needed to "adjust" to crises that are not attributed to capitalism as an economic system. This contrasts with SAPs imposed on the countries in the south that were designed to bring so-called peripheral economies into the capitalist world economy. The problem of debt, which is produced, in large measure, by relations of ruling and inequality of access to resources and economic sustainability, surfaces as the driving force justifying the need for structural adjustment and austerity policies.

The shift in discourse from structural adjustment as the dominant framing for economic restructuring to austerity elides the parallels between economic policy in the south and the north. In effect, it produces the image that, for the most part, countries in the north are structurally sound economically and that the problems that erupt are unusual and are a consequence of failure of governance or weaknesses in economic competitiveness rather than a failure of neoliberal economics. While structural adjustment held out neoliberal economics as the solution to economic failure in the south, contemporary austerity policies applied in the northern context masks the failure of neoliberal economic policy.

Neoliberal Structural Adjustment of Women's Lives

Feminist economics has long noted the negative effects on women's lives. In fact, female-headed households were the most negatively affected by the IMF's and World Bank's imposition of structural adjustment on states in the global south. Julius O. Ihonvbere (1995) summarizes the findings from studies of SAPs in Africa. He found that structural adjustment "increased social and economic burdens of vulnerable groups—women, youths, children, and the unemployed" (134–35). These effects were felt in diverse countries such as Nigeria, Zambia, and Trinidad and Tobago. Some of the current findings about growing inequality within northern countries and the ongoing vulnerability of women and others who are economically marginal to the capitalist economy were presaged in feminist economic analysis. Lourdes Benería and Breny Mendoza (1995) discuss the effects of structural adjustment in Honduras, Mexico, and Nicaragua and note that the international financial community declared the financial crisis, which was the basis for structural adjustment in Latin America, over in the early 1990s. However, they conclude, "the legacy of the crisis continues to be felt in countries with improved economic indicators, such as Mexico, Chile and Argentina" (54) in the mid-1990s.

Feminist analysis of structural adjustment reveals the diversity across nations in the implementation and effects of economic and social policy that mirror contemporary implementation of austerity policies. For example, Jennifer Ball (2004) highlights the diversity of approaches to structural adjustment that contributes to variations in women's relative employment, among other measures. She also focuses attention on Latin America and found that "countries with less orthodox adjustment policies appear to have had greater growth in women's relative employment than countries with more orthodox [neoliberal] policies" (974).[6] She concludes that "SAPs are not gender neutral"; however, "it is possible to choose policies that will promote economic growth while not making the most vulnerable groups in society worse off, and this may mean that the extreme neoliberalism in structural adjustment—as has long been suspected by feminist and other heterodox economics—is inappropriate" (984).

Despite the lessons that could be learned from these and many other feminist analyses of SAPs in the south, governments and neoliberal economists turned to similar policies when faced with the economic crisis that occurred in the United States and Europe during the late 2000s. The comparative approach reveals the extent to which discourse is relational, in that certain local or national economies are constructed as more or less economically vulnerable, not as a function of a broad failure of neoliberal economic policy but as individual failures of governance or ineffective engagement in a neoliberal capitalist economy. These constructions are both a consequence of material relations of ruling that contour the economies in different locales and further contribute to austerity policies. These interactions intensify the material effects of the policies as they shape women's lives and those of others by the intersection of gender, race, class, and nation.

Austerity Policies: Structural Adjustment in the United States and Europe

The discursive move from SAPs to austerity decenters the neoliberal arguments for structural adjustment and foregrounds one that renders invisible or takes for granted the neoliberal economic policies that shape both forms of economic intervention. As was evident in the implementation of structural adjustment in the south, there was variation between the discourse and practices of austerity across and within the United States and the European Union. This variation both reveals and furthers the hierarchies of communities and nations as some cities (in the U.S. case) and nations (in the E.U. case) that are deemed economically unviable must seek financial assistance extra-locally. Therefore, some cities and nations are forced by economic necessity to submit to harsh austerity measures in exchange for assistance from external forces while others are able to retain more central control over what type of measures are needed and how quickly they need to be implemented.

The extent to which local states in the United States could resist adopting austerity measures whole cloth was shaped by previous fiscal challenges. Imposition of austerity policies affected the ability of some major U.S. cities to function. In addition to the most notable case of Detroit, which filed bankruptcy in 2013, at least eight other municipalities have declared bankruptcy since 2010, including San Bernardino and Stockton, California; Harrisburg, Pennsylvania; and Boise County, Idaho (Governing the States and Localities 2016). Many more have experienced financial emergencies (BlackNews.com 2013) that lasted well past the "recovery." Little has been made of the link to discrimination that has fueled the precarity of those living in these urban areas.

The banking and housing crises in the United States and the growing national debt, coupled with the inability of the U.S. Congress to manage it, led to the downgrading of its triple A credit rating (Blyth 2013). This event had ripple effects elsewhere in the world, given the centrality of the U.S. currency to the world economy (see, e.g., Schneider 2013). The European market was facing similar challenges that might be easily traced to the global integration of finance, although each European country has its own unique history and unequal standings within the European Union. Debates about the expense of the welfare state in many

European states were well underway at this point; however, fiscal conservatives used this new economic crisis as an opportunity to further these efforts.

Circular reasoning and rationalizations for cuts in government services and social assistance have been mobilized in different contexts to further the devolution of the state's role in providing a social safety net or ensure the health and well-being of its citizenry. Single mothers, the elderly, and people with disabilities are among the most vulnerable under this scenario (see, e.g., Estes and Newcomer 1983). It is inextricably tied to the neoliberal agenda that, along with the cutbacks in social support, includes deregulation of capital, acceleration of the privatization of public services, and attacks on unionization. Austerity discourse draws strength from the discursive frames that have propelled neoliberalism to a hegemonic approach to economic globalization and many national policy agendas (Blyth 2013).

For this analysis, I began by identifying all newspaper articles and editorials in twelve major English-language newspapers using the terms "structural adjustment," "austerity," "debt crisis," "housing crisis," and "bail-out" for the years 2005–15. I did a second search to see when and in what context protests were reported in articles that mentioned these terms.[7] While these observations were illuminating in their own right, it was necessary to closely analyze the context and application of "austerity" as a discursive accomplishment within different articles. In order to do so, a sample of articles was chosen for close analysis. Given its international coverage, I chose to limit the in-depth analysis of austerity discourse to the *International Herald Tribune* (renamed the *International New York Times* in 2013).[8]

While governments across Europe adopted austerity policies in response to the Great Recession, the shape and depth of the cutbacks varied across the continent, much as SAPs did in Latin American and Africa (Ball 2004; Carmody 1998; Emeagwali 1995). However, relatively few articles surveyed in the *International Herald Tribune/International New York Times* used the term "structural adjustment" anywhere in the text during the time frame 2005–15. When the term was used, it was generally not the leading framework but, rather, one among a list of general features that needed to be reformed in order to respond to financial crisis.

Greece is one of many European countries that exist at the periphery of the European Union (see, for example, Castle 2010). Despite popular protest against austerity measures, Prime Minister Alexis Tsipras reluctantly accepted economic changes required by Greece's creditors (Alderman 2015). In return for a three-year bailout, the writer reported, the terms included "a series of new taxes and *structural adjustments* throughout the Greek economy" (10; italics added). Greek citizens faced increasing cuts in the pension system, rising age of retirement, phasing out of support for poor pensioners, and increased pensioners' contributions to health insurance. However, in contrast to demands that were possible for countries in the south, it was reported that Tsipras also pressed for an increase in the corporate tax rate. Despite the general similarity to Latin American and African SAPs and the inclusion of "structural adjustment" in the narrative, the article is framed through the lens of "austerity policies."

The discursive framing of structural adjustment for European countries with a stronger economic base differs in both tone and content. For example, in a 2015 article in the *International New York Times*, the journalist Neil Irwin differentiates Finland from Greece as follows: "Like Greece, it is geographically far from the core West European powers of Britain, France and Germany. And like Greece, it uses the euro currency. But unlike Greece, it is a model of sound governance and responsible use of debt" (Irwin 2015, 18). However, Irwin notes, "Finland's economy is also not doing so great, with an 11.8 percent unemployment rate and with its gross domestic product contracting in each of the last three years" (18). He reports that "a number of commentators have looked at Finland's current economic troubles as a clear sign that what ails the Eurozone is far deeper than profligate spending by the Greeks" (18).

Devaluation of the currency is among the strategies that were being considered to deal with the downturn in Finland's economy. However, as reported in the article, the minister responded, "Devaluation is a little like doping in sports," he said. "It gives you perhaps a short-term boost, but in the long run, it's not beneficial. Just like anyone else, we need structural reform, structural adjustment; we need to increase our competitiveness, and a little bit of luck" (19). In contrast to structural adjustment as a master frame that drove a series of major changes in the economy in Latin American and Africa under externally imposed structural adjustment polices, it functions rhetorically in this article on Finland with little specificity. "Structural reform" leads the sentence implying more modest interventions. The two strategies mentioned (increasing "competitiveness, and a little bit of luck") are also far from the structural changes imposed by the IMF and World Bank on African and Latin American economics.

The diagnosis of weakness in competitiveness (rather than a weakness of neoliberal capitalism) surfaced in a number of articles. In a central bankers' conference in Jackson Hole, Wyoming, in 2011, Jean-Claude Trichet, president of the European Central Bank (E.C.B.) from 2003 to 2011, asserted "that Europe's problems are fundamentally a question of which governments have taken steps to become competitive and which have not" (Ewing 2011, n.p.). States are positioned against one another in levels of competitiveness as one manifestation of how relations of ruling construct inequalities of nations. According to reporter Jack Ewing, Trichet highlighted this complicated relationship among European states and explained that "Greece, Portugal and Ireland, in particular, had progressively lost competitiveness vis-à-vis their main trading partners in the euro area" (Ewing 2011, n.p.). He pointed out that "Germany is now an example of how big the dividends of reform can be if structural adjustment is made a strategic priority and implemented with sufficient patience" (Ewing 2011, n.p.). His explanation foregrounds the ruling relations within the European Union and the complicated relationship between member states that reinforces inequalities among nations. Consider another example. Christine Lagarde, managing director of the IMF, stressed the need for governments to take quick action "to find a balance between cutting debt and promoting growth" and argued that "banks, whose fragility is a key element of the crisis in Europe, should be recapitalized—forcibly and with public funds, if need be" (Ewing 2011, n.p.). Largarde's assertion, however, does not address the effect on people's lives.

The erasure of the effect of such policies on people's lives is reinforced by particular public narratives on austerity that emphasize personal responsibility for debt and other "bad" financial decisions, a theme that elides easily to state actors (see, e.g., Schram 2015). In a 2015 article on neoliberalism, debt, and austerity, Shawn Cassiman paraphrases *New York Times* conservative columnist David Brooks by saying that "a failure to pay debts is evidence of moral failure." Cassiman notes that according to Brooks "this failure exists at both the national and personal level and is a result of profligate spending at the government level, and living beyond one's means at the individual level" (20).[9]

Discursive Constructions of the "Debt Crisis"

In *Austerity: The History of a Dangerous Idea*, Mark Blyth cogently argues that neoliberal and libertarian policy makers in Europe and the United States have convinced many of the polity on both sides of the Atlantic that government spending is reckless and wasteful and has contributed to the current economic crisis. Those economic and political elites who believe in the need to ensure that the free market remains free from any oversight used the economic crisis to justify cutting government budgets and to shift concern from the fiscal crisis prompted by unregulated and unchecked banking practices to the state's budget deficit.

Construction of the so-called debt crisis in the United States and the United Kingdom as one of the driving forces for austerity measures created the grounds for swift government action to cut expenses through withdrawal of support for social welfare and public employment, and increased privatization of government programs and services. One of the first arguments used to justify cutting government expenditures was that rising deficits would undermine the economic viability of national governments. However, as Blyth (2013) points out, as recently as 2002, the Italian public-sector debt "was 105.7 of GDP and no one cared," and "in 2009, it was almost exactly the same figure and everyone cared" (5). What changed? In the U.S. context, attention was initially focused on a housing crisis that was then tied to a banking crisis and the financial collapse of Wall Street. These interrelated crises were overshadowed by what became known as the "debt crisis." How did managing the debt (which in the United States was accumulated, not in small part by fighting two wars abroad and tax exemptions for corporations and wealthy Americans) become the problem? Many critical analysts argue that the economic crisis became a new opportunity to rechannel neoliberal fiscal practices and focus new attention on the deficit as a potential site for intervention (Cassiman 2015; MacLeavy 2011; Miller and Hokenstad 2014).

External pressure on Italy to lower their debt came with expectations of harsh austerity measures. In a 2011 article in the *International Herald Tribune*, Landon Thomas Jr. (2011) reported that despite ongoing austerity measures undertaken in Italy, the European Union had reasons for concern: "Italy's overall debt level of 126 percent of G.D.P. is one of the highest in the world and its failure to emerge from a decade-long slump suggests it will be harder than ever for Rome to service that debt. But, as Stephen King, chief economist at HSBC, points out, Italy is one of the few countries whose debt levels have remained essentially unchanged since the onset of the euro in 1999" (14). The fact that Italy had already imposed severe austerity measures on their population and stabilized its debt while other countries experienced an increased debt during this period did not exempt it from undergoing "an [additional] austerity cure" (14). As Thomas reported, economists did point out the danger in pushing for more austerity measures: "Some economists warn that making them cut even further could push their teetering economies over the edge. And unlike Greece or Portugal, Italy and Spain are so big that any default would probably shatter the euro zone for good" (14). The contradictions in austerity discourse logic pointed out in this short article include the following:

> Italy is on track to bring its deficit down to 3.9 percent of gross domestic product this year and, under further pressure from Germany and the E.C.B. last week, Prime Minister Silvio Berlusconi said more cuts would be brought forward with the aim of balancing Italy's budget by 2013. When taking into account its financial position apart from interest on existing debt, the Italian budget is actually in surplus, to the tune of 2 percent of G.D.P. This so-called primary budget status is generally considered the most useful way of measuring the financial health of a country. (14)

After acknowledging the inconsistencies in the application of austerity measures, the reporter concludes that the economies of Italy and Spain "have been hurt by their coddled, high-cost labor forces" (14). Since the goal is set at "restor[ing] industrial competitiveness" and having a balanced budget is defined as central to this goal, "there is no way for such countries to avoid a painful deflationary adjustment in wages"

(14). In this case, it is clear that neoliberal economic logic is a driving force in justifying austerity measures even when contradictions are acknowledged. The needs of industry trump the needs of the workers. Furthermore, achieving a balanced government budget is defined as essential to "industrial competitiveness." In closing, the reporter also affirms the hierarchy of nations within the European Union and the danger that Italy and other southern European countries pose to the stability of the eurozone.

> "There is this fear in Germany that countries like Italy are just not stability oriented," said Peter Bofinger, a German economist who is on a panel of experts advising the German government. The feeling is, he added, "that they just need more market discipline." In his monthly news conference in Frankfurt last week, Jean-Claude Trichet, president of the E.C.B., lost his usual central-banker cool to deliver an impassioned message to Italy and other countries about cutting spending. "The key to everything is that governments stay ahead of the curve—with fiscal policy and structural reforms," he said. "It is absolutely essential. Governments that do this and control their costs will be rewarded." (14)

Here blame is cast on the lack of market discipline and overpaid workers rather than on the deregulation of markets and banking in the north, most especially in the United States, that helped drive the "fiscal crisis."

While many feminist and progressive economists identified the link between the measures adopted to deal with the recession in the United States and the decades-long march of neoliberal policy making, fiscal conservatives and their well-financed think tanks developed discursive strategies that, in many quarters, successfully delinked the current efforts from the past. The construction of the debt ceiling as a "crisis" was one of many interconnected themes that discursively distracted from focus on the continuity of the neoliberal agenda. One clear illustration of the contradiction within austerity discourse and the relations of ruling that the discourse supports is the resistance to increasing taxes on wealthy individuals and corporations. Instead, faced with the need to increase the debt ceiling in the United States, one of the discursive strategies used to gain wider support or at least minimize opposition was that as a nation we needed to balance our national checkbook much like households should in order to become fiscally responsible. Note this ad from the 2014 campaign to reelect Ohio State Republican Representative Dave Hall: "Balancing Ohio's budget is essential to Ohio's economic health and strength. It's why I supported closing an unsustainable $8 billion hole in Ohio's budget. By tightening our belts and making the tough decisions, Ohio's 'Rainy Day Fund' successfully grew from $0.89 cents to $1.5 billion. In our recovering economy, if families are required to live on a tight budget, so should our government." Despite this message, many economists pointed out that the U.S. government operates in a much different fashion than individual families. As individuals, we can't print our own money when we are running short of funds or raise additional funds through taxes, or manipulate interest rates. Furthermore, Jeffrey Michler (2013) notes, "While household austerity only affects the household, government austerity affects all households." For example, he explains, the loss of government jobs makes these workers "austere" and cuts their ability to consume and, in turn, lowers their contribution to the gross domestic product (GDP).

> While the adoption of austerity by a single household has no noticeable effect on GDP, the adoption of austerity at a national level can drive a country back into recession. When a household adopts austerity it reduces expenditure with no effect on its income. When a government adopts austerity, the resulting recession reduces the income of a nation, thus reducing tax revenue (government income), and requiring further austerity measures in order to balance the books. National austerity can become a race to the bottom, as austerity in expenditure results in reduced taxes or income, which leads to further austerity measures. (N.p.)

Critical economic analyses also conclude that austerity measures do not do what they are supposed to do—namely, provide economic stability. For example, Greece's debt to GDP ratio increased from 106 to 170 percent in 2012 despite the imposition of austerity budget cuts (Blyth 2013).

One of the other discursive strategies that also justified the passage of austerity policies in the United States was the construction of a collective "we," as in "we must all sacrifice for the greater good." In one clear example, New Jersey Governor Chris Christie suggested that teachers "chip in" a portion of their salaries to help balance the state's budget.

> Christie is the Hot New Thing in the group [called "the austerity caucus"] because he not only has ideas to cut deficits but he's found a political strategy to enact them, even with a Democratic Legislature. One of the keys to cutting budgets, he says, is that "almost nothing can be sacrosanct." Inheriting an $11 billion deficit, he spread cuts across every agency. He even had to cut education spending by $820 million but said any individual district could avoid cuts if the teachers there would be willing to chip in 1.5 percent of their salaries to help pay for health benefits (few districts took advantage of this). (Brooks 2010)

Such calls for economic sacrifice that presume a collective "we" target less privileged social groups and elide the role of the state in securing economic stability for the citizenry.

Who and What Are Heard in the Economic Debates?

The shift from a Keynesian or corporatist framing of the role of the state to one that diminishes the state's role in ensuring citizens' basic economic needs was hastened by the work of two Harvard economists, Carmen Reinhart and Kenneth Rogoff (2009), who produced a study in which they concluded that countries with debt burdens over 90 percent of their total economy have slower economic growth. They describe their findings in an *International Herald Tribune* article: "In May 2010, we published an academic paper, 'Growth in a Time of Debt.' Its main finding, drawing on data from 44 countries over 200 years, was that in both rich and developing countries, high levels of government debt—specifically, gross public debt equaling 90 percent or more of the nation's annual economic output—was associated with notably lower rates of growth" (Reinhart and Rogoff 2013, 7). Many U.S. politicians enthusiastically cited Reinhart and Rogoff's study in support of the budget cuts (Waldron 2013). For example, Republican Representative Paul Ryan of Wisconsin exclaimed in June 2011, "Economists who have studied sovereign debt tell us that letting total debt rise above 90 percent of GDP creates a drag on economic growth and intensifies the risk of a debt-fueled economic crisis" (n.p.).

But Reinhart and Rogoff's research was methodologically flawed (Lowrey 2013). University of Massachusetts, Amherst, economists

Thomas Herndon, Michael Ash, and Robert Pollin (2014) ran the analysis a second time and corrected for numerous mistakes by Reinhart and Rogoff, including leaving off a few countries at the beginning of the alphabet (Australia, Austria, Belgium, Canada, and Denmark) and a few significant years. Their revised analysis demonstrates that "the most spectacular results from the Reinhart and Rogoff paper disappear" (Alexander 2013, n.p.). High debt is still statistically correlated with "somewhat lower growth" but is much less than Reinhart and Rogoff found, and "there are lots of exceptions to the rule" (n.p.). Herndon, Ash, and Pollin (2014) conclude that the "combination of the collapse of the empirical result that high public debt is inevitably associated with greatly reduced GDP growth and the weakness of the theoretical mechanism under current conditions, . . . render the Reinhart and Rogoff point close to irrelevant for current public policy debate" (n.p.). In their defense, Reinhart and Rogoff (2013) explain: "The politically charged discussion, especially sharp in the past week or so, has falsely equated our finding of a negative association between debt and growth with an unambiguous call for austerity" (14). They argue further that instead of a clarion call for austerity, "Our consistent advice has been to avoid withdrawing fiscal stimulus too quickly, a position identical to that of most mainstream economists." They conclude that, "in short: Many countries around the world have extraordinarily high public debts by historical standards, especially when medical and old-age support programs are taken into account. Resolving these debt burdens usually involves a transfer, often painful, from savers to borrowers. This time is no different, and the latest academic kerfuffle should not divert our attention from that fact" (14). However, what they saw as "academic kerfuffle" was taken up by influential policy makers to support austerity measures that had negative material effects on diverse individuals, families, and communities. Pollin (2013) summarizes his critique of political decisions based on Reinhart and Rogoff's faulty analysis, noting, "Many austerity hawks in the United States view this historical moment as an opportunity to eviscerate the public sector, labor unions, social insurance, and other basic social protections. To date, as we have seen, the austerity agenda has succeeded over the 2010–2011 'recovery' years in delivering sharply rising incomes for the richest one percent of households while incomes for everyone else have stagnated or declined" (776). In response to the revised findings, University of London economist Daniel Hamermesh observed, "I don't think jobs were destroyed because of this but it provides an intellectual rationalisation for things that affect how people think about the world. And how people think about the world, especially politicians, eventually affects how the world works" (Alexander 2013). However, it is not just any science or any academic research that gets the kind of traction that Reinhart and Rogoff's study did. It is, rather, a matter of how well their findings and interpretations (regardless of how close to the actual, and possibly more nuanced, conclusions) resonated with a wider political discourse on government spending and the role of the state.

In the United States, policy prescriptions for reduction in government debt replaced past government and economic policy responses to recessions. As Kevin Drum (2013) notes, "After every other recent recession, government spending has continued rising steadily throughout the recovery, providing a backstop that prevented the economy from sliding backward. . . . yet government spending at all levels—state, local, and federal combined—has declined 7 percent since the publication of Reinhart and Rogoff's paper" (n.p.).[10] Drum (2016) extends the analysis and explains that the United States is now spending 5 percent less than in 2009: "It's now 26 quarters since the official end of the Great Recession and total government spending is *still* below its 2009 level. This is entirely unlike previous recessions, in which we spent our way to recovery. After 26 quarters, Reagan was spending 19 percent more than in November 1982, when his recession ended. Clinton (and the Gingrich congress) were spending 6 percent more. Bush was spending a whopping 26 percent more" (n.p.). Cutbacks in government spending do not land evenly in the lives of all U.S. residents. The specific individuals, communities, and populations whose lives are economically restructured by the loss of government services, direct support, and public employment are less visible in aggregate reports of inequality and poverty. In the next section, I highlight the ways in which austerity discourse and policy deepens ongoing inequality.

Inequality in Austerity

Broad, sweeping analyses that do acknowledge the limits of austerity policy and neoliberalism more generally fail to address the specific inequalities that they produce. For example, another publication that received significant attention far beyond policy and academic circles was Thomas Piketty's (2014) book, *Capital in the Twenty-First Century.* Timothy Patrick Moran (2015) notes the limits of Piketty's analysis for capturing the complexity of the inequalities that follow from capitalism: "For a book 'seeking to understand the global distribution of wealth,' *Capital* is really a book concerning inequality within rich countries, and even more narrowly about the rapidly rising inequality occurring within the very top of the income distribution in rich countries" (868). Moran points out that "the vast majority of wealth differentiation in the world exists between countries, not within them" (869). But even within countries, different groups pay different prices for capitalist economic policies. The elderly, women, racial minorities, immigrants, and others who live at the periphery of capitalist economies are especially hard hit by both structural adjustment and austerity policies.

The globalizing narrative about austerity and the "debt crisis" too often masks the way in which these cuts disproportionately land in the lives of certain workers, women, the elderly, and youth. For example, according to a report by the Council of Europe, "young people have been one of the groups hardest hit by the economic crisis in Europe" (n.p.). Youth unemployment doubled from the highest average in the European Union, and countries like Greece and Spain showed unemployment levels over 50 percent. The working class was also hard hit by austerity measures (see, e.g., Hersh 2013). However, the middle class took center stage in many of the debates on the housing crisis and debt crisis in the United States. Of course, they had long disappeared as a legitimate political concern. In a previous article (Naples 2013), I reviewed the shifting frames from the 1960s to contemporary debates on social welfare programs. For the most part, the poor are nowhere to be found in arguments about the social and economic costs of fiscal crises. As I conclude,

This "symbolic annihilation" (Gerbner and Gross 1976) invites indifference to the structures of economic inequality. Except in the organizing efforts of anti-poverty organizations, discourses centered the middle class without addressing concerns of the poor. The discourses on the U.S. housing crisis reflect this finding. For example, foreclosures received significantly more attention than evictions. Some evictions occurred as a result of middle class landlords' bad investments (Desmond 2012). Even progressive legislators failed to include Medicaid as a program they sought to preserve (see, for example, Franken 2011). As Raymond Williams (1976) explains, the stratifying class discourse places the middle class in a hierarchal relationship to the poor, which limits the ways middle class citizens understand shared interests with working class citizens. (141).

The effect of austerity measures is acutely evident in urban areas that were already reeling from deindustrialization, high rates of unemployment, racial segregation, decline in the value of housing stock, and crumbling infrastructure (Jimenez 2009; Miller and Hokenstad 2014). In July 2012, the mayor of Scranton, Pennsylvania, cut the salary of all the city's employees to the minimum wage of $7.25 per hour.[11] The measure was necessary, officials said, due to the decline in the tax base and decrease in revenue from the state (Larson 2012). As *Dissent* reporter Ann Larson (2012) notes, "Increasing debt loads, along with other neoliberal policies demanding that municipalities do more with less, put cities under enormous pressure to promote private economic growth in lieu of spending public funds on public goods" (n.p.). These strategies contributed to "controversial development strategies such as declaring a parcel of land 'blighted' to allow it to be seized by eminent domain and auctioned to the highest bidder" and "leasing public assets to the private sector" (n.p.).

Consequences for Women

Along numerous measures, researchers find that women in both so-called developed and developing countries face the most negative consequences from state-imposed austerity measures (Deen 2013). Yet, gender analysis is most prominently missing from most economic analysis of the effects of austerity measures (Abramovitz 2012; Asthana 2010). When gender analyses are conducted, however, it is unsurprising that they find gender effects. For example, in ten European countries, women's unemployment was greater than men's in August 2012. The countries surveyed included Spain, Greece, Slovakia, Italy, France, Poland, Slovenia, Czech Republic, Malta, and Luxembourg (Deen 2013). Female unemployment in Greece and Spain was greater than 25 percent.

Women's disproportionate employment in the public sector further increases their vulnerability to austerity measures. The European Women's Lobby (2012) notes that "women constitute on average 69.2% of public sector workers in the EU." In the United Kingdom, "four in 10 working women are in public sector jobs" (Asthana 2010). This sector has suffered massive cuts due to austerity measures (see also Fawcett Society 2012). Austerity measures include cuts in wages, pensions, and social services and higher taxes on consumption which all increase women's economic vulnerability. Black women and ethnic minority women face even greater marginalization as a result of austerity measures. For example, while African Americans represent 10.9 percent of the private sector workforce, they are 12.8 percent of the public sector workforce; since this sector is dominated by women, African American women are further disadvantaged in this regard (Cooper, Gable, and Austin 2012). According to the United Kingdom's All Party Parliamentary Group on Race and Community's (APPG 2012) inquiry into ethnic minority female unemployment, unemployment rates for Black, Pakistani, and Bangladeshi heritage women have been higher than for white women and ethnic minority men for the decades proceeding the Great Recession. They are especially vulnerable to discrimination in the job interview process and in the workplace. Their unemployment and discrimination have accelerated as a result of the austerity measures adopted during the recession.

Women's care work responsibilities lead to their vulnerability from both sides of the work-family equation; as workers they are more likely to lose their jobs as a result of austerity measures, and as unpaid caretakers their workload has increased by cutbacks in child care, elder care, and disabilities services. Feminist geographer Julie MacLeavy (2011) further points out how the gendered rhetoric of "duty of care to civil society and the voluntary sector" was used to justify austerity measures (36). The elderly, a disproportionate percentage of whom are women, have also been a target of austerity measures with the imposition of pension reforms and cuts to elder services (Messia 2011).

Another significant dimension that is often missed by more traditional economic analyses relates to the loss of funding for efforts to address gender equity and to support women's organizations (see, e.g., Emejulu and Bassel 2013). The European Women's Lobby (2012) reports that "Gender equality institutions/bodies have been abolished (ES, RO), merged with other institutions (TK, DK, IE, CZ), or had their funding cut in a drastic manner (UK, GR). The erosion of gender equality machinery is an infringement of E.U. and international commitments to women's rights and gender equality" (2).[12] Gains made in establishing programs to fight gender discrimination and domestic violence as well as those providing support for survivors have been rolled back under austerity measures. One of Mimi Abramovitz's most shocking observations of the gender effects of austerity measures was what she describes as the near decriminalization of "domestic violence because the cost of prosecuting it was too high" (2012, 33). This sharply reveals the relations of ruling manifest in austerity policy as the intersection of class dynamics, racial inequality, and gender oppression contribute to women's greater reliance on state programs and state employment and therefore their increased precarity under regimes of austerity. Again, women of color are disproportionately disadvantaged as a result of these intersectional relations of ruling.

Inequality and Resistance in Recovery

Austerity discourse not only justified the restructuring of the state through the continued dismantling of public programs and social support and rendered invisible the increased precarity of many people living in different regions around the world, it also laid the discursive grounds for a focus on a limited measure of economic recovery rather than the structural conditions that produced the crisis. This shaped both public and state responses to the crisis. Instead of viewing the economic crisis as a product of neoliberal economic policy, austerity discourse shifts focus to circumscribed evidence for a presumed recovery from what is defined as an unusual and short-term economic crisis. Limited evidence of a state-defined "recovery" from the 2008–9 crisis includes the reliance on unemployment rates that disappear those who have stopped looking for work, consumer spending indexes that fail to take into account the limited "recovery," and debt repayment that fails to recognize that the price tag was increased precarity for millions of people.

In an article in the *Financial Times* (Bolan and Moore 2014), the reporters note that as Ireland was on the cusp of repaying the debt they owed to the IMF, the "ministers at home queued to deliver the message every Irish person wanted to hear—that seven years of austerity are coming to an end" (n.p.). The deputy prime minister explained that the budget for 2015 "would put 'the historical period of austerity arising from the [bailout] behind us'" (n.p.). These statements increase expectations of recovery that may not be met.

The expectation of a "recovery" and the disappointment at the slow speed by which it is occurring and for whom it benefits has received the attention of some of the most prominent economists, like Larry Summers, who directed Obama's National Economic Council until 2010. He noted that "even if the economy creates 30,000 jobs a month and grows at 4 percent, it would take several years to restore normal conditions" (quoted in Galbraith 2013). The expectation here is that there is something called "normal conditions." As James Galbraith (2013) notes, the use of the word "normal" "signifies a belief that Summers shares with many economists" that the market system trends naturally toward an end state of full production and high employment" (36). Then he asks, "Rather than 'abnormal,' is the present, miserable state of the economy exactly what we should expect from now on?" (37). He concludes that "normality . . . is an economists' illusion, fostered by our exceptional run of happy history over three-quarters of a century, since the Great Depression—coupled with sloppy habits of economic thought" (38). But even in his critique, Galbraith fails to note that there were many people living during the decades following the New Deal who were not so economically "happy."

Both Keynesian and neoliberal economic analyses fail to acknowledge that many households did not share in the economic growth that built a middle class in America. However, as governments declared that the economic crisis was coming to an end, many people expressed frustration at what they saw as a recovery that did not reflect their experiences. In many cases, this contradiction between state-defined recovery and everyday life translated into protests and other forms of resistance.

In the Irish case, newspaper accounts depict a population initially resigned to the austerity measures imposed on them. After years of economic hardship experienced by many sectors, the narrative of resignation shifted as protests erupted following repeated assertions of recovery (see, e.g., Boland and Moore 2014). The contradiction between the claims of recovery and the ongoing hardship experienced by many, followed by the imposition of taxes on basic needs, ignited resistance across Ireland. In March 2015, Suzanne Daley reported, "As the Irish economy rebounds, the [water] tax has stirred nationwide protests at a time when the government has assured them that austerity is over" (1).

> Miranda Lumsden, 43, a single mother of four, had never protested against anything before the Irish government introduced new water fees last summer.
>
> But the prospect of yet another bill arriving in the mail made her angry enough to join a cluster of demonstrators outside Dublin's City Hall recently, even as sleet turned their homemade "We Won't Pay" posters soggy.
>
> "I'm scrimping from week to week as it is," said Ms. Lumsden, pulling her jacket closer. "I've only got my bus fare home to last me the rest of the week." (1)

Daley notes that after expressing "little resistance as their government, grappling with huge debts from the country's failed banks, introduced new taxes and increased old ones, even while laying off workers and cutting health and welfare benefits," the Irish increased their public protest (1). "The prospect of paying for water, which many see as yet another new tax at a time *when the government has assured them that austerity is over*, has prompted a series of mass protests across the country, from Dublin to Cork. Many demonstrators say they have no intention of paying the new fees" (1; italics added). Unlike the optimistic picture painted by Irish politicians, Daley reports, "The most recent figures available show that nearly a third of the population in 2013 was suffering from 'enforced deprivation' characterized by a lack of two or more basic requirements for a comfortable standard of living, such as adequate food, heating or a warm winter coat, up from 13.7 in 2008, before the financial crisis and the recession" (1). Daley concludes her article with the following quote from Paul Murphy, a member of Parliament from the Socialist Party: "A lot of people now see the bailouts of the banks as an ongoing crime." He added, "There is a real sense out there of, 'O.K., is there going to be any recovery for us?'" (1).

Women's resistance was prominent in numerous accounts of protests as illustrated in the following excerpt:

"They're bigger than us but we're angrier," said Despina Kostopoulou, 53, who worked at the Finance Ministry as a cleaning woman for 22 years before she was laid off last fall. In May, a court ruled that she and 396 of her fellow workers were unfairly dismissed. Since then, she has been sleeping in a tent outside the offices, demanding along with her co-workers that the ministry rehire them.

The David and Goliath-style standoff, which features mostly middle-aged women brandishing mops and heckling government officials, has turned the cleaning women into an unlikely symbol of resistance to the austerity measures that Mr. [Antonis] Samaras [prime minister from 2012 to 2015] insists have gradually allowed Greece to resume control of its finances, return to bond markets and report a primary surplus—a budget in the black before debt payments—of some (EURO) 1.5 billion. (Kitsantonis 2013, 1)

Again we see that despite Prime Minster Samaras's assertion of a modest recovery as filtered through the budget and financial sector, it has not trickled down or appeared in the lives of most Greek workers. In fact, this protester lost her job as a direct result of austerity policy that targeted government employees.

Women's Activism and Feminist Interventions

Women have been highly visible in protests against austerity before and after "recovery" was declared (PressTV 2013). In the United States, women mobilized to protest their low wages, lack of benefits, and other workplace inequities in the fast food and retail industries (see, e.g., DeBode 2014). In London, mothers came out to protest closures of child care facilities and related services. Kerrie Hales, single mother of a five-year-old son, explained her decision to join the protest against the proposed shutdown of her son's public day care center: "'I don't know what I'm going to do,' she said. She works full time at a design company, relying on the Camden Square Play Center to pick her son up from school and look after him until 6 p.m. for £4.80 a day because she cannot afford a private nanny. Like many other mothers campaigning against the closure, she does not want to reduce hours at work but acknowledges she might have to" (Benhold 2011, 2). Women also took to the streets in Paris and several other cities across France to challenge austerity measures and workplace discrimination against women, which they argue has intensified "due to the tough government austerity measures" (n.p.). The demonstrators also called for increases in women's salaries and noted the large number of jobs lost by women through cuts "in the traditionally female-dominated government and social service sectors" (n.p.).

Feminist interventions are reported in several newspaper articles sampled. For example, Anna Bird, speaking on behalf of the Fawcett Society, the women's advocacy group in London was quoted on women's negative experiences with austerity: "This is not just individual categories of women losing out, this is structural: This is rolling back gender equality" (Benhold 2011, 2). The problems reported include the finding "that women are likely to bear the brunt of austerity: as public sector employees, as retirees who live longer than men and thus rely more on health care and social security, and as mothers whose decision to work depends on affordable child care." Benhold included results from a British Women's Budget Group's study that "the average British household will lose public services worth 6.8 percent of its income to austerity"; "single female retirees will lose 11.7 percent, and single mothers 18.5 percent" (2). "In those parts of the public sector so far more sheltered from the cuts, nearly three in four of those subject to a pay freeze are women, according to the Women's Budget Group, an independent organization that has been analyzing the gender implications of British budgets since the 1990s. This will probably increase the pay gap, which last year stood at 15.5 percent for women in full-time employment" (2).

As Cynthia Enloe (2013) explains, "taking feminist analysis *seriously* ... means asking where women are in each corner of each recession and why—and *then* continuing to ask those questions month after month, as the economy takes its twists and turns—and *then* translating the investigatory findings into a basis for realistic economic policies" (86). This is a tall order that requires concerted efforts by feminists inside and outside of state and economic institutions. Enloe includes numerous examples of the important work of feminist scholars, activists, and politicians in challenging austerity proposals and policies. After the 2008 economic crash, Icelandic women gained positions in parliament. They worked to elect a feminist as prime minister and promoted women-friendly policies in government and business (80). Feminists working with think tanks such as the Institute for Women's Policy Research (IWPR) in Washington, DC, and the Fawcett Society in Great Britain documented the effects and translated them into policy recommendations. For example, IWPR founder and president, Heidi Hartmann, in collaboration with feminist policy advocates and scholars, effectively intervened in the proposed U.S. federal stimulus package to add a focus on health care and education (93). The original proposal focused only on spending for infrastructures like roads and bridges, which they argued were "masculinized" areas that would not lead to many jobs for women. The relations of ruling within austerity discourse as well as who and what were defined as targets for state "stimulus" is revealed through feminist analysis and challenged through feminist praxis. However, resistance took different forms, reflecting politically right and left responses to state imposed austerity measures, debt relief, and stimulus packages.

Challenging Contradictions between Discourse and Everyday Life in Protests on Left and Right

Austerity measures implemented in Europe and the United States fueled resentment among residents who had either experienced a decline in their standard of living or lost hope in ever achieving it (see, e.g., Flesher and Cox 2013). As standards of living declined for many and many more lost hope that recovery would improve their chances of regaining lost footing or any footing at all, protests expanded and fueled populist movements on the left and right. Nationalist parties and other groups that shifted blame for continued joblessness or underemployment toward immigrants or refugees gained momentum in local and national elections. Left movements also experienced a resurgence and brought to the fore other heated issues such as urban disinvestment, stagnant wages, unemployment, and racial profiling. Starting with similar grievances at the state's management of the economic crisis, protesters channeled their concerns into divergent demands on the state.

Urban protesters in places like Ferguson, Missouri, and Detroit, Michigan, among other cities, have effectively linked collective responses against disinvestment in their cities to police brutality, unemployment, and racism to channel the frustration of Black residents whose lives have become even more austere following the Great Recession (Barone 2014; *Huffington Post* 2011). Labor union activists in Scranton, Pennsylvania, successfully challenged the policies that undermined their ability to earn a living wage (Morgan-Besecker 2013). Demands for the increase of the minimum wage to $15 per hour gained traction and resulted in the increase in wages for workers in California and New York State.

Some municipalities were also able to resist the rollback of local government during this period. In a study of 1,700 U.S. localities, Linda Lobao, Lazarus Adua, and Gregory Hooks (2014) conclude, "When comparing business attraction, social service delivery, and privatization from 2008 to 2011 we did not find that localities are moving toward a wider embrace of market-oriented policies." They conclude that "neoliberal policy has [not] been uniformly ascendant across the United States," and "local states [do not] systematically prioritize business goals and retreat from programs promoting human welfare" (668).

The bailout of U.S. banks and other businesses "too big to fail" was also seen by many people as contradicting the call to balance the federal budget by cutting spending. At the same time, the call for raising taxes on the wealthy (that even some of the wealthy were willing to support [see, for example, Buffett 2011]) failed to gain sufficient support in a divided Congress. Of course, this contradiction did not go unnoticed as both the Occupy movement and Tea Party activists pointed out (see, e.g., Schram 2015). Despite the drastic differences in their approach to taxes and state intervention in the economy, the Tea Party and Occupy movements shared many themes that contributed to mobilization. Both movements expressed anger over the bailouts of banks and other corporations, U.S. tax policy, and the handling of the debt crisis. While the Tea Party called for decreasing debt by cutting entitlement programs, Occupy argued for an increased government investment in addressing economic inequality, including taxing the wealthy. How each movement constructed the problem of debt is instructive in teasing out the different popular responses to austerity and the debt crisis. Occupy's approach calls attention to the structural conditions contributing to debt, while the Tea Party adopts the hegemonic view of debt that holds irresponsible governments and individuals culpable for it (Schram 2015).

Occupy Wall Street protests begun in Manhattan captured the popular imagination of many and quickly spread. Within two months, resistance was evident in cities across the United States. For example, on November 17, 2011, Occupy Detroit conducted "a day of action against austerity measure" with protests against tax breaks for the wealthy and austerity measures (*Huffington Post* 2011, n.p.). The spokesman for Occupy Detroit, Lee Gaddies, told the Detroit radio station WWJ: "When you have a mayor who hasn't created any jobs, but gives tax breaks to millionaires and billionaires to move their businesses to the city and then don't pay any taxes for 15 years—how's that fair to residents who've lived here and are footing that bill for the police and fire and garbage pick-up?" (n.p.).

The Tea Party grew out of a response to President Barack Obama's plan to assist homeowners with mortgages they had taken on and could not pay following the declaration of the housing crisis. Speaking from the Chicago Mercantile Exchange, TV reporter Rick Santelli "burst into a tirade against the Obama administration's nascent foreclosure relief plan: 'The government is rewarding bad behavior!'" and "he invited America's 'capitalists to a Chicago Tea party' to protest measures to 'subsidize the loser's mortgages'" (Skocpol and Williamson 2013, 7). The movement grew through social media and expanded to include calls to police immigrants, protect Second Amendment gun rights, and promote "prolife and traditional family values" (4). They successfully mobilized voters to elect Tea Party members to Congress during the midterm elections in 2010. This election gave the Republican Party control of both houses of Congress and led to blocking judicial nominees and legislation promoted by the Obama administration. Tea Party members of the U.S. Congress fought against government spending and through their anti-state political position, for the most part, promoted an austerity agenda. This is also evident in their anti-immigrant stance, which constructed a scarce economic environment that was threatened by a perceived influx of "illegal aliens" unlawfully accessing public welfare and displacing citizen workers.

Despite its success in the United States, the Tea Party movement did not inspire similar mobilizations in other countries. However, Occupy-inspired movements emerged in different countries across Europe and elsewhere. For example, unlike the narrative told about the lack of resistance in Ireland, as early as 2011 Irish activists engaged in anti-austerity resistance:

> The Irish are not prone to protest, but now more are being organized, inspired by the Occupy movement in the United States.
>
> On a recent frosty night in Dublin, David Johnson, 38, an I.T. consultant, stepped outside a makeshift camp set up by the Occupy Dame Street movement in front of the Central Bank of Ireland.
>
> "This is all new to Ireland," he said, pointing to tarpaulins and protest signs urging the government to boot out the International Monetary Fund and require bondholders to share Irish banks' losses, which have largely been assumed by taxpayers. "The feeling is that the people who can least afford it are the ones shouldering the burden of this crisis," he said. (Alderman 2011, 15)

Mary Naughton (2015) explored the diverse responses to the bailout by the Irish between November 2010 and February 2013. She found that the nature of the protests differed from what was reported on Greece, Portugal, and Spain:

> The majority of protests targeting the bailout have been part of a small, sustained local campaign, taking place in a village in Cork where it is less likely to attract the attention of national and international media due to the proximity effect. The majority of the larger protest events that took place (those numbering about 10,000) tended to address the social consequences of the bailout, such as cuts to hospital services (Save Waterford), third level funding and the difficulties experienced by certain industries. (304)

She explains the difference between the actuality of Irish protest during this period and the general media coverage: "It would be more difficult for journalists writing about Ireland from the outside, lacking an understanding of the nature of participation and protest in Ireland to make the link between these protests and the bailout, and to perceive the Irish as passive" (304).

Resistance also erupted in other cities and towns across Europe and posed a challenge to the short-term view and so-called abnormality of the recent economic crisis (Connolly and Chrisafis 2015; Pfanner 2012). Some activists claimed that the fundamental and faulty assumptions of austerity discourse and policies and, by extension, neoliberalism destabilized the hegemony of global capitalism. The case of Greece seems to illuminate the short-lived effectiveness of mass protests that erupted in 2010, which forestalled the government from signing on to IMF and eurozone nations' demand for the implementation of drastic austerity measures, but when "Athens, staggering under a €300bn debt, found itself locked out of capital markets because of prohibitively high borrowing costs," the government was forced to accept the inevitable (Smith 2010). Yet, resistance continued despite the previous failure to halt the imposition of austerity measures. On November 27, 2014, thousands of Greek workers protested new austerity measures by holding a twenty-four-hour strike (Kitsantonis 2014). With unemployment at 24 percent and household income down by one-third since the IMF, European Central Bank, and the European Commission imposed austerity measures as a condition of financial bailouts, the workers organized against the proposed 2015 budget released by Greece's government. Kitsantonis (2014) notes that the protesters felt "that Greece is being held to tight restrictions while countries like France and Italy were allowed to adopt 2015 budgets that bend or break the rules" (n.p.). Again, we see the way in which relations of ruling shape the hierarchy of nations within Europe and in the context of austerity.

Conclusion

This materialist feminist analysis of austerity demonstrates that discourse does matter but so does the material context in which it is generated and marshalled. It matters how policy debates are framed and who is ignored, marginalized, or demonized in the process. It is also important to track the shifts in discourse to identify the underlying assumptions and themes that are woven together in order to identify contradictions and tensions within divergent discursive contexts and to chronicle these material effects of the discourse. In explaining why gender analysis is so vital to challenging austerity and misogyny, Enloe

(2013) argues that both structure and culture matter. She emphasizes that gender analysts must attend to "who owns what, which regulations determine who is required to do what, who has the authority and tools to enforce those regulations," and "who has to answer to whom" in political and economic organizations (58–59). Enloe also notes that culture matters in terms of "collectively shared conscious beliefs, implicit assumptions, and commonly held (and fostered) selective memories and forgettings" (59). But how do these beliefs, assumptions, and memories take shape and contour the policies and practices that structure or restructure social, political, and economic life? In order to understand these processes, analysts must attend to the interaction between the discourses that become hegemonic and their material effects and the silences in both discourse and policy. Analysis of silences in discourse reveals the taken-for-granted dimensions of the political claims and practices that, in this case, mask the relations of ruling that contour the construction of the problem (for example, "the debt crisis" or the "fiscal cliff"), the solution ("cut spending"), and the success of the government intervention ("recovery"). I conceptualize these processes not only as discursive politics but also in terms of the intersection of economic, political, cultural, colonial, and historical structures and practices.

Constructions of austerity and less structural understandings of structural adjustment effectively detract from the failings of global capitalism. However, as a consequence of austerity measures, the lives of countless individuals, families, and communities were fundamentally restructured, resulting in increased precarity of many who, in turn, are rendered invisible or disposable in both discourse and economic policy. Differences between the United States and Europe also make visible how the larger political and economic fields intersect to create different contexts for the ways in which austerity discourse and policy function to contour everyday life. Economic and political differences within Europe and within the United States further shape the autonomy of different European countries and U.S. cities to resist extra-local pressure to adopt austerity measures and reveals both general patterns and differences in the relations of ruling in diverse contexts.

The measures enacted in the name of austerity have increased the already deep economic divisions within and across countries. It has also helped deepen the trend away from state programs designed to temper the impulses of capitalism to put profits before people. According to Schram (2015), the shift in discourse on contemporary neoliberal globalization and capitalism to a "debt crisis" fed what he calls a "debt phobia." He explains: "Debt phobia continues even as the government imposes austerity on itself (which ends up holding back spending that could help reenergize the economy" (42). This phenomenon illustrates the extent to which neoliberalism has become "the new normal" (42). In other words, neoliberalism has become such a taken-for-granted tapestry for everyday economic and social life that it no longer needs to be named or made visible in discourse and policy.

While austerity measures left an elite few unscathed (the 1 percent in the terms of the Occupy movement), millions of others have suffered increased poverty, displacement, and structural violence (see, for example, Healy 2017).[13] Women have been disproportionately affected by these dynamics as they bear the brunt of the responsibilities for the health and daily sustenance of their households. Their disproportionate lack of access for working-class and immigrant women to jobs paying a living wage intensifies their disadvantage as they face the dissolution of their social support systems and communities. Furthermore, as Julie MacLeavy (2011) notes, "Those most at risk—the young, women, and those with low skills—tend to have reduced political influence in terms of political participation, serving on political bodies and government organizations, and in labor movements" (360). However, women activists and feminist policy analysts have found myriad ways to challenge austerity discourse and practices.

Diverse modes of resistance coupled with the failure of the state-defined neocapitalist view of "recovery" to improve the lives of many people who have been expelled from or marginalized in the global economy will continue to haunt those who promote neoliberalism as a discourse and practice. How activists experience and define their precarity leads to divergent political analyses and can fuel populism of the right and left. The material context in which protest is expressed further limits its effectiveness for achieving fundamental and lasting change.

As this chapter demonstrates, discursive formations such as austerity are shaped by cultural tropes, myths, and ideologies but are productive in masking structural dynamics upon which they depend and are reinforced. A feminist materialist discourse analysis reveals how hegemonic cultural beliefs and practices are both produced by and construct ruling relations and structures. It also generates an important resource for resistance strategies and mobilization.

NOTES

1 An earlier version of this chapter was presented at the symposium, "Understanding the Neoliberal State: Feminism, Inequality, Social Change," held at the University of Michigan, October 24, 2014. A previous version was also presented in the session on "The Current Crisis from the Perspective of Gender" at the conference on "The Crisis in EU and USA," University of Pisa, June 13, 2014. Thanks to Leela Fernandes and Mary Bernstein for their extremely helpful comments on earlier drafts of the chapter.

2 In keeping with feminist materialist discourse analytic strategies, I also treat neoliberalism as both a discourse and practice. When I refer to neoliberal agendas, I am referring to the policies and practices associated with neoliberalism.

3 The British voted to leave the European Union with a margin of 52 percent to 48 percent on June 23, 2016. In fact, according to a poll conducted by Ipsos MORI in 2016, one-third of people surveyed in seven countries (Belgium, France, Germany, Hungary, Italy, Poland, Spain, and Sweden) reported they would vote to leave the European Union if given the opportunity to vote on it.

4 Dorothy Smith (1999) uses the term "relations of ruling" to identify "a complex of organized practices, including government, law, business and financial management, professional organization, and educational institutions as well as the discourse in texts that interpenetrate the multiple sites of power" (2).

5 This approach is especially powerful for foregrounding the shifts in both discourse and government policies as they intersect with media accounts, debates among political elites, and economic analyses. As I discuss elsewhere,

Many feminists who analyze discourse and are interested in the relationship between power and knowledge utilize Michel Foucault's (1972) approach, which describes how powerful discourses shape institutional practices and construct subjects. Foucault's critics argue that his analysis of discourse "turns away from the subject" (Gutting 1989, 244). Foucault's approach also masks the important feminist insight that social policies target gendered, racialized, and sexualized subjects (Naples 2003, 28). Therefore, we need a feminist theoretical approach to discourse that brings materialist and non-discursive practices into focus and recognizes the agency of the subject. A materialist feminist approach to discourse centers the dynamics of gender, race, culture, sexuality, and class more effectively than a non-feminist Foucauldian approach. (Naples 2013, 135)

6 Ball (2004) explains that women in countries that adopted a "more neoliberal" approach such as Chile and Mexico experienced greater hardship than those who lived in Costa Rica, Ecuador, and Venezuela, where a less aggressive set of

SAPs were adopted. In particular, the "cutbacks in public expenditures and selling of public enterprises" increased women's relative employment when not offset by a shift in public spending. For example, although Mexico did adopt a strong neoliberal approach, "privatization allowed government funds to be redirected to health, education, social security, and welfare, areas in which women are highly represented in employment" (981), but this shift did not necessarily offset the loss of clerical jobs through privatization.

7   The following newspapers were searched: *International Herald Tribune/International New York Times, Korea Times, New York Times, Times of India,* the *Australian, Daily Mail* (U.K.), *Globe and Mail* (Canada), *Guardian* (U.K.), *New York Post* (U.S.), *Times of London,* and *USA Today.*

8   There were 3,617 articles in which the term "austerity" appeared somewhere in the text. To further narrow down the search, I focused on the 321 articles with "austerity" in the headlines from 2005 to 2015 and analyzed them using the qualitative software program NVivo. Since there were comparatively fewer items that used the term "structural adjustment" (2005–15), all 46 articles using the term anywhere in the text were downloaded as well. The articles were coded for themes and for country comparisons.

9   In this vein, Judith Butler (2015) argues that "Neoliberal rationality demands self-sufficiency as a moral ideal at the same time that neoliberal forms of power work to destroy that very possibility at an economic level, establishing every member of the population as potentially or actually precarious, even using the ever-present threat of precarity to justify its heightened regulation of public space and its regulation of market expansion" (14).

10   Christian Proaño (2013) also demonstrates that "fiscal austerity cannot be considered a useful policy agenda to promote economic growth" (870). Instead, he reports that a simulation study of the European Union using the global econometric model of Oxford Economics found that the logic of austerity "is based on faulty grounds" (870). Instead, researchers conclude that "economic growth is a necessary condition for fiscal consolidation and not the other way around" (870). In his working paper on "Trends in Income Inequality and Its Impact on Economic Growth" (2014), Federico Cingano argues that the path to economic growth comes from lessening inequality.

11   Following a strike by Scranton's municipal unions in 2012, the workers' wages were restored (Larson 2012).

12   ES = Estonia, RO = Romania, TK = Turkey, DK = Denmark, IE = Ireland, Cz = Czech Republic, UK = United Kingdom, and GR = Germany.

13   Blyth (2013) argues that austerity is a dangerous idea, noting that "it doesn't work in practice, it relies on the poor paying for the mistakes of the rich" (10).

REFERENCES

Abramovitz, Mimi. 2012. "The Feminization of Austerity." *New Labor Forum* 21, no. 1: 32–41.

Alderman, Liz. 2011. "After Harsh Debt Cure, a Fragile Ireland; Austerity Plan Has Won Praise from Europe, but at High Cost to Taxpayers." *International Herald Tribune*, December 7, 15.

———. 2015. "Comparing Greece's Plan to the Demands It Rejected: Minister Alexis Tsipras of Greece Largely Capitulated to Austerity Demands by His Country's Creditors." *International New York Times*, July 11.

Alexander, Ruth. 2013. "Reinhart, Rogoff . . . and Herndon: The Student Who Caught Out the Profs." *BBC News*, April 19. www.bbc.com.

All Party Parliamentary Group on Race and Community (APPG). 2012. *Ethnic Minority Female Unemployment: Black, Pakistani and Bangladeshi Heritage Women*. First Report of Session 2012–2013. London: Runnymede Trust, 1–27.

Asthana, Anushka. 2010. "Thousands of Women Fear Bleak Future as They Bear the Brunt of Public Sector Cuts." *Guardian/Observer*, August 7.

Ball, Jennifer A. 2004. "The Effects of Neoliberal Structural Adjustment on Women's Relative Employment in Latin America." *International Journal of Social Economics* 31, no. 9/10: 974–87.

Barone, Michael. 2014. "Ferguson: Not Nearly as Daunting as the 1960s Riots." *Washington Examiner*, August 20.

Bello, Walden F., with Shea Cunningham and Bill Rau. 1994. *Dark Victory: The United States, Structural Adjustment, and Global Poverty*. London: Pluto.

Benería, Lourdes, and Breny Mendoza. 1995. "Structural Adjustment and Social Emergency Funds: The Cases of Honduras, Mexico and Nicaragua." *European Journal of Development Research* 7, no. 1: 53–76.

Benhold, Katrin. 2011. "Austerity Turns Tables on Women; The Female Factor." *International Herald Tribune*, April 27, 2.

BlackNews.com. 2013. "Not Just Detroit: 7 Other U.S. Cities Have also Filed for Bankruptcy since 2010." *New Pittsburgh Courier*, December 29. www.newpittsburghcourieronline.com.

Blyth, Mark. 2013. *Austerity: The History of a Dangerous Idea*. New York: Oxford University Press.

Boland, Vincent, and Elaine Moore. 2014. "Seven Years of Irish Austerity Nears End amid Signs of Recovery." *Financial Times*, September 12. www.ft.com.

Brooks, David. 2010. "The Austerity Caucus." *International Herald Tribune*, September 20.

Buffett, Warren E. 2011. "Stop Coddling the Super-Rich." *New York Times*, August 14. http://www.nytimes.com/2011/08/15/opinion/stop-coddling-the-super-rich.html.

Butler, Judith. 2015. *Notes toward a Performative Theory of Assembly*. Cambridge, MA: Harvard University Press.

Carmody, Pádraig. 1998. "Constructing Alternatives to Structural Adjustment in Africa." *Review of African Political Economy* 25, no. 75: 25–46.

Cassiman, Shawn. 2015. "The Discursive Axis of Neoliberalism: Debt, Deficits, and Austerity." In *The Routledge Handbook of Poverty in the United States*, edited by

Stephen Nathan Haymes, María Vidal de Haymes, and Reuben Jonathan Miller, 19–31. New York: Routledge.

Castle, Stephen. 2010. "E.U. Backs Greek Plan for Austerity; Approval Includes Pledge of Strict Oversight to Keep Deficit Cutting on Track." *International Herald Tribune*, February 4, 14.

Cingano, Frederico. 2014. "Trends in Income Inequality and Its Impact on Economic Growth." OECD Social, Employment and Migration Working Papers, no. 163. OECD Publishing. www.oecd-ilibrary.org. doi:10.1787/5jxrjncwxv6j-en.

Connolly, Kate, and Angelique Chrisafis. 2015. "Anti-Austerity Movements Gaining Momentum across Europe." *Guardian*, June 20. www.theguardian.com.

Cooper, David, Mary Gable, and Algernon Austin. 2012. "The Public Sector Jobs Crisis: Women and African Americans Hit Hardest by Job Losses in State and Local Government." Economic Policy Institute, Briefing Paper #339. www.epi.org/publication/bp339-public-sector-jobs-crisis.

Council of Europe. 2014. "Youth Human Rights at Risk during the Crisis." Council of Europe, June 3. www.coe.int/en/web/commissioner/-/youth-human-rights-at-risk-during-the-crisis.

Daley, Suzanne. 2015. "Water Fees End Patience of Irish with Austerity; As Economy Recovers, Resistance Spreads in the Face of Yet Another Levy." *International New York Times*, March 26, 1.

DeBode, Lisa. 2104. "Walmart's Image Problem under Scrutiny at Annual Shareholder Meeting." www.America.Aljazeera.com.

Deen, Thalif. 2013. "Q&A: Women Hardest Hit by Growing New Austerity Measures." *IPS—Inter Press Service* (Montevideo), June 10. www.ipsnews.net.

Desmond, Matthew. 2012. "Eviction and the Reproduction of Urban Poverty." *American Journal of Sociology* 118: 88–133.

Drum, Kevin. 2013. "How Austerity Wrecked the American Economy." *Mother Jones*, September 23. www.motherjones.com.

———. 2016. "Chart of the Day: Here's Why Our Infrastructure Is Crumbling and Our Recovery Is So Weak." *Mother Jones*, May 25. www.motherjones.com.

Emeagwali, Gloria. 1995. Women Pay the Price: Structural Adjustment in Africa and the Caribbean. Trenton, NJ: Africa World Press.

Emejulu, Akwugo, and Leah Bassel. 2013. "Between Scylla and Charybdis: Enterprise and Austerity as a Double Hazard for Non-Governmental Organisations in France and the UK." Briefing paper for the Centre for Education for Racial Equality in Scotland. University of Edinburgh, no. 2, March.

Enloe, Cynthia. 2013. *Seriously! Investigating Crashes and Crises as If Women Mattered.* Berkeley: University of California Press.

Estes, Carroll L., and Robert J. Newcomer et al. 1983. *Fiscal Austerity and Aging: Shifting Government Responsibility for the Elderly.* Beverly Hills: Sage.

European Women's Lobby. 2012. *The Price of Austerity—The Impact on Women's Rights and Gender Equality in Europe.* Brussels: European Women's Lobby.

Ewing, Jack. 2011. "More Action Sought to Revive World Economy." *International Herald Tribune*, August 29, 14.

Fawcett Society. 2012. "The Impact of Austerity on Women." London: Fawcett Society (March). www.fawcettsociety.org.uk.

Flesher Fominava, Cristina, and Laurence Cox. 2013. *Understanding European Movements: New Social Movements, Global Justice Struggles, Anti-Austerity Protest*. New York: Taylor and Francis.

Foucault, Michel. 1972. *The Archaeology of Knowledge and the Discourse on Language*. New York: Harper and Row.

Franken, Senator Al. 2011. The Attack on America's Middle Class, and the Plan to Fight Back. *Netroots Nation*, June 23. www.alternet.org.

Galbraith, James K. 2013. "Cloudy with No Chance of Normal: A Full Recovery Is Nowhere in Sight. So Beware Economists Who Use a False Dawn to Push Awful Policies." *Pacific Stander* (January/February): 36–38.

Gerbner, George, and Larry Gross. 1976. "Living with Television: The Violence Profile." *Journal of Communication* 26: 172–99.

Gladwin, Christina H. 1991. *Structural Adjustment and African Women Farmers*. Gainesville: University Press of Florida.

Governing the States and Localities. 2016. "Bankrupt Cities, Municipalities List and Map." www.governing.com.

Gutting, Gary. 1989. *Michel Foucault's Archaeology of Scientific Reasoning*. Cambridge: Cambridge University Press.

Healy, Jack. "Rights Battles Emerge in Cities Where Homelessness Can Be a Crime." *New York Times*, January 9. www.nytimes.com.

Heatherton, Christina. 2014. "When Your Only Tool Is a Hammer, Every Problem Looks Like a Nail: Neoliberal Problem Solving from Ferguson, Skid Row, and Beyond." Paper presented at "Understanding the Neoliberal State: Feminism, Inequality, and Social Change," Institute for Research on Women and Gender, University of Michigan, October.

Herndon, Thomas, Michael Ash, and Robert Pollin. 2014. "Does High Public Debt Consistently Stifle Economic Growth? A Critique of Reinhart and Rogoff." *Cambridge Journal of Economics*. doi:10.1093/cje/bet075.

Hersh, Adam. 2013. "Fiscal Austerity Is Undermining Long-Term U.S. Economic Prospects." *Center for American Progress*, June 6. www.americanprogress.org.

Huffington Post. 2011. "Occupy Detroit Joins Nov. 17 Day of Action." November 17. www.huffingtonpost.com.

Ihonvbere, Julius O. 1995. "Economic Crisis, Structural Adjustment, and Africa's Future." In *Why Women Pay the Price: Structural Adjustment in Africa and the Caribbean*, edited by Gloria Thomas-Emeagwali, 133–53. Trenton, NJ: Africa World Press.

Ipsos MORI. 2016. "Half of People in Nine European Countries Believe UK Will Vote to Leave the EU." May 9. www.ipsos-mori.com.

Irwin, Neil. 2015. "Looking at Long Run, Finland Sees Euro's Value: The Upshot." *International New York Times*, July 22, 18.

Jimenez, B. S. 2009. "Fiscal Stress and the Allocation of Expenditure Responsibilities between State and Local Governments: An Exploratory Study." *State and Local government Review* 41, no. 2: 508–29.

Judis, John B. 2016. *The Populist Explosion: How the Great Recession Transformed American and European Politics.* New York: Columbia Global Reports.

Kitsantonis, Niki. 2013. "Court Cases Threaten Greek Overhaul; Rulings Risk Punching Big Holes in Government's Broad Austerity Agenda." *International New York Times*, June 13, 1.

———. 2014. "Greeks Go on Strike over New Austerity Measures." *New York Times*. www.nytimes.com.

Larson, Ann. 2012. "Cities in the Red: Austerity Hits America." *Dissent*, November 16. www.dissentmagazine.org.

Lobao, Linda, Lazarus Adua, and Gregory Hooks. 2014. "Privatization, Business Attraction, and Social Services across the United States: Local Governments' Use of Market-Oriented Neoliberal Policies in the Post-2000 Period." *Social Problems* 61, no. 4: 644–72.

Lowrey, Annie. 2013. "Challenging Austerity's Rationale; New Study Finds Flaws in Research that Linked High Debt to Low Growth." *International Herald Tribune*, April 18, 14.

MacLeavy, Julie. 2011. "A 'New Politics' of Austerity, Workfare and Gender? The UK Coalition Government's Welfare Reform Proposals." *Cambridge Journal of Regions, Economy and Society* 4: 355–67.

Messia, Hada. 2011. "Italy Approves Austerity, Berlusconi Resigns." *@CNNMoney*, November 13.

Michler, Jeffrey D. 2013. "Austerity and the Metaphors that Bind." *Red Egg Review* (April). www.redeggreview.org.

Miller, David B., and Terry Hokenstad. 2014. "Rolling Downhill: Effects of Austerity on Local Government Social Services in the United States." *Journal of Sociology and Social Welfare* 41, no. 2: 93–108.

Moran, Timothy Patrick. 2015. It's Good to Be Rich: Piketty's *Capital in the Twenty-First Century. Sociological Forum* 30, no. 3: 865–69.

Morgan-Besecker, Terrie. 2013. "Minimum Wage Earners Struggle to Survive." *Times Tribune*, December 22.

Naples, Nancy A. 2003. *Feminism and Method: Ethnography, Discourse Analysis, and Activist Research.* New York: Routledge.

———. 2013. "'It's Not Fair!': Discursive Politics, Social Justice, and Feminist Praxis." *Gender and Society* 27, no. 2: 133–57.

Naughton, Mary. 2015. "An Interrogation of the Character of Protest in Ireland since the Bailout." *Interface: A Journal for and about Social Movements* 7, no. 1: 289–308.

Piketty, Thomas. 2014. *Capital in the Twenty-First Century.* Cambridge, MA: Belknap Press.

Pfanner, Eric. 2012. "May Day Protests Target Europe's Austerity Stance." *International Herald Tribune*, May 2, 3.

Pollin, Robert. 2013. "Austerity Economics and the Struggle for the Soul of U.S. Capitalism." *Social Research* 80, no. 3: 749–80.

PressTV. 2013. "Women in France Protest Austerity Measures, Gender Inequality." June 10. www.presstv.com.

Proaño, Christian R. 2013. "On the Potential Pitfalls of the EU Fiscal Pact: A Simulation Study of the International Dimensions of Fiscal Austerity." *Social Research* 80, no. 3: 855–82, 978.

Reinhart, Carmen M., and Kenneth S. Rogoff. 2009. *This Time Is Different: Eight Centuries of Financial Folly.* Princeton, NJ: Princeton University Press.

———. 2013. "The Austerity Debate." *International Herald Tribune,* April 27, 7. www.nytimes.com/2013/04/26/opinion/debt-growth-and-the-austerity-debate.html.

Sassen, Saskia. 2014. *Expulsions: Brutality and Complexity in the Global Economy.* Cambridge, MA: Harvard University Press.

Schneider, Howard. 2013. "IMF Warns that U.S. Uncertainty Could Scramble World Markets." *Washington Post,* October 9. www.washingtonpost.com.

Schram, Sanford F. 2015. *The Return of Ordinary Capitalism: Neoliberalism, Precarity, Occupy.* New York: Oxford University Press.

Sims, Alexandra. 2016. "Austerity, Not Immigration, to Blame for Inequality Underlying Brexit Vote, Argues Oxford Professor." July 9. www.independent.co.uk.

Skocpol, Theda, and Vanessa Williamson. 2013. *The Tea Party and the Remaking of Republican Conservatism.* New York: Oxford University Press.

Smith, Dorothy E. 1999. *Writing the Social: Critique, Theory and Investigations.* Toronto: University of Toronto Press.

Smith, Helena. 2010. "Greece Approves Sweeping Austerity Measures." *Guardian,* May 6.

Thomas, Landon Jr. 2011. "The Reward for Good Deeds? More Austerity; Both Italy and Spain Pushed to Cut Deeper Despite Progress Made." *International Herald Tribune,* August 10, 14.

Waldron, Travis. 2013. "11 Republicans Who Cited a Faulty Study to Push for Drastic Spending Cuts." *Think Progress.* www.thinkprogress.org.

Williams, Raymond. 1976. *Keywords.* New York: Oxford University Press.

3

After Rights

Choice and the Structure of Citizenship

UJJU AGGARWAL

"Choice works, and it works with a vengeance. . . . Choice in education is the wave of the future because it represents a return to some of our most basic American values. Choice in education is no mere abstraction. Like its economic cousin, free enterprise, and its political cousin, democracy, it affords hope and opportunity."
—Ronald Reagan, from workshop on education convened by the White House, 1989

"[Myths] represent in narrative form the resolution of things, which can't be resolved in real life. What they tell us about is about the 'dream life' of a culture. But to gain a privileged access to the dream life of a culture, you had better know how to unlock the complex ways in which narrative plays across real life. Once you look at any of these popular narratives, which constantly in the imagination of a society construct the place, the identities, the experience, the histories of the different peoples who live within it, one is instantly aware of the complexity of the nature of racism itself."
—Stuart Hall, *The Origins of Cultural Studies*

Introduction

It's a Tuesday afternoon in February 2012 and Tasha has arrived early for a workshop that is organized at the Head Start center where her four-year-old child attends preschool. The workshops are held every Tuesday afternoon and focus on public school access for low-income parents.

This is Tasha's first time in attendance. There's a drip in the classroom sink that, alternating with the "bloop" of the small fish tank, provides a percussion-like background as she waits. Soon, two more women trickle in. Like Tasha, both Nicole and Edith have children who currently attend the Head Start center. Next year, their children will exit the Head Start center and enter kindergarten. In preparation, both women also regularly participate in the weekly workshops. They have been meeting together since October.

This Tuesday, the rose-colored tiles that cover the floors take on a darker hue, as there is not much sun that makes it through the cinder block glass windows. Outside is Aberdeen Avenue, and the thick glass provides a barrier between the small children inside and the "big kids" outside who attend the two middle schools across the street. The middle schools are housed in one building, Adam Clayton Powell (ACP), which takes up the radius of an entire block. Edon is the honors middle school program for Community School District 3 in New York City.[1] The other school, STRIVE, otherwise known as ACP, serves a "general" student population. As a reviewer for a popular education website put it, "A single middle school serving two different student populations, Adam Clayton Powell School . . . at times seems to have a split personality." The mental health prognosis results from the structures inside the school, which ensure that Black and Latino students are separated from their largely white and also Asian counterparts; a separation that is rationalized by standardized tests, which are said to measure academic ability.

And so it happens, on Aberdeen Avenue as elsewhere in the United States, more than half a century after *Brown v. Board of Education* (1954), that these two groups of students, who see each other every day, rarely meet. They don't eat lunch together, and more recently, after complaints from Edon students and their parents resulted in different dismissal times for the two schools, the chance for interacting out of school has been further elided. Aberdeen Avenue, once deemed a "gang" area and associated with STRIVE students, has been changing over the past years as the neighborhood has gentrified. Yet remnants of earlier years remain, and there are still security cameras outside the preschool, providing a veneer of safety. And it is the precariousness, or lack of security, for the futures of their children that has brought Tasha, Nicole, Edith, and the other mothers from the Head Start center together.

While they wait for others to arrive, the women settle themselves into the small wooden chairs made for the three-year-olds who occupy the room during the day, and start sharing updates with one another about the school tours they have attended. After listening to Nicole and Edith's detailed assessments, Tasha interjects, "Wait a minute, can I ask a question? What are these meetings *about*?" In response, Nicole and Edith share what they do together every week. The members of the group work to help one another find good schools for their children and to make sure all schools are good and serve the community. They learn about their rights and about the schools in the district. They share their observations and frustrations and also develop ways to support one another. For example, one method they developed was going to visit schools in teams, imagining that school staff and administrators might think differently about dismissing a group as opposed to an individual, and that by going together they might find greater strength and defend one another. "Going together is better," Nicole explains, "because the schools in the district are racism and discrimination [*sic*]. They do not want families who are not rich and white—they do not want our children." Tasha responds, "So ... what's new ... I mean haven't they *always* done that? I mean, you know ... that's the way it's always been ... So are they doing something *different now*?"

Over the course of several years of conducting outreach as a community organizer, I met many parents who asked similar questions as Tasha: *Why care? What's new? Isn't that the way it's always been?* Throughout the course of this work, one lesson I learned was the need to understand what questions like these were actually explaining rather than asking: how rather than signaling an apathetic disposition, they required close attention. Tasha's question is also indicative of Ruth Wilson Gilmore's observation that "for African Americans there is nothing new in realizing, once again, second-class status (Du Bois [1935] 1992; Fields 1990; Sykes 1988). But while repetition is part of the deadly drama of living in a racial state, the particular challenge is to work out the specific realignments of the social structure in a period of rapid change" (Gilmore 2007, 214).

Taking a cue from Gilmore, and from Tasha, in this chapter I draw on ethnographic research, federal, state, and municipal policy mandates, and feminist and critical race theory to track the realignment that took place in the post–civil rights social structure and how it animates the present day to ensure the repetition of a confined and restricted citizenship. That is, if *Brown v. Board of Education* signaled the redistribution of citizenship rights, how can we assess what these rights came to mean, and why? As we will see, tracking this realignment is critical to (1) understanding how freedom, citizenship, and rights were imagined, structured, and constrained in the post–civil rights period; (2) a more capacious understanding of neoliberal restructuring; and (3) more clearly identifying the terrain of struggle and what we fight *for*.

Why Public Education?

Public education provides a useful way to think through some of the contradictions presented by postracial logics.[2] Thinking *through* education is useful for at least two primary reasons. First, education has, historically, been a key site and method of struggle for liberation movements. In the United States, this cartography can be charted by Black freedom struggles. Indeed, as Ernest Green, a participant in one of the most famous desegregation efforts and the first Black student to graduate from Little Rock High School, recounted in our interview, "education was a critical site of struggle because it was a key instrument to changing the rest of American society" and to shifting the ways that second-class citizenship was administered. Yet, as news reports declare every May 17 as the anniversary of *Brown* approaches, students in STRIVE and Edon and in public schools across the United States continue to be separated by race and income. As such, thinking *through* public education in the post–civil rights period— one of the most universally accessible institutions in the United States, and yet one of the most unequal—can help us understand more broadly, as Wendy Brown suggests, what rights *do*. That is, what political culture is created through the restructuring of rights and how does such restructuring within the liberal capitalist state work to depoliticize and obscure economic and political power (1995, 125)?

Over the past decade, education scholars and activists have identified privatization as the key and leading cause of inequality in public schools. Drawing heavily upon David Harvey's articulation of *accumulation by dispossession*, these scholars and activists have provided important and timely analyses of how neoliberal restructuring in education works (through, for example, the reinvigoration and expanded use of mechanisms such as charter schools and voucher programs) to structure the dispossession and increased segregation of low-income communities of color (see, for example, Buras 2011; Lipman and Hursh 2007; Saltman 2007).[3] The rapid pace of school closings in cities such as Chicago, Detroit, New Orleans, and New York, which has occurred at the same time as the expansion of charter schools, neoliberalism, and inequality in education more broadly, have largely been equated with privatization. Central to this storyline is the Reagan administration's 1983 report, *A Nation at Risk: The Imperative for Educational Reform* (Gardner 1983), which is generally located as the key turning point toward neoliberal restructuring in education.[4] As education scholar Michael W. Apple (2001) notes, *A Nation at Risk* encouraged the production of a new political rationale in education where democracy was increasingly equated with a marketplace and citizens came to be understood to be consumers. Likewise, Lesley Bartlett, Marla Frederick, Thadeus Gulbrandsen, and Enrique Murillo (2002) argue that *A Nation at Risk* signaled a shift to market principles: "The goal of social equity through education, codified as *Brown v. Board of Education* in 1954, the Elementary and Secondary Education Act of 1965, and desegregation policies, was gradually eclipsed by economic uses of schools" (5). As they elaborate, since the publication of *A Nation at Risk*, public education has become increasingly marketized, which, they note, "signified the intensified injection of market principles such as deregulation, competition, and stratification into schools" (1). Such analyses, then, identify two key characteristics of neoliberalism as including a consumer-oriented citizenship and the organization of publicly owned assets or goods according to market-based logics. Yet a closer look at educational policy reforms demonstrates that these characteristics are decidedly not reliant on privatization mechanisms but, rather, have been deeply entrenched within the realm of the public long before the 1980s and *A Nation at Risk*.

In this chapter I trace a genealogy of choice—as a key principle of reform and management in education that appeared in the post-*Brown* context—in order to dislodge accepted categories and historical timelines having to do with rights and citizenship, on the one hand, and neoliberal restructuring, on the other.[5] In doing so, I build on the work of critical race theorists (Bell 2004; Harris 1993; Ladson-Billings 2004) who have examined the limitations of *Brown* in achieving justice. As the genealogy I trace illustrates, the structuring of rights won by Black freedom struggles as individual, private choices is integral to working out the realignment that took shape among the state, the market, and rights in the post–civil rights social structure. As we will see, the framework of choice has ensured the reconstitution of a hierarchical citizenship and of racialized exclusion despite juridical inclusion. In addition, this genealogy illustrates that two key characteristics of neoliberal restructuring, the cultivation of a consumer-oriented citizenship and the use of market-based assets to organize public goods, are deeply entrenched within the realm of the public and are not reliant on privatization mechanisms.

This chapter attempts to address the need, as identified by Leela Fernandes in the introduction to this volume, to shift from a singular focus on privatization to deeper examinations of the public in order to identify, with greater precision, the continuities (and distinctions) of how inequality is produced, and how state power is exercised in the post-liberalization period that also accounts for place-based and historical specificity. Likewise, Jamie Peck, Nik Theodore, and Neil Brenner (2009) remind us that what neoliberal restructuring actually looks like in a given place is *path-dependent*. That is, already-existing political and economic structures as well as cultural contexts and histories impact what is *rolled back* and *rolled out* in different places at different times. We might then consider Jim Crow as the path that neoliberal restructuring follows in the United States. Extending this timeline temporally and analytically can help us understand, more generally, how neoliberal restructuring in the United States emerged in tandem with and as a response to the winning of civil rights, is directly tied to the structuring of universal rights to public goods as individual private choices, *and* does not only have racialized outcomes but, rather, is organized through race.

Finally, this chapter draws on feminist theory both analytically and methodologically. Between 2009 and 2012 I conducted eighteen months of ethnographic research in one school district in New York City. The district, Community School District 3 (CSD3) is one of the most racially and economically diverse districts in New York City and yet is also one of the most segregated and unequal (Kucsera and Orfield 2014). CSD3 is also among the districts that offer the most choice or options for parents when deciding where to send their child to public elementary school.

During the period of my research, choice-based programs in CSD3 include magnet programs, dual-language programs, gifted and talented programs, districtwide choice schools, and charter schools. With choice-based admissions, schools choose parents and, likewise, parents choose schools. I conducted interviews, focus groups, and extensive participant observation with low-, middle-, and upper-middle-income parents and with teachers, principals, administrators, policy experts, and district and elected officials. I also attended a number of school tours (during the time of my fieldwork, schools required that prospective parents attend a school tour to obtain an application to apply to the school). As a practice, school tours were indicative of the consumer-oriented citizenship that choice policies cultivate. My research focuses on women-as-mothers to account for the ways that women have historically been, and continue to be, central protagonists in struggles surrounding schools. I also focus on the ways that social policies have identified mothers, and the ways that they care for children, as both the cause of and potential solution to inequality. I examine the ways that rights, inequality, and choice are negotiated and narrated through intersecting positions of race, class, and gender within a context where all participants are supposed to have the same rights.[6] Theoretically, feminist theory helps us think through the limits of reform and the contradictions of inclusion while also asking us what situated knowledge might illuminate about how power works and, related to this, what is necessary to *transform* rather than *reform*. That is, how might the experiences and *motherwork* (Collins 2002) of low-income women of color, as excluded political subjects who inhabit the cracks of liberalism's contradictory universalism, direct us toward *nonreformist reforms*, or changes that do not work to realign or solidify the infrastructures of hierarchical citizenship and racialized exclusion (Gilmore and Gilmore 2008; Loyd, Mitchelson, and Burridge 2013)?

Neoliberalism Reconsidered: Milton Friedman's Third Alternative, the Right to Choose, the Freedom to Exclude

As is well known, in 1954 the U.S. Supreme Court determined that separate but equal schools could never be equal. Yet the question still remained as to how and when desegregation would be carried out. As such, the Court's decision signaled the possibility of two paths: one that could have required the state to redistribute resources, and another that allowed for freedom to be reconciled otherwise. This second path, as I chart below, allowed for a redistribution of rights that were decidedly not tied to resources but, rather, guided by the logic of choice and predicated by the co-constitutive relationship between freedom and capitalism that grounds the liberal democracy of the United States.

In 1955, in *Brown v. Board of Education II* (1955), the Supreme Court failed to provide any clear guidance about how desegregation should take place. Instead, states and municipalities were granted the right to develop their own implementation plans at their own pace and *with all deliberate speed*. As has been widely critiqued, "deliberate" was subjective and determined at the discretion of those who already had political and economic power.

The same year as *Brown II*, Milton Friedman (1955) put forth a vision for the restructuring of public education.[7] Central to his plan of how schools should be organized was his argument that choice, rights, and freedom are inextricably linked. The timing of Friedman's prescription for public education was not by chance. Rather, Friedman framed his plan as a response to *Brown*, which, he argued, presented the problem of reconciling desegregation with a liberal version of freedom understood as individual liberties. If state-sanctioned segregation was morally wrong, was not, he queried, state-enforced desegregation equally problematic, as it impeded an individual's right to choose the most appropriate means of educating their child? Friedman suggested that this conundrum could be fixed through the principle of choice, or rights structured as *flexible*. This fix, he argued, could preserve the democratic process by ensuring that parents who were unhappy with a particular school would have the freedom to withdraw their child and reinvest in a range of options—private, public, religious, or even segregated—that better suited their needs. Universal rights structured as flexible, individual private choices would provide what Friedman called a "third alternative" to state-enforced desegregation or segregation. As we will see, Friedman's framework of choice as a third alternative has animated a range of policy reforms in the post-*Brown* era that have relied on the coupling of the freedom to choose and the right to exclude.

Critical race theorist Cheryl Harris reminds us that the right to exclude is critical to the workings of what she terms "whiteness as property": "the ways that parallel yet distinct histories of U.S. slavery and genocide are continually inscribed into 'racially contingent forms of property and rights,' which are consistently articulated by the *right to exclude*" (Harris 1993, 1714). Indeed, as she notes, the right to exclude is the common nucleus for both whiteness *and* private property as legal categories. Significant to how *whiteness as property* works, Harris explains, is its persistence over time, its ability to maintain this nucleus of exclusion as characteristic and function, even as definitions of race and property have changed. That is, while *Brown* overturned *Plessy v. Ferguson* (1896), which defined whiteness as defendable property through the disassociation—or exclusion—of those that the state defined as nonwhite, in failing to redistribute resources, *Brown* ratified a new iteration of *whiteness as property*. This new version was grounded not in the right to disassociate per se, but in the right to protect institutionalized and historically accumulated assets tied to status and privilege, thus sanctioning a status quo of "substantive disadvantage . . . as an accepted and acceptable baseline" grounded in—yet masking—racial domination and exclusion (Harris 1993, 1753). In the post–civil rights period then, and beginning with *Brown*, *whiteness as property* has been administered and maintained through judicial inclusion.

And so it happened that with *Brown II* the redistribution of universal rights as individual private choices elided the question of resources and thus ensured the right to exclude along with the continued protection and production of whiteness. Enlivened, then, by the right to exclude, *whiteness* as *property* was given continued shape, form, and force through the principle of choice. Thus, while *Brown* signaled a different structure of citizenship than Jim Crow, as the genealogy of choice policies that I provide below demonstrates, the same ends were achieved through the joining of rights and choice, a joining that was predicated on exclusion. As Karl Marx reminds us, the right to private property is, in essence, the right to self-interest and, as such, "leads every man to see in other men, not the realization, but rather the limitation of his own liberty" (1978, 42). Drawing on this insight from Marx, Jodi Melamed advises that we might understand racial capitalism as systemic violence on collective life through the "production of social separateness" (2015, 78). As we will see in what follows, the structuring of universal rights as individual private choices ensured the market's embeddedness into the public and required the cultivation of a consumer-oriented citizenship predicated on exclusion, making it so that the commons—represented by public education in this case—was always already characterized by the production of social separateness that is integral to racial capitalism.

Tracking Choice, Tracking the State: A Genealogy of Choice after *Brown v. Board of Education*

In the years following *Brown II*, several states (including Arkansas, Alabama, Georgia, Louisiana, Mississippi, North Carolina, South Carolina, and Virginia) developed what came to be known as Freedom of Choice plans. The term "segregation academies" (Champagne 1973; Ladson-Billings 2004; Walder and Cleveland 1971) has aptly been used to describe the development of these plans that ensured the continued race-based segregation of students through a variety of means and mechanisms that ranged from local student assignment plans to the development of publicly funded all-white schools to the development of voucher systems. Yet diverse as their tactics were, the unifying element of Freedom of Choice plans was that they were enlivened by Friedman's vision of choice as a third alternative supported by the state and were grounded in the right to exclude. State support included monetary funds, in-kind donations, and legal and policy support (see, for example, Alexander and Alexander 2004; Gordon 1994; Turner 2004). As Helen Hershkoff and Adam S. Cohen (1992) observe, in the case of Choctaw County, Alabama, where private school enrollment rose from 25,000 to 535,000 within just six years (1966–72), "many governmental entities throughout the South provided buildings, donated educational supplies. . . . The movement's rhetorical commitment was to 'individual freedom in choosing public or private schooling'" (3). Likewise, in the well-known case of Prince Edward County, Virginia, a series of state laws cut off funds to the local school board, thus forcing all public schools to close for five years between 1959 and 1964. The schools that developed in the wake of these closings were voucher supported and all white.[8]

It took nearly ten years for the Supreme Court to determine that these voucher-driven segregation academies were unconstitutional. Yet even after the Court's findings in *Griffin v. County School Board* (1964), which declared, "there has been entirely too much deliberation and not enough speed in enforcing the constitutional rights which we held in *Brown v. Board of Education*," various state and municipal governments continued to use or reconstitute choice-based plans to preserve segregated education through separate schools (quoted in Turner 2004, 1689). In the case of New Kent, Virginia, for example, the county devised a plan that included two public schools: one white and one Black. The infrastructure of the all-white schools was thus maintained by using tactics that included various forms of persuasion, such as proactive school-based counseling of Black students to "choose" white schools (Gordon 1994). Like Friedman's defense of individual liberties, the school board of New Kent claimed it could not be held culpable for the fact that individual choices resulted in separate schools.

The local school board defended the plan and contended that it had fulfilled its obligation mandated by *Brown II* by adopting a plan in which every student, regardless of race, could "freely choose the school he or she would attend" (Alexander and Alexander 2004, 1139). When the case of *Green v. County School Board of New Kent County* was brought before the Supreme Court in 1968, the Court determined that the so-called neutrality of choice that guided Freedom of Choice plans was no longer satisfactory. Although the Court did not prohibit such plans, it mandated that other methods of desegregation—which were both speedier and more effective—should be first considered and devised.[9]

If the aftermath of *Brown* in the South was characterized by new tactics developed by those with power to preserve the structures of Jim Crow, the North was also characterized by its own brand of continuity in racialized exclusion. Throughout northern cities, Black and Latino communities worked to dismantle what they understood to be state-engineered—not de facto—segregation. In New York City, the movement for desegregated schools had been steadily mounting, and in 1958, nine Black mothers were charged with illegally keeping their children home from school (Back 2003). The group of women, who later became known as the Harlem Nine, refused to send their children to public schools that they believed would harm them. Ironically perhaps, the mothers' campaign was called Freedom of Choice for Junior High Schools, and resulted in the first court decision that recognized the structured character of de facto segregation (Back 2003).[10] The struggle waged by these mothers became a precursor for the movement for community control of schools, a movement that less than ten years later was able to galvanize working-class parents of color across New York City to keep their children home from school and, at the same time, create and implement freedom schools that modeled what education could be.[11] Likewise, Black mothers in Boston, propelled by the comparable conditions, engaged in a similar fight. Groundwork laid by Ruth Balson and Ellen Jackson as well as the Black Student Union was critical to the 1974 federal ruling that the structures of segregation in Boston's public schools needed to be undone (Theoharis 2003). The decision, which called for a mandatory desegregation plan, was met with massive resistance and violence as white communities defended their right to exclude. Years later, the violence of these years is still remembered and referenced in discussions about desegregation, and the outcomes of these joined struggles—in New York City and Boston—waged in the post-*Brown* North are critical to understanding the trajectory of national education reform policies in the years that followed.

The same year as U.S. Federal Judge W. Arthur Garrity issued an order requiring that Boston's public schools desegregate, the Midwest city of Detroit also caught the nation's attention with *Milliken v. Bradley* (1974) in what would come to be one of the most significant court cases after *Brown*.[12] The NAACP had sued Michigan Governor William Milliken for the development and implementation policies that maintained and further entrenched school and housing segregation, asserting the need to desegregate schools *across* district and county lines by consolidating the districts into one school district and desegregating schools therein. In *Milliken*, the Supreme Court determined that municipal governments could not be required to desegregate across district lines unless segregation was explicitly outlined as an *intentional* and affirmative policy. As a result, desegregation in the post-*Brown* era—exemplified by plans such as those developed in Detroit to address inequities among school districts—were found to be *wholly impermissible* unless the explicit intent to segregate could be demonstrated. Indeed, as Harris observes, the Court's decision in *Milliken* interprets the state and the market to be neutral and innocent. In doing so, the Court then ratified the right to protect historically accumulated assets tied to institutionalized status and privilege—thereby ensuring the continued protection and production of *whiteness as property*—predicated upon the right to exclude.

Subsequent to *Milliken v. Bradley* (1974), in the wake of violence that erupted from the Boston desegregation plan, and in response to increased white flight from urban areas, the creation of the Federal Magnet Program provided yet another iteration of choice-based policies. Magnet schools were first developed in the 1960s and 1970s but were widely implemented throughout the 1980s and 1990s (Beal and Hendry 2012). The goals of magnet schools/programs are twofold: (1) to *magnetize* or make attractive—through the development of curriculum, resources, and learning themes—schools that might otherwise not be chosen; and (2) thereby encourage students and their families to *choose* a school that lies outside of their neighborhood (West 1994). Both goals are supposed to result in desegregation outcomes, or more specifically, the reduction of racial isolation.[13] As such, magnet schools rely on a market-driven framework of choice, one that places the onus for desegregation on families (and the choices they make) rather than on school districts or municipal governments. More specifically, magnet schools have consistently been targeted for implementation in urban areas where municipal governments have identified the need to make public schools more attractive to white parents *and* as a way to circumvent mandatory student assignment plans (Carl 1994). As has been widely documented, magnet schools and programs have been limited in their stated goals of reducing racial isolation, and some magnet schools and programs have actually exacerbated segregation (Beal and Hendry 2012; Carl 1994; West 1994).

In 1990 another experiment in school choice—the Milwaukee Parental Choice Program—which revisited the mechanism of voucher programs, gained national attention. The program had strong state-based support from Governor Tommy Thompson (who also became widely known in the 1990s for his welfare-to-work, otherwise known as workfare program); federal support (from the George H. W. Bush administration); and private backing (from the Bradley and Heritage Foundations, two conservative policy organizations that were, at the time, entrenched in lobbying for voucher programs nationally). Further, as Jack Dougherty (2004) as well as Thomas Pedroni and Michael W. Apple (2005) document, the voucher program was also undergirded by an unlikely alliance between these primarily white and conservative forces and some sectors of the Black community who called for the creation of a separate Black school district (a call that grew out of an assessment that integrated education had not and would not advance the needs and well-being of Black families). When it began, the voucher program in Milwaukee provided low-income students with a $2,446 voucher that was redeemable as full tuition at a state-approved private school. Five years later, by 1995, Republicans had gained control of the Wisconsin state legislature and raised the voucher amount to $4,600 while also expanding the range of schools included in the program (which would come to include religious schools). As the voucher program continued to expand (by 2003 it served over 11,000 children), the majority of participants in the program were almost exclusively Black and Latino, thus raising critiques that the voucher program worked to increase segregation (Alexander and Alexander 2004). Moreover, Walter C. Farrell Jr. and Jackolyn E. Mathews (2006) find that in addition to increasing segregation, voucher participants were often subjected to inferior schools with fewer resources and poorer facilities and made "no consistently significant improvement in academic achievement" (527).

In 2002, proponents of the No Child Left Behind Act (NCLB) appropriated what had been a demand for greater accountability made by low-income communities of color. NCLB advocates, such as those who had advocated for the voucher movement in Milwaukee years before, made particular reference to the ways that public education has historically abandoned low-income communities of color. In particular, the Bush administration promised that NCLB—with provisions that allowed for local governments to penalize schools, teachers, parents, and students for poor academic outcomes—would close the achievement gap for low-income students and students of color by increasing accountability for schools, and provide opportunity and choice for parents and students. A common sound bite of the Bush administration was that NCLB would bring an end to the *soft bigotry of low expectations* (Bush 2000) by requiring that the data used to determine student achievement be disaggregated. Indeed, part of the Bush administration's brilliance was in marketing NCLB as a policy that would finally account for the ways that race *did* matter.[14] Vouchers were initially written into NCLB but were later removed as the legislation worked its way through various committees. The concept of choice, however, remained in the form of a transfer program: students at schools that failed to demonstrate Adequate Yearly Progress (through the measure of mandatory high-stakes tests) for two consecutive years were em-powered to choose to transfer to a better performing public school in their district.[15]

Yet as Monty Neill (2003) and Roslyn Arlin Mickelson and Stephanie Southworth (2005) note, given the infrastructure of many school systems, the transfer option simply did not work. In most cases the seats were not available to transfer *to*; and so, as the long history prior to NCLB demonstrates, the right to choose did not work for poor families. Further, the so-called accountability provisions of NCLB were not tied to requirements for the state to re-invest in "failing" public schools. Rather, the organized abandonment (Gilmore 2008) that had character-ized and produced such schools became only further entrenched. The right to choose under NCLB, then, was merely a hollowed-out statutory right for most. Those with political and economic power already benefit-ted from the right to choose; those to whom Bush claimed this right was extended experienced little change in accessing a more equitable educa-tion for their child. And so, while NCLB did not bring greater choice (or resources) to communities who, since *Brown*, have continued to be historically underserved by public education, the legislation did solidify a new freedom: one for markets of private enterprise within the public. That is, the structuring of universal rights as individual private choices embedded the market within the realm of the public. In this context, NCLB extended the structures through which state monies were fun-neled to private contractors in ways that further entrenched the prin-ciple of market competition proposed by Friedman within the state.[16]

Less than a decade later, in 2009, the same principle of market competition within the state was further consolidated with President Obama's Race to the Top Fund (otherwise known as the "education stimulus"). Part of the Obama administration's American Recovery and Reinvestment Act of 2009, Race to the Top promised $4.35 billion in federal funding for education (Aggarwal and Mayorga 2016). However, there was a catch: funds were not evenly distributed among the states or school districts. Instead, Race to the Top required that states compete against one another. In order to be eligible to compete for funds, states were required to meet a number of guidelines that included amending policies that limited the number of charter schools that could exist at a given time. Moreover, states were required to remove policy provisions that prohibited teachers' salaries from being determined by student performance on high-stakes tests. As such, Race to the Top can be understood as akin to the structural adjustment programs associated with the global south, which require states to restructure public goods and services as conditions in order to receive much-needed loans. And like structural adjustment programs carried out abroad, the policy changes required by Race to the Top have resulted in intensified processes of disinvestment, state abandonment, and inequality.

As we have seen, the post-Brown structuring of rights has resulted in the continued structuring of a hierarchical citizenship. Yet after over sixty years of reforms that failed to undo separate and unequal education, the logic of choice as the panacea to inequality and perquisite of freedom persists. On one hand, as one CSD3 elected official who I interviewed put it, you can't have freedom without choice, it's as "American as apple pie." Yet joined to this particular qualifier of liberal freedom is what could be argued to be just as American: the right to exclude, the defining logic of *whiteness as property*. Friedman appears to have understood this twinned character of choice as it operates within capitalism. Indeed, while *Brown I* indicated the end of state-enforced segregation, *how* universal rights came to be structured as individual private choices ensured that the same ends, built into the realm of the public, would be achieved through different means: through choice.

The Post-*Brown* Present: Choice, Differential Rights, and Exclusion

As the genealogy I have outlined above demonstrates, choice provided a theory and method for the state to elide undoing the second-class citizenship referenced by Ernest Green. Indeed, as we have seen, in the post-*Brown* period choice became the conduit that would guarantee the modern form of *whiteness as property* and the repetition and reconstitution of a hierarchical citizenship that Tasha recognized so immediately. This reconstitution was perhaps nowhere more apparent than in CSD3, the district where Tasha, Nicole, Edith, and other women from the Head Start center take time out of their daily lives to meet together every week to navigate public elementary school admissions. While choice-based policies in CSD3 included some charter schools, the women spent the majority of their time trying to access noncharter public elementary schools, many of which, in CSD3, also used choice-based admissions policies (these included, for example, magnet programs, dual-language programs, gifted and talented programs, and district-wide choice schools). The case of CSD3 illustrates that the structuring of universal rights as individual private choices embedded the market in the public in ways that cannot be reduced to simple mechanisms of privatization. In what follows, I examine how a reinvestment in the public schools of CSD3 resulted not in a stronger commons but, rather, in a commons characterized by intensified exclusion and segregation.[17] This unfolded through the production of the social separateness required by racial capitalism and the production of competitive consumer citizens who, in making differential rights claims to the shared resource of public schools—as Marx warned—came to see in their fellow citizen only the limits to their own freedom.

It was a warm and sunny Saturday morning in October 2011, and the cafeteria at P.S. 54 was bustling. It was the annual CSD3 elementary school fair. As part of the district's policy of school choice, the fair was designed to provide an opportunity for schools to showcase their programs to prospective families. At the fair, each school had a table or two allocated to them where they had laid out promotional materials, usually including colorful banners and informational brochures. There were long lines at some tables, while others seemed to lack interest from prospective parents. Unlike most days at P.S. 54, a school comprised of nearly 95 percent students of color and approximately an 80 percent free and reduced lunch rate, the parents who filled the cafeteria were mostly white.[18] More striking, however, was that a number of parents made similar comments as they explained themselves to one another and to school representatives. The refrain that bound their divergent lives together went something like this: these parents were first-time public "customers": some had older children who were attending private schools, and some had their child enrolled in a private pre-K. But one thing was true for many of them—they had not considered public schools before, and they were making a switch.

I first met Rebecca, a white woman in her mid-thirties, in line at the table for P.S. 15, one of the most sought-after schools in CSD3. Parents at P.S. 15 raise hundreds of thousands to millions of dollars annually. These funds pay for enrichment programs, school aides, facilities, and class-room resources, all of which have become scarcer in the years following the financial crisis when funding for public schools and other public services was dramatically cut. Together, these resources—unsurprisingly— make a significant impact on students' academic achievement. Like many of the other parents at the school fair that day, Rebecca had only come to gather information about P.S. 15. Rebecca and her husband had recently moved back to the United States after living abroad. After returning to New York, they shopped around for schools and opted for DeCamp, an elite private school in the area. Thanks, in part, Rebecca believes, to the fact that they had a friend on the board, her child was granted admission. But after a rocky first year, along with the continued impact of the financial crisis, Rebecca and her husband decided they were not happy with the services they were paying for. As Rebecca reflected, "There are probably three or four good teachers, but for that kind of money I want extraordinary teachers." Given also that their second child was getting to be preschool age, and after much deliberation, the family decided to go public.

Rebecca and her family were not alone. In CSD3 and in school districts across the country, the years following the financial crisis were marked by a migration of middle- and upper-middle-class families into the public system. While an increased investment in public schools might sound like an ideal scenario, in the case of CSD3, choice-based policies facilitated heightened exclusion, and as a result, families migrating to public schools were largely investing only in *certain* schools (Aggarwal 2014).[19] The exclusions that choice-based policies result in are often explained as having to do with a lack of information, empowerment, know-how, or savvy from the part of poor and working-class parents and parents of color. Yet as I explore below, Tasha, Edith, Nicole, and the other mothers at the Head Start center were well informed of the options available and their rights. Too, they had developed strategies to support and advocate for one another. As the experiences of the mothers from the Head Start center illuminates, the exclusionary results of choice-based policies had very little to do with a lack of information or empowerment. It is not that "marginalized" parents need to become better consumers; rather, as the genealogy of choice explored earlier demonstrates, consumer citizenship produces marginalization.

The post–financial-crisis migration to certain public schools resulted in a surge of interest in P.S. 15, and in 2010 the waiting list at the school (125 children for kindergarten seats) was the longest in the city. Although other schools in CSD3 didn't experience the same increase in numbers, and although some schools were underutilized (and had empty seats), an active group of parents on the waitlist decided that the appropriate remedy would be a new school for their children. And so, in the midst of a time of austerity measures, when the city was closing a number of schools, the would-be parents of P.S. 15 were able to lobby the New York City Department of Education (NYCDOE) to create a new school for their families. The creation of a new, almost all-white school sounds like a relic of the post-*Brown* South's segregation academies. Yet the ability of a minority power bloc of parents to get the city to create a new school for their families came be narrated as the consequence not of segregation but, rather, of concerned and active parents.

Samantha Karl was one of the founding parents of the new school. Samantha moved to the district soon after she and her husband had a child. I met Samantha, a white woman in her mid-thirties, on warm afternoon in June. She was coming from a yoga class. As we sat together at a café, she recalled that as her son grew, she would walk him by the school every day, "I would tell him, that's going to be your school. And I'm sure everybody else did the same thing." But as her son neared kindergarten age, Samantha started hearing rumors that there was not going to be enough space at the school for her child. She started researching private schools, but she was not hopeful, "knowing it would be a stretch for us . . . the one I liked was extremely hard to get into, and we didn't have any connections." After attending informational meetings about the overenrollment and space squeeze at P.S. 15, Samantha joined the group of parents who were organizing for a new school. She reflects on what it was like to be part of the inaugural group of parents at P.S. 301: "I wanted to be part of something new and help create it. It's been fantastic. We're happy, very impressed with the principal and the way he puts a lot of thought into everything . . . it was like a small group of people who were creating something together. It felt really important to be involved with. Not many people get to do that." Samantha's reflection is telling. There is a sense of activism, urgency, and a "can-do" spirit that informs Samantha's reflections and the actions of the parents with whom she organized. To be sure, throughout my research, amid a time of growing inequalities, those in the minority power bloc invoked themes of *inclusion, democracy, community,* and *grassroots activism* (often with reference to the civil rights movement) to rationalize, explain, and defend the segregated structures from which they benefited; and a central frame guiding their efforts was the moral significance of investing in public schools. Within this context, then, race- and class-based exclusions were made less visible. However, with a closer look it becomes increasingly apparent that this particular group of parents is not driven by the impetus to improve all schools or transform public education as a whole. Rather, there is an increased myopia that characterizes their brand of populism, one that can be understood as resulting from the structuring of universal rights as individual, private choices, which encourages and requires the cultivation of a consumer-oriented citizenship and a commons characterized by and producing social separateness.

Less than two miles north of P.S.15, Tasha, Edith, and Nicole and other mothers from the Head Start center—including Stephanie, Carla, and Marie—had also recently heard about P.S. 15. Apparently, the school was part of the federal magnet grant that CSD3 had won in 2010. The grant, which awarded $11.3 million to the district, was supposed to work to reduce racial isolation by creating even more choices for families, and the district had identified P.S. 15 as a school that needed to *diversify.* The mothers learned P.S. 15 was also the school that got the most money from federal funds received. When the question of visiting P.S. 15 was raised, the women questioned what would happen to their children's self-esteem in a majority white and wealthy school setting. Still, some of the women were also curious to see what a public school like P.S. 15 was like on the inside. They were told that there would be a special tour for potential magnet applicants at the school. They found the idea of a separate tour to be odd; other schools included in the magnet grant just told prospective parents to sign up for a regular tour. Upon finding out about the separate tour for prospective magnet parents, Stephanie, a Black mother who had herself attended an elementary school in CSD3 commented, "Wait a minute . . . let me get this straight, because I must not be understanding. . . . They are going to give us a segregated tour?! Well, we can give them what they expect; we can all go there in costume . . . give them what they expect!" Stephanie was disturbed by what she understood to be a contradiction: a separate, or segregated, tour for a magnet program, the goal of which was to reduce racial isolation.

When the day of the P.S. 15 tour came, Stephanie was not able to attend as her daughter was sick with asthma. Tasha could not make it either, due to her work schedule. I attended the tour, along with Nicole, Edith, Carla, Laura, and Marie. As we walked around the school on the guided tour, Edith dryly commented, "the Blackest thing in the school is the student's artwork on the walls." Midway through the tour, we found ourselves in the music room where a teacher, after having led the students in demonstrating their talents, spoke to the prospective parents: "We are really fortunate here at P.S. 15, and seem to have an embarrassment of riches . . . thanks to our parent association, which is *unstoppable*, we have been able to avoid the budget cuts and, unlike most schools, keep our music and art programs . . . making us one of the few schools in the City to still offer both." As we wound our way through the corridors of the school, the women popped their heads into classrooms and were astounded by the resources they saw: smart boards, microwave ovens, Apple computers, large-screen TVs. But Carla was concerned for the fate of a young Black boy, the only child of color in his classroom, who was separated from the rest of the class and sat reading alone. She surmised that he was being subject to some kind of disciplinary procedure. And while the little Black boy sat apart from the class in one classroom, we passed a yoga and meditation room and made our way to the gym, where we found a room bursting with excitement and play. Students were clustered at different stations where they each did different activities. "You really only see these resources in private schools," commented Carla.

By the time we got to the auditorium for the question and answer session, Laura was definitely interested in sending her child to the school, as was Marie. But the magnet application was confusing. Laura noted that there wasn't anything mentioned about help with the costs of transportation. If they wanted families from outside the residential area to choose the school, how were they supposed to accompany their children there without transportation assistance?

But more confusing was the fact that P.S. 15, unlike any of the other magnet schools, had two options that you could apply to: (1) Dual-

Language Kindergarten and (2) Dual-Language or Monolingual Grades 3–4. After several parents asked questions, the principal, who had appeared for the question and answer session, explained: the school was only seeking Spanish-speaking applicants for the kindergarten dual-language program. Apparently, they didn't have enough Spanish-speaking children to make the program work. In contrast to traditional bilingual programs that are meant to transition English Language Learners to English, dual-language programs reposition language learning by encouraging all students to become both linguistically and culturally biliterate. As Sandra Del Valle notes, when dual-language programs first started in the 1980s, they revived the vision put forward in the 1960s by groups like the United Bronx Parents, which was part of the Movement for Community Control of Schools (Del Valle 1998).

In recent years, in CSD3, programs such as those at P.S. 15 and elsewhere are increasingly in high demand by middle- and upper-middle-class white and English-speaking families. P.S. 15's need for "diversity" worked for Laura (who is from Ecuador) but not for Marie (who is from Côte d'Ivoire) or many of the other families in attendance. "I guess I don't have anything for them," Marie reflected, as she pushed through the auditorium swing door to exit the building. Susan, who directs a preschool in CSD3 that serves largely middle- to upper-middle-income families, believes that there is an attitude among middle-class parents about bilingualism that is indicative of a new trend: "People think it'll make their kid smarter. They'll do anything that will give their kids a competitive edge, that'll do something for their brain. And it's the flavor of the month." Likewise, Lizette, also a mother from the Head Start center, who grew up in CSD3 and whose family is from the Dominican Republic, reflects on how the contemporary embracing of bilingualism in CSD3 stands in stark contrast to her own experiences as a bilingual child growing up in an immigrant household:

> It was really very much a lot of segregation around language. And speaking your own language was a bad thing, embarrassing at times, because you'd be at the supermarket or at the store and have to explain something to your mom and have to translate or you'd have to go to a doctor's appointment and explain to your mom what it was the doctor was saying and you had to learn how to be a doctor and a teacher and a nurse be-

cause you were the one responsible for getting the message across to your parent and that, that was embarrassing back then to me. . . .

. . . and now, I see people wanting to learn Spanish and people who were the ones who made me feel ashamed for even speaking Spanish now wanting their kids to learn Spanish. But I feel like their motives are not necessarily good motives . . . just wanting their kid to be smarter, or, not necessarily learning this language so they can relate to any other culture or anyone else the way we use language to relate to each other, to communicate with each other . . . more of, "I want to expose them to this cause it's like a fad."

As Lizette's reflection makes clear, repositioned as a fashionable *choice*, what gets lost amid the growing trendiness of bilingualism is the oppositional politics forged out of histories of organized abandonment (Gilmore 2008) that drove groups like the United Bronx Parents to fight for dual-language programs in the first place.

Lizette's assessment was echoed at a citywide educational forum for parents on how to choose an elementary school, where Robin Arinow, who provides private consulting services to parents on how to select a public private school, advised that "dual language is the new Gifted and Talented [G and T]."[20] Yet, taking full advantage of the enrichment that dual language has to offer, Arinow explained, requires a commitment from parents to finding the right sources for language tutelage outside of school settings that might include a doorman or nanny. The assumption here is that the same the families who benefit from segregated structures such as gifted and talented programs and who might also benefit from the labor of global help, have now found a different way to extract additional value from the cultures and languages of their laborers. In this context, the dual-language programs in the district—exemplified by P.S. 15's—had shifted from their radical roots as places that might inculcate and embody an oppositional politics to the form and function of *whiteness as property*. Reconfigured as such, Laura provided a certain value to whiteness that allowed for conditional inclusion. In contrast, Marie understood that her difference brought no value to maintaining the status quo, and was thus excludable.

Back at the Head Start center, it is June, and the women have gathered in the parents' room where an overworked window air conditioner hums in the background. Some of the women have brought their younger children—not yet old enough to join the Head Start classroom—who sit on their laps along the long plastic folding table that takes up much of the room and around which the women meet. As they share their next steps and plans for the fall, Carla reflects, "I thought it was going to be a little easier, they say it's supposed to be really good to be able to choose . . . I don't like the idea that they say you have a choice. It's not so easy as they say. It's kind of like they somehow make you segregate even when you try to go places or open up." Edith shares that she went to over twenty school tours: "I went to almost all of them, I maybe missed two. I went to public schools, I went to private. At the end of it all, I was tired. And now I'm not sure if I have the best choice, but I have a second plan—I have a second plan, a third plan, and . . . [laughs] . . . Catholic school is my second plan . . . I'm broke, but it's my second plan." Marie imagined the possibility of a better life outside of the city; others reluctantly decided that they would try their chances at charter schools; and still others understood that their only option, their only choice, was to enroll their children in what they understood to be inferior public schools, where the relative value that the state placed on their children's lives was clearly marked by the depreciation, despite rights. What becomes crystal clear when surveying the case of CSD3 is that the exclusions that arise from the policies of choice (which join together the magnet programs, the creation of new segregated enclave schools, and the appropriation of dual-language programs) have little to do with empowerment or know-how, or the need of so-called marginalized communities to become better or more savvy consumer citizens. Rather, as we have traced historically and as the case of CSD3 demonstrates, guided by market logics, choice policies cultivate a consumer citizenship within the realm of the public that anticipates inequality, produces margins, and ensures the protection of *whiteness as property*, or the protection of institutionalized and historically accumulated assets tied to status and privilege.

Conclusion

This chapter began with a vignette from a Head Start center where a group of Black and Latina mothers of limited economic means were trying to navigate access for their soon-to-be five-year-old children within the most diverse, yet segregated and unequal, district in the nation's largest school system. The women are from different places but, by virtue of the positions of race and class that they occupy in the United States, find themselves in the same predicament, one that Tasha cautions us is far from new. Rather, the constraints that they confront are indicative of a realignment, as Gilmore reminds us, in the social structure (Gilmore 2007, 214). As we have seen, the post-*Brown* structuring of universal rights as individual private choices secured this realignment, which, predicated on the right to exclude, elided the redistribution of resources and ensured the continuity of a hierarchical citizenship, organized through race. Our examination has demonstrated that as a result of this elision, the organization of equal rights in the post-*Brown* period preserves, protects, and consistently produces *whiteness as property* while obscuring the organization of political and economic power required to do so. Furthermore, by embedding the market in the realm of the public, the post-*Brown* realignment ensures the cultivation of a consumer-based citizenship and a commons that is characterized by and that produces social separateness. To return to Nicole's description: the schools *are* racism and discrimination.

But every day Tasha, Nicole, and Edith and the others who have joined them work to secure what is not guaranteed and often not received: a decent education for their children. Informing their labor is a particular knowing that is inculcated as a result of inhabiting the cracks of a contradictory universalism, one that invokes a clear awareness of the historical continuity, of a future that is not secured, filled with hope and caution and circumscribed love and the daily work of care.[21] This situated knowledge is confirmed by the findings of a study from the Robert Woods Johnson Foundation: that premature death is significantly determined by access to education, which is stratified by race and class (Tavernise 2012). Likewise, Ruth Wilson Gilmore (2007) defines racism as "the state-sanctioned or extralegal production and exploitation of group-differentiated vulnerability to premature death" (247). In such a formulation, education becomes representative of life while unequal, or segregated, education becomes representative of differentially valued life.

As these mothers work to fasten the futures of their children within the structured legacies and *longue durée* of organized abandonment, embedded in their struggles is a fight for life, for freedom of a different kind, one that might gesture an alternative to the exclusion that *whiteness as property* requires and guarantees—and one that invokes a different kind of public (Gilmore 2008). As such, Tasha, Nicole, Edith, and other mothers from the Head Start center, who are now organizing to desegregate CSD3 schools, are involved in a not new but renewed fight. It is a fight for the very same things that the Harlem Nine engaged in nearly sixty years ago. Indeed, as Nikhil Pal Singh (2005) reminds us:

> Black freedom struggles have not only been about obtaining market access, equal citizenship, or integrating black people into common national subjectivity. Rather, they represent the counter-statements of political subjects who have struggled to widen the circle of common humanity. To put it another way, if American universalism has been marked by its persistent degeneration into racial exclusion, black political life has been marked by the opposite movement: the generation of new universals form the forcible enclosures of racial stigma. (44)

While these women do not share a common or formal politics per se, as excluded political subjects they fight from the margins for their children. And here, context makes a difference. Almost every teacher at the Head Start center is a former parent of the program, so many of the women at the center have raised their children together. As co-workers and neighbors they are also part of one another's lives. They have been *co-madres*, confidants, friends, and aunties to each other's children. They take up collections for one another when family members pass away and have supported one another in fighting off evictions and the Administration of Children's Services, or the prospect of the state taking their children. They also gather to celebrate their children's graduations, weddings, and journeys into parenthood. Indeed, like the extended kin systems of exchange and care that Carol Stack (1975) documents, the community at the Head Start center operates much like an extended family: there are differences that arise among its members (some of these differences are short lasting while others are more entrenched), and some members get along with each other more than others do; not many leave, and there is a sense of shared responsibility for and toward one another. Wendy Brown (2015) notes that one of the greatest dangers of neoliberalism is its capacity to transform our political subjectivities in such a way as to make the marketplace the only political imaginary we are able to construct.

Yet it is within this context (bounded also by income and geography)—where children are understood to represent more than one family's future, and more than one or two parents' responsibility— that the consumer citizenship and market logics that neoliberalism relies upon, fails. Here, motherhood becomes a political foundation for collective action rather than a descriptive category of individual women's experiences, requiring us to extend our political horizon (Collins 2000; Gilmore 2007). And so it is from this shared space, which stretches both temporally and spatially and yet is grounded in the quotidian of a particular place and time, that we find an immanent architecture of rights and belonging that gestures the contemporary echoes of the Black radical tradition, and as such presents the possibility of reaching beyond the repetition of confined citizenship—where in each other we might be able to recognize the possibilities for a different kind of freedom.

NOTES

1 I have provided pseudonyms for all schools, people, and references (such as street names).

2 According to Ian F. Haney López (2010), postracialism is a dominant ideology that can be associated with the 2008 election of President Barack Obama. According to López, as ideology, postracialism refers to race rather than racism, refers to race as historical artifact, and identifies individual bigotry as the problem that must be overcome.

3 David Harvey (2003) describes accumulation by dispossession as the process by which "assets held by the state or in common were released into the market where overaccumulating capital could invest in them, upgrade them, and speculate in them. New terrains for profitable activity were opened up. . . . Once in motion, however, this movement created incredible pressures to find more and more arenas, either at home or abroad, where privatization might be achieved" (158).

In 2014, charters represented 6 percent of schools nationally; 4 percent of schools in New York State, and in New York City 1 percent. In New Orleans, the post-Katrina era has translated to the entire erasure of traditional public schools, while in New York and Chicago there has been rapid growth. In New York City, this has been especially true after New York State lifted the city's cap on the number of charter schools that could exist at a time in order to compete for Race to the Top funds in 2009. However, the majority of schools in New York City, and in Community School District 3 (CSD3), remain public. Within this context, in CSD3, the same minority power bloc of almost entirely white, middle- and upper-middle-class parents has pushed back against the privatization of education (via charter schools), while also working to protect the segregated structures within the public schools from which they benefit. To add, CSD3 is known for its liberalism, which education scholar and activist Jonathan Kozol commented on in his book, *Amazing Grace*. As Kozol notes, while CSD3 is a place where civic responsibility and the concept of the public are revered, is also a site filled with the contradictions of liberalism when it comes to citizenship and public schools (Kozol 1996). I examine these contradictions elsewhere (Aggarwal 2014).

4 *A Nation at Risk* was released just a few years after 1979, a year that Harvey (2003) notes ushered the "dramatic consolidation of neoliberalism as a new economic orthodoxy" (22). In 1983, the year preceding the report's release, the United States was in the midst of an economic recession and unemployment had reached 10.8 percent. In this context, and also in the midst of the Cold War, education became a key dumping ground to blame for a worsening economic situation. At the same time, education was the emblem of U.S. democracy.

5 As Úna Crowley (2009) explains, for Foucault "genealogy is a historical perspective and investigative method, which offers an intrinsic critique of the present. It provides people with the critical skills for analysing and uncovering the relationship between knowledge, power and the human subject in modern society and the conceptual tools to understand how their being has been shaped by historical forces" (341). I also draw on Lisa Lowe's (2015) insights: "By genealogy I mean that my analysis does not accept given categories and concepts as fixed or constant, but rather, takes as its work the inquiry into how those categories became established as given, and with what effects. Genealogical method questions the apparent closure of our understanding of historical progress and attempts to contribute to what Michel Foucault has discussed as a historical ontology of ourselves, or a history of the present" (3).

6 In New York City, property taxes do not dictate school funding.

7 Friedman is often identified as a leading figure in the development of neoliberal policies and is known for having trained a number of economists at the University of Chicago, including a group of Chilean economists who came to have a pivotal role in the development and implementation of neoliberal policies in the aftermath of the U.S.-backed coup in 1973. These policies privatized nearly the entirety of state assets. As such, the case of Chile has come to be central to how we understand and locate neoliberalism analytically and temporally. Yet, as I explore in this chapter, what might the earlier interventions of Friedman indicate and illuminate about the variegated paths of neoliberal restructuring—and the dialectical relationship of neoliberal restructuring with place-based freedom struggles (which in

Chile would be the election of Salvador Allende, while in the United States would be Black freedom struggles and the long civil rights movement)?

8   And in Prince Edward County, as was the case elsewhere, the consequences of segregation academies extended beyond that of education. Indeed, as Black families were forced to determine if and how their children would go to school, many children went without schooling, many siblings were separated from one another, some children were sent to live with relatives in nearby counties or far away, and some children attended separate schools that their families and others tried to construct out of necessity. As Kara Miles Turner (2004) documents, the impact on Black children of this era—who have come to be termed the "lost generation"—ranged in scale and scope and included intergenerational social, emotional, and physical health.

9   In *Green*, the Court established six "*Green* factors" that could be used to assess whether a school districted was *unitary* and to ensure that the following factors were not being used to separate students: (1) student assignment, (2) faculty assignment, (3) staff assignment, (4) transportation, (5) extracurricular activities, and (6) facilities. However, as Derrick Bell Jr. (2004) notes, the scope and impact of *Green* (and subsequently *Swann*) were limited since the appearance of dual separate school systems was altered but not eliminated, and new measures (such as dual systems within schools) were created. *Green* was followed by a significant desegregation win three years later, with *Swann v. Charlotte-Mecklenburg Board of Education* (1971). Building on *Green* and the broader momentum of movements for racial justice, *Swann* further chipped away the freedom to exclude that had ensured the continued production of *whiteness as property*. The Charlotte-Mecklenburg district of North Carolina had essentially been operating Freedom of Choice plans until 1968 when, in response to challenges in court (brought by the NAACP), the school board developed a geography-based plan, which also continued structures of segregation. A third plan, dubbed the "Finger plan" for its architect, John Finger, called for a metropolitan-wide busing plan as a method to achieve desegregation. The school board failed to implement the plan, and the case eventually reached the U.S. Supreme Court. In his opinion, Chief Justice Warren E. Burger noted that busing could be a "remedial technique" to achieve desegregation, a piece that was picked up by the press given the significant white resistance to desegregation and given the fact that President Nixon, who supported Freedom of Choice plans and strongly opposed integration, had introduced a moratorium on busing. In the wake of *Swann*, Nixon came down hard on Chief Justice Burger, who insisted that *Swann* in fact placed significant limits on busing (Orfield 2015). Too, other advisors to Nixon observed the decision safeguarded racial imbalance or de facto segregation (Delmont 2016). Four months after Swann, in the desegregation case of Winston-Salem (*Winston-Salem County Board v. Scott*, 1971), Chief Justice Burger issued a stay application that significantly reframed and diluted the potential impact of *Swann* (Orfield, 2015; Swindler 1974, 451).

10 The court found the mothers not guilty; moreover, Judge Justine Polier, in her opinion, condemned the New York City Board of Education, noting that four years after *Brown*, "the Board of Education of the City of New York has done substantially nothing to rectify a situation it should never have allowed to develop, for which it is legally responsible, and with which it has had ample time to come to grips," and "the Board of Education of the City of New York can no more disclaim responsibility for what has occurred in this matter than the State of South Carolina could avoid responsibility for a 'Jim Crow' State Democratic Party which the State did everything possible to render 'private' in character and operation" (*Matter of Skipwith*, Legale.com, accessed July 5, 2016; quoted also in Back 2003). These mothers, then, were challenging what Matthew Lassiter and Joseph Crespino (2009) term the "myth of southern exceptionalism," or the ways that a supposedly backward South rampant with racism is positioned against an enlightened and civilized North, free of Jim Crow and legal segregation. Indeed, as Jeanne Theoharis and Komozi Woodard (2003) note, such portrayals overlook the fact that in the North and the West, "schools, housing and jobs operated on strict racial hierarchy with whites at the top and blacks at the bottom. And many public spaces, while not explicitly marked for 'whites only,' practiced that just the same," and do not account for the intention, efforts, or policy structures that ensured the continued production of segregation (3).

11 These northern movements illustrate the contradictory history of choice in education. Further, as Theoharis (2003) and Delmont (2016), among others, have pointed out, efforts to desegregate in northern cities were significantly hindered by the racial imbalance clause of the 1964 Civil Rights Act, which stated: "'Desegregation' means the assignment of students to public schools and within such schools without regard to their race, color, religion, or national origin, but 'desegregation' shall not mean the assignment of students to public schools in order to overcome racial imbalance."

12 As Matthew Delmont (2016) points out, in Detroit as in Boston, and nationally, the idea of busing became a trope used by politicians and media to provide a palatable way to push back against desegregation without sounding explicitly racist.

13 The term "racial isolation" in education policy can be traced backed to the Coleman Report of 1966, which like the Moynihan Report identified a culture of poverty and, specifically, Black cultural inferiority, as a leading cause of the continuance of race-based inequality. The Coleman Report, then, reframed the problem of inequality in education as being rooted in the "initial deficiency" that poor students of color start out with: namely, the ways that poverty impacts the "cultures"—defined as the practices, attitudes, and values—of their families (Coleman 1966, 21). If left uninterrupted, the authors of the report reason, this deficiency would translate to low aspirations and greater educational inequality due to a limited capacity to believe in one's ability to change one's destiny; or, in other words, to pull one's self up by the bootstraps. The Coleman Report thus claims that the concentration of students of color—or racial isolation—results

in the replication of harm espoused by the Court's decision in *Brown I*: that students believe less in their own individual worth and less in their abilities to control their own destinies. These beliefs, the authors assert, negatively impact the educational aspirations and motivations of students of color and result in lower academic achievement levels. Accordingly, the continuance of race-based unequal educational outcomes is exacerbated, the report claims, if students of color are surrounded by one another and, conversely, is minimized by greater contact with white and middle-class students.

14 Craig Willse (2015) provides a useful critique of the claims made by social scientists and policy experts regarding what disaggregating data accounts for and does. As he examines, the mere act of disaggregating data has been positioned as accounting for race, yet does very little to account for the ongoing conditions that continue to produce racism and, as Gilmore (2007) puts it, "group differentiated vulnerability to premature death."

15 In 2012, at least thirty-three states were granted NCLB waivers, which many cite as an indication of the legislation's failure.

16 In New York City, for example, findings indicate that the combination of a lack of infrastructure and confusing bureaucracy made the transfer provision ineffective at best, while in many cases it actually exacerbated problems. According to a 2008 *New York Daily News* article, of the 181,000 students eligible to transfer to better schools, less than 2 percent did (Melago 2008).

17 By "commons" I mean the public infrastructures that might materially operationalize what Melamed refers to as "collective life" (2015, 78), the potential of which, I argue, was abbreviated in the post-*Brown* realignment among the market, the state, and rights. Understood as such, the fight for public education is a fight for a commons that does not yet exist and is tied to the larger unfinished project of the long civil rights movement.

18 The brochures reference the informational materials at the school fair (these included flyers, pamphlets, glossy printed materials, etc., that differed from school to school. The data references state data sets for P.S. 54 specifically, where the fair was held. The data set is found in the New York State School Report Card Accountability and Overview Report, 2010–11. However, I have not included additional information on the state data set as it would undo the anonymity of the school.

19 In CSD3, this meant that between 2008 and 2013, the number of kindergartens grew by approximately 250. Further, In CSD3, despite significant gentrification and displacement, low-income communities of color remain, largely due to a sizable public housing stock. As such, in the afterlife of gentrification and in the aftermath of the financial crisis, public schools became one of the few spaces where parents from different race and class backgrounds met, struggled, and fought over a shared public resource and the rights and futures of their children.

20 February 7, 2012, forum on "How to Apply to Public Elementary School," organized by the New School's Milano School International Affairs, Management, and Urban Policy and by Inside Schools.

21 Indeed, as Patricia Hill Collins (2002) reminds us, this epistemology is critical to understanding how power works, and how it might be challenged.

REFERENCES

Aggarwal, Ujju. 2014. "The Politics of Choice and the Structuring of Citizenship Post–*Brown v. Board of Education*." *Transforming Anthropology* 22, no. 2: 92–104.

———. 2016. "The Ideological Architecture of Whiteness as Property in Educational Policy." *Educational Policy* 30, no. 1: 128–52.

Alexander, K., and K. Alexander. 2004. "Vouchers and the Privatization of American Education: Justifying Racial Segregation from Brown to Zelman." *University of Illinois Law Review*, no. 5: 1131–53.

Apple, Michael W. 2001. "Comparing Neo-Liberal Projects and Inequality in Education." *Comparative Education* 37, no. 4: 409–23.

Back, Adina. 2003. "Exposing the "Whole Segregation Myth": The Harlem Nine and New York City's School Desegregation Battles." In *Freedom North: Black Freedom Struggles Outside the South, 1940–1980*, edited by Jeanne Theoharis and Komozi Woodard. New York: Palgrave Macmillan.

Ball, Stephen J., and Vincent Carpentier. 1998. "I Heard It on the Grapevine: 'Hot' Knowledge and School Choice." *British Journal of Sociology of Education* 19, no. 3: 377–400.

Bartlett, Lesley, Marla Frederick, Thadeus Gulbrandsen, and Enrique Murillo. 2002. "The Marketization of Education: Public Schools for Private Ends." *Anthropology and Education Quarterly* 33, no. 1: 5–29.

Beal, Heather K. Olsen, and Petra Munro Hendry. 2012. "The Ironies of School Choice: Empowering Parents and Reconceptualizing Public Education." *American Journal of Education* 118, no. 4: 521–50.

Bell, Derrick A. Jr. 2004. *Silent Covenants: Brown v. Board of Education and the Unfulfilled Hopes for Racial Reform*. New York: Oxford University Press.

Brown v. Board of Education, 347 U.S. 483, 74 S. Ct. 686, 98 L. Ed. 873 (1954).

Brown v. Board of Education, 349 U.S. 294, 75 S. Ct. 753, 99 L. Ed. 1083 (1955).

Buras, Kristen. 2011. "Race, Charter Schools, and Conscious Capitalism: On the Spatial Politics of Whiteness as Property (and the Unconscionable Assault on Black New Orleans)." *Harvard Educational Review* 81, no. 2: 296–331.

Bush, George W. 2000. "George W. Bush's Speech to the NAACP." *Washington Post*, July 10. www.washingtonpost.com/wp-srv/onpolitics/elections/bushtext071000.htm. Accessed July 7, 2016.

Carl, Jim. 1994. "Parental Choice as National Policy in England and the United States." *Comparative Education Review* 38, no. 3: 294–322.

Champagne, Anthony M. 1973. "The Segregation Academy and the Law." *Journal of Negro Education* 42, no. 1: 58–66.

Coleman, J. S., E. Q. Campbell, C. J. Hobson, J. McPartland, A. M. Mood, F. D. Weinfeld, and R. York. 1966. *Equality of Educational Opportunity*. Washington, DC: U.S. Department of Health Education and Welfare, U.S. Government Printing Office.

Collins, Patricia Hill. 2002. *Black Feminist Thought: Knowledge, Consciousness, and the Politics of Empowerment.* 2nd ed. New York: Routledge.

Crowley, Úna. 2009. "Genealogy Method." In *International Encyclopedia of Human Geography,* vol. 4, edited by Rob Kitchin and Nigel Thrift, 341–44. Oxford: Elsevier.

Delmont, Matthew F. 2016. *Why Busing Failed: Race, Media, and the National Resistance to School Desegregation.* Berkeley: University of California Press.

Del Valle, S. 1998. "Bilingual Education for Puerto Ricans in New York City: From Hope to Compromise." *Harvard Education Review* 68, no. 2: 193–217.

Dougherty, Jack. 2004. *More Than One struggle: The Evolution of Black School Reform in Milwaukee.* Chapel Hill: University of North Carolina Press.

Du Bois, W. E. B. 1935. 1992. *Black Reconstruction in America, 1860–1880.* New York: Atheneum.

Farrell Jr., Walter C., and Jackolyn Mathews. 2006. "The Milwaukee School Voucher Initiative: Impact on Black Students." *Journal of Negro Education* 75, no. 3: 519–31.

Fields, Barbara Jeanne. 1990. "Slavery, Race and Ideology in the United States of America." *New Left Review* 181: 95–118.

Friedman, Milton. 1955. *The Role of Government in Education.* New Brunswick, NJ: Rutgers University Press.

Gardner, David P. 1983. *A Nation at Risk: The Imperative for Educational Reform. A Report of the National Commission for Excellence in Education.* Washington, DC: Department of Education.

Gilmore, Ruth Wilson. 2007. *Golden Gulag: Prisons, Surplus, Crisis, and Opposition in Globalizing California.* Berkeley: University of California Press.

———. 2008. "Forgotten Places and the Seeds of Grassroots Planning." In *Engaging Contradictions: Theory, Politics, and Methods of Activist Scholarship,* edited by Charles R. Hale, 31–61. Berkeley: University of California Press.

Gilmore, Ruth Wilson, and Craig Gilmore. 2008. "Restating the Obvious." In *Indefensible Space: The Architecture of the National Insecurity State,* edited by Michael Sorkin, 141–61. New York: Routledge.

Gordon, William M. 1994. "The Implementation of Desegregation Plans since Brown." *Journal of Negro Education* 63, no. 3: 310–22.

Green v. County School Board of New Kent County, 391 U.S. 430, 88 S. Ct. 1689, 20 L. Ed. 2d 716 (1968).

Harris, Cheryl I. 1993. "Whiteness as Property." *Harvard Law Review* 106, no. 8: 1707–91.

Harvey, David. 2003. *The New Imperialism.* Oxford: Oxford University Press.

Hershkoff, Helen, and Adam S. Cohen. 1992. "School Choice and the Lessons of Choctaw County." *Yale Law and Policy Review* 10, no. 1: 1–29.

Kozol, Jonathan. 1996. *Amazing Grace: The Lives of Children and the Conscience of a Nation.* New York: Harper Perennial.

Kucsera, J., and G. Orfield. 2014. *New York State's Extreme School Segregation: Inequality, Inaction, and a Damaged Future.* UCLA: The Civil Rights Project / Proyecto Derechos Civiles.

Ladson-Billings, Gloria. 2004. "Landing on the Wrong Note: The Price We Paid for Brown." *Educational Researcher* 33, no. 7: 3–13.

Lassiter, Matthew D., and Joseph Crespino, eds. 2009. *The Myth of Southern Exceptionalism*. Oxford: Oxford University Press.

Lipman, Pauline, and David Hursh. 2007. "Renaissance 2010: The Reassertion of Ruling-Class Power through Neoliberal Policies in Chicago." *Policy Futures in Education* 5, no. 2: 160–78.

López, Ian F. Haney. 2010. "Is the Post in Post-Racial the Blind in Colorblind." *Cardozo Law Review* 32: 807.

Lowe, Lisa. 2015. *The Intimacies of Four Continents*. Durham, NC: Duke University Press.

Loyd, Jenna M., Matt Mitchelson, and Andrew Burridge, eds. 2013. *Beyond Walls and Cages: Prisons, Borders, and Global Crisis*. Vol. 14. Athens: University of Georgia Press.

Marx, Karl. 1978. "On the Jewish Question." In Karl Marx and Friedrich Engels, *The Marx-Engels Reader*, edited by Robert C. Tucker. New York: Norton.

Matter of Skipwith, 14 Misc. 2d 325, 180 N.Y.S.2d 852, 180 N.Y.2d 852 (Dom. Rel. Ct. 1958).

Melago, Carrie. 2008. "Left in Dark over No Child Left Behind." *New York Daily News*. www.nydailynews.com.

Melamed, Jodi. 2015. "Racial Capitalism." *Critical Ethnic Studies* 1: 76–85.

Mickelson, Roslyn Arlin, and Stephanie Southworth. 2005. "When Opting Out Is Not a Choice: Implications for NCLB's Transfer Option from Charlotte, North Carolina." *Equity and Excellence in Education* 38, no. 3: 249–63.

Milliken v. Bradley, 418 U.S. 717, 94 S. Ct. 3112, 41 L. Ed. 2d 1069 (1974).

NAPCS—New York City Department of Education. dashboard2.publiccharters.org. Accessed May 18, 2016.

Neill, Monty. 2003. "Don't Mourn, Organize! Making Lemonade from NCLB Lemons." *Rethinking Schools* (Fall): 9–11.

Orfield, Myron. 2015. "Milliken, Meredith, and Metropolitan Segregation." *UCLA Law Review* 62: 363.

Peck, Jamie, Nik Theodore, and Neil Brenner. 2009. "Neoliberal Urbanism: Models, Moments, Mutations." *SAIS Review of International Affairs* 29, no. 1: 49–66.

Pedroni, Thomas, and Michael Apple. 2005. "Conservative Alliance Building and African American Support of Vouchers: The End of Brown's Promise or a New Beginning?" *Teachers College Record* 107, no. 9: 2068–2105.

Saltman, Kenneth J., ed. *Schooling and the Politics of Disaster*. New York: Routledge, 2007.

Singh, Nikhil Pal. 2005. *Black Is a Country: Race and the Unfinished Struggle for Democracy*. Cambridge, MA: Harvard University Press.

Stack, Carol B. 1975. *All Our Kin*. New York: Basic Books.

Swann v. Charlotte-Mecklenburg Board of Education, 402 U.S. 1 (U.S. Supreme Court, 1971).

Swann v. Charlotte-Mecklenburg Board of Education—North Carolina History Project. www.northcarolinahistory.org. Accessed May 17, 2016.

Swindler, William F. 1974. "The Court, the Constitution, and Chief Justice Burger." *Vanderbilt Law Review* 27: 443.

Sykes, Mary. 1988. From 'Rights' to 'Needs': Official Discourse and the 'Welfarization' of Race." In *Discourse and Discrimination*, edited by Geneva Smitherman Donaldson and Teun A. van Dijk, 176–205. Detroit: Wayne State University Press.

Tavernise, Sabrina. 2012. "Longevity Up in U.S., but Education Creates Disparity, Study Says." *New York Times*, April 3, A14.

Theoharis, Jeanne. 2003. "I'd Rather Go to School in the South": How Boston's School Desegregation Complicates the Civil Rights Paradigm." In *Freedom North: Black Freedom Struggles Outside the South, 1940–1980*, edited by Jeanne Theoharis and Komozi Woodard, 125–51. New York: Palgrave Macmillan.

Theoharis, Jeanne, and Komozi Woodard, eds. 2003. *Freedom North: Black Freedom Struggles Outside the South, 1940–1980*. New York: Palgrave Macmillan.

Turner, Kara Miles. 2004. "Both Victors and Victims: Prince Edward County, Virginia, the NAACP, and 'Brown.'" *Virginia Law Review* 90: 1667–91.

Walder, John C., and Allen D. Cleveland. 1971. "The South's New Segregation Academies." *Phi Delta Kappa*, 53, no. 4: 234–39.

West, Kimberly C. 1994. "A Desegregation Tool That Backfired: Magnet Schools and Classroom Segregation." *Yale Law Journal* 103, no. 8: 2567–92.

Willse, Craig. 2015. *The Value of Homelessness: Managing Surplus Life in the United States*. Minneapolis: University of Minnesota Press.

4

The Production of Silence

The State-NGO Nexus in Bangladesh

LAMIA KARIM

In the early 1980s, Bangladesh emerged as the heartland of microfinance nongovernmental organizations (NGOs) with some of the most "innovative NGOs in the world" (World Bank Report 1996). It is home to the 2006 Nobel Peace Prize winner, the Grameen Bank and BRAC, the largest NGO in the world and the second largest employer after the state in Bangladesh (Ahasan and Gardner 2016, 4).[1] The country's early induction into market liberalization was the result of a combination of forces––policies of international development organizations, the state, and NGOs––that predated both the Washington consensus and the Thatcher-Reagan policies. Neoliberalism in Bangladesh did not unfold according to a conventional narrative of the dismantling of the welfare state but through a historically specific relationship between the state, donors, and NGOs that centered on market-oriented welfare solutions for impoverished communities (see introduction to this volume). This relationship, I argue, centered on ideas of women's empowerment promoted by the World Bank and the United Nations, and this development-oriented focus has had critical implications for women's activism in Bangladesh.[2] Recent programs have built on and accelerated earlier policies of neoliberalism that were deployed by the state and donors, and through a particular role that NGOs have played in Bangladesh. My analysis foregrounds this complex relationship between development ideologies, state practices, and market liberalization policies.

When the United Nations declared 1975 as the Year of the Woman, and the U.S. Percy Amendment (1973) made women's role central to all aspects of development, Bangladeshi NGOs and women's organizations found an avenue through which they could mobilize resources to ameliorate the conditions of rural women. Neoliberal policy makers emphasized open markets and export-orientation and this model was adopted by the state. In this respect, the figure of the self-employed woman through microfinance activities, and the female wage laborer in the ready-made garment industry became the quintessential marker of women's development in Bangladesh. It should be underscored that in both sectors women operate under the hegemony of corporate capital promoted by the World Bank and the World Trade Organization (WTO).

This chapter examines this distinctive pattern of neoliberalism in Bangladesh that began under military rule in 1975, and analyzes the discursive silences that neoliberal development policies have produced within the NGO sector. I analyze three major strands: (1) how policies of market liberalization were historically promoted by successive military and democratic governments since independence; (2) the impact of this confluence of market liberalization on the state, NGOs, and the framing of women's agendas; and (3) how policies and ideologies of neoliberalism discursively shaped public discourses about NGOs, women, and development. This chapter addresses this conundrum regarding the silence of feminist critiques of market reform policies of the Bangladeshi state, and how women's groups organized as NGOs are shaped by a particular historical relationship between the state and NGOs. This relationship positions these groups as circumstantial allies of the capitalist state.

I use silence as an analytical tool to examine the landscapes of development. Silences in development documents reveal existing power hierarchies and what forms of speech can be heard in donor/NGO-dominated places. "Foucault's insight into how truth and power operate in the representation of social reality, and how they make certain constructs more intelligible than others, is an analytic frame through which we can analyze 'how a certain order of discourse produces permissible modes of being and thinking while disqualifying and even making others impossible'" (Karim 2011, 164). Within the NGO sector in Bangladesh, speech that criticizes NGOs, donors, and market reform policies is routinely silenced, and class as an analytic category is seldom addressed in their conferences and reports (Karim 2011, 163–70). Instead, class has been replaced by the terms "poverty" and "extreme poverty," which lump together a diverse group of people (marginal farmers, sharecroppers, women, and indigenous people) who are differentially situated and for whom poverty is produced through multiple structures of inequality without examining how class, gender, ethnicity, lineage, caste, and other identities intersect. In NGO conferences and meetings, people self-censor their critiques if they wish to have a relationship with NGOs as consultants and experts. NGOs also censor critical voices from their public events, voices that would disrupt their narratives of development and progress. Silence as speech operates as an instrument of co-optation and discipline.

The research is based on my work in Bangladesh over twenty years, my ongoing ethnography of development and women's issues, and conversations with local activist circles. In 2011, my book *Microfinance and Its Discontents* was published, and it critiqued the neoliberal paradigm followed by the four NGOs I had studied (Grameen Bank, BRAC, Association for Social Advancement [ASA], and Proshika). I draw on this extensive research and have also interviewed four feminists (two NGO leaders and two academics) and several leftist activists to get their perspectives on the absence of feminist critiques of neoliberalism in Bangladesh.[3] I develop my argument about feminist silences through three sections in this essay. I begin with an analysis of historical patterns that have shaped the relationship between the state and the NGO sphere in Bangladesh. I then examine the implications this relationship has had for women's groups and their relationship to the NGO sphere. Finally, I analyze the production of silences through recent changes in state-NGO relations that have unfolded through the politics surrounding the Grameen Bank and the removal of its founder, and I point to some emergent sites of critical feminist discourse on neoliberalism and the state in Bangladesh.

Historical Patterns: Market Liberalization and the State-NGO Nexus

Sovereignty and nationalism are considered to be two enduring aspects of the modern state. Yet the modern state is no longer the sole arbiter of sovereign powers (Sharma and Gupta 2006, 7). In instances where the state is weak to begin with, state sovereignty is shared with NGOs and other transnational bodies, especially in rural and peripheral areas.

This is particularly significant in times of disaster relief due to war and natural calamities when NGOs deliver services to affected populations (Gunewardena and Schuller 2008). It is also important to remember that while the state may have outsourced some of its functions to NGOs, it does not mean that these institutions (NGOs) operate outside of national laws (Sassen 1996). In fact, with the transnational flows of capital, labor, goods, conventions, and treaties, the older definition of state equals territoriality has been reinvented to include new actors who act inside and outside of state boundaries simultaneously, and who also make claims on the ideological formation of the state. Human rights NGOs are at the forefront of holding the government's feet to the fire by reporting on human rights violations inside states to international bodies (such as Human Rights Watch and Amnesty International). This has resulted in a crackdown on human rights NGOs by many states such as China, Russia, Venezuela, and Afghanistan (Famularo 2015). Bangladesh has also clamped down on human rights organizations (*Odhikar* and *Ain-o-Salish Kendro*) that documented extra-judicial killings by the paramilitary force of the state (Odhikar 2009).

My analysis of the Bangladeshi state departs from conventional views of states as sovereign entities that have rights over their subjects, institutions, and territories. States have never been fully sovereign over their populations and territories. This is particularly true of postcolonial states that have turned to Western nations (also their former colonizers) to build their economies, thereby exacerbating existing dependent and unequal relationships. Moreover, the hegemony of a post-Fordist economy in contemporary times has increasingly challenged the sovereign powers of the state, often undermining it through several processes. Under neoliberalism, states have transferred many essential services to nongovernmental organizations (NGOs), thereby creating a "shadow state" within the state (Gilmore 2009; Wolch 1990). However, as Fernandes cautions, "An effect of these very real processes of restructuring is a danger of presuming that the state has retreated or vanished in the post-liberalization period or that the neoliberal state is marked by a clear historical break from earlier forms of modern state power. In this context, neoliberalism risks taking on a deterministic and ghostly character—acting as a primary agent that reshapes socioeconomic and cultural practices and permeates all forms of cultural, social, and political life" (see introduction to this volume).

In Bangladesh, the state played an active role in promoting market liberalization prior to the ascendancy of the models and language of neoliberalism, and that cultivated a specific state-NGO nexus. Between 1947 and 1971, Bangladesh was part of Pakistan, and under Pakistani economic, political, and cultural hegemony. Under Pakistani military rule, capital formation was in the hands of West Pakistani industrialists who had close connections with the military generals (Alvi 1972). Bangladeshis were bypassed by the Pakistani state because of ethnicity and language. At its independence in 1971, Bangladesh was 80 percent agrarian and the newly independent state faced the monumental challenge of rebuilding a broken infrastructure, resettling ten million refugees, and providing essential services to the rural poor. One of the founding pillars of Bangladesh was socialism, but its durability was compromised by the inefficiency of the new government and its dependence on Western assistance to rebuild a broken economy. In 1972, the Awami League government nationalized the jute mills, banks, and factories that were previously controlled by non-Bengalis. Although workers' wages were increased, production fell due to mismanagement and corruption under government ownership. It was in this environment of a postconflict society that the fledgling NGO sector began to work in relief and rehabilitation (Zohir 2004).

The birth of Bangladesh was coterminous with a growing embrace of market liberalization that would eventually culminate in the rise of neoliberalism in the West (and the gradual dismantling of the welfare state in the United Kingdom under Margaret Thatcher, and the United States under Ronald Reagan). Western nations that had begun to experiment with economic restructuring in their societies were also the major donors engaged in development aid to the newly independent state that came out of a nine-month bloody war of independence with Pakistan. As early as 1974, economists Just Faaland and J. R. Parkinson laid the ground rules for Bangladesh as the "test case for development" and noted the importance of a "continuing massive injection of aid" to jump-start development:

> Bangladesh is not a country of strategic importance to any but her immediate neighbors. Perhaps its only importance politically, lies in its avail-

ability as a possible test-bench of two opposing systems of development, collective and compulsive methods on the one hand, and a less fettered working of the private enterprise on the other. . . . Assistance from other countries must be seen as an endeavor to solve the world's most difficult problem of economic development. If the problem of Bangladesh can be solved, there can be reasonable confidence that less difficult problems of development can be solved. It is in this sense that Bangladesh is to be regarded as the test case. (Faaland and Parkinson 1974, 5)

Thus, soon after its birth as an independent country in December 1971, Bangladesh prefigured as an exemplar of market liberalization, and it bore an early signature of neoliberalism. Under the successive military governments in Bangladesh, two important convergences were created, the first between the state and an emergent class of business elites that helped to consolidate market reform policies, and the second between the state and the NGO sector that made NGOs quasi-sovereign in rural areas.

State and Market Reforms

The assassination of Sheikh Mujibur Rahman led to military rule in Bangladesh for the next fifteen years during which market reforms were initiated and embedded. The first military dictator Ziaur Rahman (1975–81) capitalized on the interest of Western donors in rebuilding a postconflict society. He implemented the country's first Revised Investment Policy (RIP) in 1975. After the adoption of RIP 1975, he announced that "the state would never nationalize private enterprise." The government began to denationalize state-owned enterprises. It created opportunities for foreign investors and opened the first export processing zone in Chittagong (Quadir 2000, 4).

At a macro level, Zia followed World Bank/IMF structural adjustment policies and took measures to "reduce the budget deficit, reform the public sector, withdraw subsidies on such items as food, fertilizer and petroleum, and liberalize the trade regime" (Quadir 2000, 4). The military's main focus was on consolidating its urban base by building alliances with the emerging business elites in Bangladesh. For example, in the 1979 national elections, 28 percent of the newly elected members of parliament were industrialists and traders, and 33.5 percent of Zia's

Bangladesh National Party (BNP) executive committee was composed of business elites who helped shape government policy (Quadir 2000, 6). Many of these business elites borrowed heavily from public banks and then defaulted on loans, and the clannish relationship between the government and the business elites did not allow for any formal prosecution. Zia himself noted that "corruption and misuse of power have led to the wasting of almost 40 percent of the total resources set apart for development" (6). The second military ruler, General Husain Ershad, accelerated the pace of liberalization to win the approval of the IMF/World Bank. He introduced the New Industrial Policy in 1982, which was revised in 1986. "Within a year of NIP, the military transferred ownership of 60 jute and textile industries to the private sector" (7). The military also sold profit-making public enterprises to the private sector, a number that went from 32 percent in 1981 to 78 percent in 1985 (7).

In 1990, Bangladesh transitioned to democracy and Khaleda Zia, the widow of Ziaur Rahman, came to power. Under her leadership, market reforms were further accelerated. The IMF/World Bank pushed for faster reforms and reduced their aid commitment to her government until necessary reforms were made in economic development, poverty alleviation, and employment generation (Quadir 2000, 9). The economy began to grow in the 1990s, and between 2000 and 2012 it had a growth rate of 5.5 percent and 6.12 percent by 2014–15, but inequality was exacerbated (Riaz 2016, 222–23). Growth, however, does not lead to the redistribution of wealth, and Bangladeshis continue to leave the country in large numbers in search of employment. In the agricultural sector, the state adapted to the neoliberal order through NGO-led microfinance loans, manpower export policies, and female labor in the garment industry without welfare provisioning for the marginal farmers (Guhathakurta 2015, 19).

In the 1990s, many leaders of the major NGOs often sat on national policy-making boards. Through a collaboration between the government and the NGO sector called GO-NGO that was facilitated by the World Bank, senior government officials were rotated to NGO offices on a two- to three-year deputation to increase complementarity between these two institutions and to create a harmonious working relationship. While in the 1980s some activist NGOs were labeled as adversaries, by the 1990s NGOs were heralded as partners in development and they worked closely with donors and state officials. Although two women have led Bangladesh since democratization, they have not been champions of women's rights; however, they have improved some aspects of women's lives. Both heads of state have worked to expand a stipend program for young girls to stay in school up to grade twelve in order to delay early marriage (Raynor and Wesson 2006). The current prime minister, Sheikh Hasina, has expanded social safety nets for very poor women and has invested in women's sports. Yet, neither head of state intervened to improve the wages for women in the global garment industry or to withdraw the government's reservations on Muslim women's right to equal inheritance in accordance with the Convention for the Elimination of All Forms of Discrimination against Women (CEDAW).

In its early days, Bangladesh was heavily dependent on donor money, and between 1990 and 1995, the country received USD 7,664 million, which was 48 percent of the country's development expenditure (Quadir 2000). Khaleda Zia's government was also under pressure from business elites to spur economic liberalization. However, these market reforms adversely affected Bangladeshi workers and increased inequality. In response, the Sramik Karmachari Aikka Parishad (SKOP), an alliance of fifteen trade unions, launched a massive anti-reform movement (Quadir 2000, 11; Riaz 2016). "Like Generals Zia and Ershad, the civilian BNP regime neglected the importance of both generating popular support in favor of its liberalizing program and developing a broad political consensus "on major reform issues by organizing dialogues with relevant actors. . . . it did not initiate any programs for educating people as to the costs and benefits of market reforms" (Quadir 2000, 11).

Although trade unions spoke out against the adverse effects of market reforms on labor, trade unions in Bangladesh were concentrated within a small labor market, and they do not represent the majority of people. While it led to widespread discontent in the population, there was no organized movement that could bring market reform issues to the fore for a national discussion. The national discontent with Khaleda Zia's handling of liberalization policies resulted in the people voting in the Awami League in 1996. In the two-party political system of Bangladesh, the public vote in one party in one election, and in the following election, the other party. Thus, the votes are not an endorsement of the platform of any party. Instead, they are a vote against the party that had ruled the country in the previous few years.

By the early 2000s, Bangladesh had three elections, with Awami League winning one and BNP winning two. These two party leaders, Khaleda Zia and Sheikh Hasina, have a particularly acrimonious relationship. In 2007, the political situation became extremely volatile when the two party leaders could not agree on the head of the caretaker government. The Bangladeshi constitution had a caretaker provision for holding transparent elections that would be acceptable to all parties. This amendment was later removed in 2011 by the Awami League government (Liton and Hasan 2011). According to this provision, the ruling party was expected to step down two months before the national elections and hand over the reins of the state to a caretaker government that was formed of civil society members who would oversee a fair election. The situation became so toxic that on January 11, 2007, a military-backed coup installed a caretaker government to run the state. The coup, supported by Western governments, installed a former World Bank official as the head of the caretaker government. The caretaker government put both leaders of Awami League and BNP under house arrest, but they were later released. During this time, there were discussions about sending both leaders into exile, a strategy known as the Minus Two Policy, to clean up the political culture in Bangladesh (*Economist* 2007). After two years, the caretaker government handed over the reins of the government to the Awami League, which came to power in a landslide victory. Since 2010, the Awami League has been in power. It won the December 2013 election uncontested because the opposition (BNP) boycotted the elections, calling them "rigged."

State and NGOs

The NGO movement in Bangladesh was spearheaded by a small group of international NGOs (Red Cross, Caritas, Oxfam, Care, World Vision). In 1970, Bangladesh faced a devastating cyclone that killed over 500,000 people. This was the first time that this fledgling NGO sector came to the attention of international aid organizations. When the war ended in December 1971 and aid flowed in to help rehabilitate the ten million returning refugees, these NGOs were able to step in as rural service providers. Within a short time, the NGO movement became indigenized and Bangladeshis began to form NGOs (BRAC, Proshika, Gonoshasthyo Kendro, Gono Shahajjo Sangstha [GSS], Nijera Kori, Association for Social Advancement, and Grameen Bank, which is registered as a bank but operates as an NGO). It was in this environment of an urgent human need that the Western development agencies and the fledgling NGO sector formed an alliance.

In the 1970s, the local NGO movement was inspired by an ideology of patriotism and sacrifice for the newly independent country. Many NGO leaders and workers had fought for the freedom of the country. Many considered working for the poor to be a noble sacrifice for their country. A substantial number were members of leftist political parties who had turned to the NGO sector for employment, and they saw the NGO as a way of transforming the rural social structure. After 1971, many left political party members joined the NGO movement as an alternative way to transform rural power structures and to bring resources and development to 80 percent of the population that was agrarian.

In its early days, NGOs such as BRAC, Proshika, GSS, ASA, Caritas, and Nijera Kori focused on the conscientization model developed by Brazilian sociologist Paolo Freire. The idea was to empower subsistence farmers and women with the tools to transform their destiny. One such powerful handbook was *The Net* by BRAC, which illustrated how rural power dynamics functioned in villages. However, facing stiff opposition from rural elites who interfered with development activities, BRAC soon abandoned this model and became a service provider. Grameen Bank was an outsider to the conscientization model all along. It had never veered from microfinance loans as a way to empower rural women and integrate them into the market economy.

In rural Bangladesh, the Left was marginalized by the mid- to late 1980s. The military, when it came to power, sought to eviscerate the Left by introducing a resource-rich NGO to work with rural people who were in need of cash and employment. In order to consolidate its power base in the urban areas, it allowed NGOs to operate independently in rural areas as long as they did not openly criticize the state. This move also enabled the NGO to invent itself as an ally of the poor. This brought the NGO and the Left into conflict. Both fought over the same constituency: the rural poor. Within this dynamic, the rural people chose the NGO because it could offer them services, loans, and employment, whereas the leftist political parties offered them ideology. Rifts within the leadership of the Left further exacerbated the prevailing situation, and after the fall of the Soviet Union, the leftist parties became even more weakened as a political entity. Consequently, there was no viable political alternative that could critique development policies and offer solutions that would be considered legitimate in policy circles.

Leftist intellectuals, most notably Anu Muhammad and Badruddin Umar, have critiqued the market reform policies of the state in their writings, and trade unions are vocal critics of market liberalization policies (Muhammad 1998). In an interview, Badruddin Umar of Bangladesh Krishak-o-Kheth Majoor Federation (Bangladesh Peasant and Agricultural Workers Federation) noted, "To the rural people, they [NGOs] preach a kind of economism instead of a political progressive consciousness. Their goal is the extension of credit instead of industrial development. In this way, political outlook is hijacked" (Karim 2011, 16). Another former leftist activist recalled, "NGOs saw the landless as an economic unit, we saw them as a relational unit . . . NGOs did anti-left propaganda. They would tell villagers, 'Why go to them? What can they give you?'" (16). However, the Left is in an extremely precarious position in Bangladesh. Its views are largely dismissed within mainstream civil society and in NGO donor circles.

Caught between NGOs that could offer employment and loans and the leftist political parties that offered them an ideology but no material goods, rural people made pragmatic choices, and most went to the NGOs for resources. In the eyes of rural people, the fact that many of these resource-rich NGOs spoke the language of rural poverty and oppression also lent more credibility to the NGO's work. A majority of the writers on NGO-state relations in Bangladesh view NGOs as purveyors of modernization for the country, as efficient resource delivery mechanisms, and the path forward for its rural poor and women (Riaz 2016, 226; Zohir 2004). From their perspective, Western donor support, specific state policies that target female education, and NGOs were integral in moving the country from large-scale illiteracy, malnourishment, gender inequality, and the unemployment of the 1970s to a historical place where some of these basic indicators of life at the margin could be met (*Prothom Alo* 2014).

In the 1990s, donors began to focus on programs that were more self-sustaining. The Grameen Bank's phenomenal success in collecting loans from poor customers at a 98 percent rate of loan recovery demonstrated a market model that the donor community strongly endorsed as sustainable. The microfinance (formerly called micro-credit) model promoted by the Grameen Bank became the gold standard for women and development. It brought together two elements sought by donors: poor women as entrepreneurs through micro-credit loans, and the ability of the NGO to recover most of its operating costs through fees and interest charged to the borrowers. Over time, such ideologies became enmeshed with the global language of women's empowerment and shifted the discourse from wage employment to entrepreneurial activities for rural women. In this context, the rural Bangladeshi woman was conceptualized not as a relational subject whose actions were circumscribed by her kinship ties, but as an autonomous subject who made independent choices about herself and her family's welfare. Similar to Rita-Ramos's (1994) notion of the "hyperreal Indian," this imagined woman took control of her life through microfinance loans and became a small entrepreneur. She was thrifty and invested in her family and her children, so investing in her meant investing in a large group of people (Mayoux 2002). Moreover, she took care of her reproductive body and kept the national birthrate low. And as a voter, she voted for progressive candidates to strengthen women's rights.

As a consequence of this shift to market principles, many NGOs, due to their dependence on donor money, had to abandon their conscientization efforts among landless farmers and adapt to the micro-credit model. Micro-credit programs emphasized fiscal responsibility and loan collections over the social organization of farmers for land and water rights, and constructed poor women as natural entrepreneurs who were financially viable. NGO work was reorganized from the earlier emphasis on political work in organizing landless farmers for higher wages and land rights (Proshika, GSS, Nijera Kori) to provisioning essential rural services. NGO managers began to speak of their beneficiaries as clients. For example, they sought "credit-worthy" borrowers as opposed to poor and vulnerable women, and gradually a corporatized model based on profits took over. The profile of NGO workers also changed from the idealistic leftists of the 1970s and 1980s to more professional workers who could keep track of financial statements and budgets, and could more easily pressure poor borrowers to recover. Institutionalization of NGOs has led to subscribers' loss of autonomy and has constrained their political voices (Feldman 2010).

The flood of 1987 was a watershed for catapulting the NGO lobby into national prominence. The devastating flood resulted in three-fourths of the country being under water. Ershad's regime was notorious for crony capitalism and widespread corruption, which the donors had become uncomfortable with. Thus, when Ershad requested assistance from Western donors, they notified him that they would release aid only through the NGO sector, which was considered to be less corrupt and more efficient. The donors also pointed out that the state did not have an infrastructure in place to deliver aid to the affected people; the NGOs did. This nexus between state and NGO was critical in the development of the NGO sector. The NGOs needed the services of the state to carry out their development mandates, and the military state needed donor patronage and relief operations.

This climate of state-NGO partnership created an opportunity for the pro-activist NGO groups (Proshika, Nijera Kori, and GSS) to pressure the government to redistribute government land (*khas*) to the poor. Zafrullah Chowdhury of Gonoshasthya Kendro worked with Ershad to implement a national drug policy in 1982 that forced multinational corporations to stop selling unnecessary and dangerous drugs, and paved the way for local manufacturing of essential drugs (Chowdhury 1995). Chowdhury also worked on a national healthcare bill that did not pass due to divisiveness within the NGO community over military rule. By the late 1980s, many NGO leaders who had fought in the liberation war went against military rule, and a group of them joined in the pro-democracy movement to oust Ershad from power in 1990.

The fact that NGOs provided many essential services to the rural poor and brought them into novel organizational structures raised the profiles of the national NGOs and transformed them into poverty eradication instruments in the minds of the urban public. NGOs opened schools, healthcare centers, and have widely expanded rural credit through microfinance programs (Zohir 2004, 3–4). Due to NGO involvement, women are visible in public places and their new roles have been socially accepted in rural society. In addition, many studies link women's engagement with NGO activities, such as taking loans, with women's greater empowerment in areas such as child welfare and decision making within households (Hashemi, Schuller, and Riley 1996; Kabeer 2005; Mayoux 1999; Zohir and Matin 2004). However, a few studies have brought attention to the adverse effects of these new social arrangements, which often tie local populations with global markets as consumers of agro-products, finance capital, and consumer goods (Ahasan and Gardner 2014; Bateman and Maclean 2017; Fernando 2011; Karim 2011; Paprocki 2017). The ties between the aid-dependent state and resource-rich NGOs are inextricably woven into a structure of dependency. The state depends on the NGO to carry out a majority of service provisioning in rural areas, which allows NGOs to operate as conduits through which capital and ideologies enter the most intimate sphere of life—home and women—and tie them to global markets.

In his analysis, Zohir notes that "the compulsion to become self reliant has encouraged many NGOs to undertake commercial activities, many such activities do not necessarily create employment for the poor" (Zohir, 2004, 4). These include a range of activities from "the production of Grameen Check . . . which employs more than 6,000 handloom workers, marketing of agricultural produce and poultry products by Grameen Kalyan Trust," and several BRAC initiatives such as BRAC University, BRAC Bank, BRAC-Delta Housing, and Aarong, its signature global handicrafts store (4). These developments in NGO activities from poverty to commerce require a reexamination of "traditional ideas of the 'private' sector development in developing countries" (4). However, with the exception of a few scholars, a critical analysis of these connections between privatization and the NGO remains largely unexamined in Bangladesh.

Women's Groups and the NGO Sphere

This pattern of state-NGO relations that emerged in Bangladesh had significant implications for women's organizations. Women's organizations became enmeshed in the underlying framework that connected the earlier state model of market liberalization and the later incarnations of neoliberalism. In Dhaka, the capital city of Bangladesh, there are multiple workshops and conferences organized by NGOs, think tanks, and universities focused on development indicators such as microfinance, reproductive healthcare, sexual harassment, gender rights, and their impact on the lives of Bangladeshi women (Karim 2011). Despite such a focus on women's lives, these workshops are framed within prevailing notions of liberal feminist thought (Jaggar 1983).[4] According to Alison Jaggar, liberal feminism refers to the equality of women in the public sphere in terms of equal pay and equal opportunity in all aspects of employment through legal provisions provided by the state. She argues, "People would be free to pursue their own interests and develop their own talents regardless of sex . . . for society as a whole there would be a larger pool of human resources to draw on" (Jaggar 1983, 39).

Rights discourse enables women to become full rights-bearing citizens who can use the instruments of democracy to transform their lives. The human rights literature that has been embraced by liberal feminists also works with a conceptual framework of an individual subject, a subject whose claim to rights transcends that of the family and community. While the right to free speech, assembly, and movement are important aspects of one's rights as a citizen in a democracy, a focus on these rights often displaces collective or group rights, and it leads to the "parcelization of social praxis and the shredding of social context" (Ronneberger 2008, 135). This individualization creates subjects who become unmoored from a social collective and who are more vulnerable to market and societal forces. In NGO discourses, the rural woman is recast as an autonomous subject who has to be liberated from rural patriarchy, and her relational links to males are marginalized and obfuscated.

Bernal and Grewal have identified the NGO as "profoundly gendered" because NGOs in many instances work with and for women in many locations (Bernal and Grewal 2014, 3). NGOs targeting women have proliferated since the 1990s, which has made many feminist groups turn to the NGO as the preferred method for reaching large numbers of women. Sabine Lang terms this process "the NGO-ization of feminism" (Lang 1997). The NGO-ization of feminism circumscribes the projects that feminists take on. In Bangladesh, almost all women's organizations are registered as NGOs, with many of them having close ties with donors for project implementation. Many of these organizations are not feminist in orientation, but women who are feminists often lead them. Thus, feminists work in a terrain that is already enmeshed in a process of privatization, transnational capital flows, and neoliberal ideologies of microfinance programs and women's entrepreneurship.

While the NGO is profoundly "gendered" as Bernal and Grewal (2014) indicate, it is important to underscore the situational specificity of how it becomes gendered, that is, what kinds of views are entertained and what views are censored. In many instances, these are woman-centric organizations that are discursively shaped by international conventions and treaties (U.S. Percy Amendment, 1973; U.N. Decade for Women, 1975; Cairo Population Conference, 1984; CEDAW, 1979; Beijing Conference, 1995) that mandated that women be included in all aspects of development work. Working with and in NGOs, donors and state, middle-class feminists have found new avenues of organizing through transnational networks that cut across state boundaries (Keck and Sikkink 1998). In this respect, NGOs that target women as beneficiaries become influential in producing feminists as experts who can provide knowledge about the grassroots and women to development organizations (Bernal and Grewal 2014, 307). These gender experts are most often drawn from the NGO sector or from researchers who worked closely on NGO projects.

Bangladeshi women's organizations were nurtured within the global discourses of women's development (Women-in-Development [WID], later called Gender and Development or [GAD]), and hence they were shaped by market-oriented ideas of women's empowerment. Not surprisingly, women's empowerment has been framed as women's development (*nari unnayan*) and not as women's emancipation (*nari mukti*) (Nazneen, Sultan, and Hossain 2010, 240). As funds for WID/GAD programs increased in the late 1970s and 1980s, many local women's groups organized as NGOs in order to garner development funds from Western donors. As such, these groups were constrained from offering a critique of liberalization that the donors sponsored through the Bangladeshi state. European countries specially mandated that NGOs increase the number of women workers in their ranks if they wanted to get resources. The NGO sector thus opened a space for feminists and women to enter the nonprofit sector both as leaders and as rank-and-file workers. Since a majority of the development NGOs worked with women as subscribers in rural areas, NGOs also found it in their interest to hire women who could meet with rural women in the privacy of their homes. Moreover, the spread of NGOs in rural areas created jobs for college-educated young women who could now find employment close to home. It also created new social identities as NGO workers for young rural women.

Despite the focus of Western donors on lifting up rural women in Bangladesh from poverty and social subjugation, and the high number of NGOs working with women in rural areas, it is surprising to find an absence of a critical feminist discourse regarding how women have been brought into the market economy, largely as entrepreneurs of microfinance loans in rural areas, and as workers in the ready-made apparel industry in urban areas (Karim 2011; Rahman 2001; Siddiqi 2009). Khushi Kabir of Nijera Kori and Farida Akhter of UNBINIG are two feminists who have spoken out on the dire effects of free market policies on shrimp farming and genetically modified seeds, respectively, but their critiques have remained within the micro-politics of shrimp and GMO cultivation, and have not become mainstreamed as a critique of the free market economy.[5] Instead, liberal feminist ideas of women's access to the economy have become grounds for the extensive acceptance of these market-driven models. Sabur noted some of the causes of the deradicalization of the women's movement in an opinion piece (Sabur 2013b). Anu Muhammad, economist and activist, notes that it is difficult to have an independent voice as an NGO because of the interpenetration of state and NGO, and the pressure on NGOs to conform to state mandates. According to Muhammad, because women are most affected by agriculture and the environment, increasing numbers of women at the grassroots are beginning to participate in social movements centered around the environment.[6] In the Phulbari movement against open-pit coal mining, for example, thousands of indigenous Santal women joined in the protest (Karim 2016). In order to comprehend the complexities of women's activism, one has to take into consideration how class, gender, and ethnicity function in these movements.

In an article entitled "National Discourses on Women's Empowerment in Bangladesh," the authors studied the literature of three major women's NGOs—Bangladesh Mahila Parishad (BMP, leftist), Women for Women (WfW, centrist), and Naripokkho (liberal feminist), and identified the following trends within these groups:

All three organizations used concepts of discrimination, inequality, deprivation, exploitation and oppression to justify the need for change. For WfW, "women's empowerment" was close to women's development and gender equality. BMP linked it to equality and emancipation, situated within a larger political vision of commitment to the secular values of the independence struggle. Naripokkho tends to use "empowerment" to refer to specific contexts and issues, rather than in relation to broader processes of transformation. For all three, "empowerment" was seen as a complex, long-term process, on which progress may be uneven or even contradictory. . . . All three organizations have taken on a rights-based approach, and rights language is prevalent in their work and publications, including explicit references to international human rights frameworks and UN conventions and declarations such as CEDAW. (Nazneen, Sultan, and Hossain 2010, 240)

According to the authors, WfW represents the mainstream World Bank development model for bringing women into a market economy. This is the model followed by a majority of the women's groups in Bangladesh, where women's empowerment results from development. BMP, a left-leaning organization, adds secularism as a foundational principle and ties it to women's emancipation. However, the question of secularism is an issue fraught with problems in Bangladesh, and many religious women there do not accept the idea of secularism.[7] Both BMP and Naripokkho incorporate ideas of increased awareness, analysis, and collective action as required skills for social transformation. Naripokkho's focus is on the woman as an individual agent: "The goal of NP is to establish women as human being [sic] with dignity with rights as citizens in the family, society and state" (Nazneen, Hossain, and Sultan 2010, 240).

Feminists who run various women's NGOs in Bangladesh (Bangladesh Mahila Samity, Bangladesh Mahila Parishad, Nijera Kori, Sammilito Nari Samaj, Ain-o-Salish Kendro, Women for Women, Nari Pokkho, to name a few) would like to see Bangladesh as a functional democracy similar to northern European countries with certain rights and guarantees for women. These urban feminists are part of the NGO sphere and are dependent on donor funds for resources to run their programs. As noted earlier, they are operationalized as "gender experts" who help facilitate and implement policies that target women in development, sexual harassment, reproductive healthcare, democratization, and education. These feminists advocate for policies, meet with donors and government officials, and implement policies through their organizations. Feminists also try to keep an independent voice vis-à-vis the state by holding the state accountable on women's issues, especially with reference to CEDAW mandates for removing all obstacles to women's full participation in society. There are human rights NGOs that conduct pedagogical training sessions for women to become leaders and run for public office. Arguably, this work is important, onerous, multidimensional, and often dangerous, but this work also faces constraints imposed by the norms embedded in global women's conventions and treaties. Feminists and women's groups have addressed the serious issues women face, such as domestic and sexual violence. They have finally succeeded with the Domestic Violence (Prevention and Protection) Act in 2010 that took almost ten years to pass. Most recently, women's groups took to the streets to protest the Child Marriage Restraint Bill in 2016 that allowed underage girls to be married off in special circumstances (Alamgir and Chaity 2017). The location of class bifurcates the NGO feminists from the garment trade union feminists. In an interview, Najma Akhter, a garment trade union leader, mentioned that middle-class feminists tend to focus on violence against women in rural society over the industrial sector because that is the Western donor mandate. As she noted, "When a woman gets killed by rural men, feminists take to the streets to demonstrate; when women burn in a factory, where are they?"[8] Another trade union activist mentioned that NGOs work with hot topics that their donors mandate and not necessarily with issues that are relevant, such as wage labor in the garment industry. Part of the reason for the vocal support for a lone rural woman being targeted is her social isolation from an organized lobby, whereas garment workers have unions to advocate for their grievances. That said, a distinction is necessary between the policy-oriented work of NGOs and activism of feminists, some of whom are members of these NGOs. In parsing out this overlap between projects and project leaders, Khushi Kabir notes that a majority of the NGOs in Bangladesh are not feminist whereas a majority of the leaders are feminist. Feminists have to navigate this fine line.

Religion also creates ambivalence and tension between feminists. Farida Akhter, executive director of UBINIG, mentioned in an interview that she had faced backlash after she publicly endorsed the view of the ultrareligious group Hefazat-e-Islam, that the free market made women into commodities (Sabur 2013a). Akhter emphasized that she had only endorsed the position that capitalism objectified women. She asked why it was that one could not agree with the clergy when they made a relevant point. While Akhter raised an important question, the feminists' reaction to Akhter was a result of the killings of the secular bloggers, which the clergy did not condemn (Barry 2015). By endorsing the clergy's viewpoint, Akhter was seen as undermining the principle of speech of the secular bloggers. Akhter's attempted critique of the neoliberal market economy and its commodification of women was subsumed under a free speech discourse, a discourse that carries more weight in contemporary times. In discussing the absence of critiques of the neoliberal state, feminist economist Farida Khan argued, "Feminism is wrapped up in the idea of women and development, and has not critiqued the notion of development as have, for example, the post-development or post-modernist theorists. 'Third World' Feminism is focused on delivering modernity to women, to have them participate in the process of modernity and thereby become 'empowered' as subjects/agents through that participation . . . such an approach is critical of neo-liberalism only to the extent that neo-liberalism does not deliver the bounties of modernization/capitalism for everyone. It is an approach or model of *exclusion*."[9] According to Khan, the focus is on "inclusion of women into the capitalist process." If women could have "well paying jobs, promotions, businesses, participated as individualized agents in the transition to capitalism," then many within the NGO sector believe that Bangladesh would be on its way to joining the global economy, and women's roles in society would be strengthened. The fact that global capitalism is a "complex historical process" that extracts wealth from workers and developing countries, and "that women are caught in a process over which they have little control," are issues that are not analyzed. I would argue that this lack of analysis is what prevents people from seeing the link between micro-credit as debt and the effects of debt on rural women's lives. Instead, most use the euphemism that credit equals trust, and therefore debt is not the extraction of wealth from the poor who are often unable to repay the loans they take on.

Speaking in a similar vein, feminist scholar Firdaus Azim mentions the lack of academic discussion about these issues in Bangladesh. She notes, "Faculty teach on neoliberalism and the free market economy at different universities, however the study of the neoliberal state is yet to develop into a serious mode of inquiry. We have many conferences on development for example, but conferences on neoliberalism and the state are largely absent. This is where an intervention can be made with feminist scholars analyzing the links between the liberalizing state and its impact on women's work." She goes onto add, "The critique that is coming out is the construction of the working-woman as a consumer, and the discourses are around advertisement of commodities to women, and how the market addresses women as consumers. Thus, our current focus tends to examine how the market may/may not empower the woman through consumerism, and not what is this *market* that is being invented through neoliberal policies."[10] What one finds then is not the absence of critique but the presence of a specific form of critique that focuses on some aspects of market liberalization, but does not extend it to a rigorous analysis of the links between the state, NGOs, and markets and their adverse effects on women's lives and livelihoods, and the erasure of alternative models such as cooperatives or collectives from debate and discussion.

Selective Speech: The Case of Grameen Bank

I now turn to an analysis of speech and silence through an examination of a critical moment for NGO-state relations that unfolded during recent political events and conflicts over the Grameen Bank. In 2010 the documentary *Caught in Micro Debt* by Danish filmmaker Tom Heinemann showed, among other issues, highly indebted Grameen Bank borrowers in Bangladesh. After the release of the documentary, the Awami League government removed Nobel laureate Muhammad Yunus as the director of Grameen Bank through a court order that was considered highly controversial both nationally and internationally. Within the Awami League, many senior politicians did not look favorably on NGOs and their leaders. For these seasoned politicians, NGOs should be engaged primarily in development activities, and elected politicians should run the state, a line that had become blurred under militarization in 1975–90. In Dhaka, I was struck by the fact that very few urban feminists—and I refer here to middle-class feminists and heads of various women's organizations/NGOs—were willing to address the situation of rural women's indebtedness through microfinance loans provided by the Grameen Bank. With the exception of one leading feminist, Khushi Kabir, most of the others that I met tended to ignore the issue of rural women's indebtedness. While the government's actions against Yunus were partially responsible for this lack of engagement, the women I spoke with, many of them associated with women's NGOs, uncritically accepted the Grameen Bank/NGO rhetoric that microfinance loans were beneficial to poor women.

In order to contextualize the government's actions against Yunus and Grameen, a set of actions require analysis. A month after the military coup of January 11, 2007, Professor Yunus went to India and met with Indian Prime Minister Manhohan Singh. Later, Yunus announced his intention to form a political party to clean up political corruption in Bangladesh. Although he soon withdrew his decision to run, his quest for political office was not lost on Sheikh Hasina (the current prime minister), who saw in Yunus a formidable force as the leader of Grameen Bank, a beloved global figure who controlled a potential vote base of eight million Grameen borrowers, and enormous resources of the fifty-four Grameen family of companies, some of which were for profit, while others were not (Srivathsan 2013). Hasina also recognized that the NGOs had developed as an autonomous political force outside of conventional political parties, and once she was back in power she took steps to stem this process from cauterizing her political party and ambitions.

After the handover of power by the caretaker government to the elected government of Sheikh Hasina in 2009, the role of NGOs began to change under her leadership. Two years later, the government of Awami League investigated Grameen Bank. Heinemann's documentary shows women who had become trapped in debt from taking microfinance loans in Bangladesh, India, and Mexico. It also alleges that in 1996 Grameen Bank had transferred 100 million Norwegian Kroner to one of its subsidiaries, Grameen Kalyan, without the authorization of the Norwegian aid organization Norad. In Bangladesh, the online newspaper *bdnews24* headlined this news as "Yunus Siphoned Tk 7bn Aid for Poor," which was a misrepresentation of the facts (Bdnews24 2010). This led to the investigation of Grameen Bank. The Norwegian government issued a statement that they had cleared the matter with Grameen Bank and they had closed the books on this issue (British Broadcasting Service 2010). The government ignored the Norwegian government's statement clearing Yunus and Grameen Bank, and instead removed Yunus as director of the bank. Although Sheikh Hasina publicly stated that Yunus was "sucking the blood of poor people through loans," her government did not address the question of rural indebtedness. In neighboring India, the Andhra Pradesh government had stopped all microfinance loans after reports of suicides linked to borrowers' inability to pay their loans to SKS Microfinance (a microfinance company in India) whereas in Bangladesh the government failed to start a nationwide investigation of microfinance NGOs to address similar patterns of rural indebtedness (Bajaj 2011). Instead, what transpired was her personal vendetta against Yunus, and that was evident to Bangladeshis.

In Bangladesh, the forced removal of Yunus on a technicality, his age, became highly controversial because Yunus is universally liked by the urban middle classes, who view him as an iconic figure who has brought fame and recognition to their country. Several prominent feminists helped to organize Grameen borrowers to protest the ouster of Yunus. Feminists in Bangladesh were unified in their condemnation of the treatment meted out to Yunus by the government and they spoke out against the breakup of Grameen Bank. In their discourse, the state was recast as "corrupt," Grameen Bank as a "Nobel Prize winner" and an icon of "national pride," and Nobel laureate Yunus as "the most important Bangladeshi known to the world." Most importantly, Yunus as member of the Dhaka's urban elite/NGO circles had brought global attention to women in Bangladesh and enabled their work. All of these are important facts that should not be discounted. But what is missing from this outrage is a feminist demand for an independent nationwide accounting of microfinance practices and their effects on women's lives. Instead, nationalism and pride triumphed over the situation of highly indebted rural women whose stories were conveniently forgotten due to the actions of the government. The state-generated Grameen/Yunus crisis was also a crisis of Bangladeshi middle-class society, and threatened the world recognition and status that Yunus and Grameen Bank brought to the nation that was once termed by Henry Kissinger as a "bottomless basket."[11] National politics, status, and class merged to create unity on this issue among feminists, and even those feminists who had in the past critiqued microfinance loans as adversely hurting women did not wish to openly speak out.

The committee that investigated the accounts of Grameen did not discover any wrongdoing but recommended the break-up of Grameen Bank and its subsidiary holdings, thereby weakening the bank's economic power ("Interim Report" 2011). After the removal of Yunus, the government cracked down on the autonomy enjoyed by NGOs. It passed a draconian Foreign Donations Regulation Act in 2014. According to the act, "The NGO Affairs Bureau in the prime minister's office would have approval authority over foreign-funded projects. It would have the authority to 'inspect, monitor and assess the activities' of groups and individuals and to close groups and cancel their registration if it sees fit." Moreover, the NGO Act required that NGO leaders had to get permission from the NGO Affairs Bureau before traveling overseas for meetings, and had to explain the purpose of those meetings. The NGO was under the intense scrutiny of the state and all aspects of its conduct were monitored. The new mandate was that NGOs should restrict their work to development activities and not engage in political activities without the approval of the party in power. The state now regulates the conduct of NGOs and their leaders, a dramatic shift in their roles.

The question is why did this attack on NGOs occur at this time? Since 2010, the space for dissent has shrunk under the Awami League government, which has become increasingly authoritarian. In this new relationship, the state and NGOs have moved to a more adversarial relationship. NGOs still work with the state but only if they follow the directives of the government. The power and influence of NGOs have not withered away; instead, they have been redrawn. The NGOs BRAC and ASA are very powerful and efficiently run entities, but they do not transgress onto the political landscape. This reversal occurred, in part, because the state is no longer dependent on donors as the source for its economic survival. With the rise of alternative revenue sources in ready-made apparel, migrant remittances, gas explorations in the Bay of Bengal, and trade ventures with China, Japan, and India, the Bangladeshi state now aspires to become a middle-income country (Riaz 2016). Within this transformed NGO landscape women's NGOs have splintered. Some have sought to remain silent, while others have spoken out against freedom of speech, corruption, and extra-judicial killings by the paramilitary forces of the state. Despite these constraints imposed by an authoritarian state and the normative liberal feminist ideals of many women's NGOs, there are also moments and spaces where alternative forms of speech emerge. My focus here is on local scholars and activists that are working outside the NGO model. Below I outline a few such organizations I found to be promising.

Inspired by left-leaning professors, students at Jahangirnagar University, a public university, are engaged in the growing environmental movement in the country against mining, destruction of the mangrove forests, and GMO cultivation. Another such group is thotkata.net, which is organized by a group of academics and activists. It is a blog that posts on vital issues that affect Bangladeshi society. "Thotkata" refers to unruly speech, that is, speech that speaks truth to power. Within the blog, one can find posts about ethnic minorities, garment workers, labor rights, capitalist exploitation, sexuality, and sexual rights—topics that are not dominant within the NGO sphere. This innovative blog has become a source of inspiration among college students in Bangladesh.

Three of the *thotkata* activists are young anthropologists who have formed a group called Activist Anthropologist after the Tazreen factory fire in 2012 that killed over 112 workers. These anthropologists conducted investigative research among the dead and missing and documented that actually 119, and not 112, workers had died in the factory fire. In the aftermath of the Rana Plaza factory collapse in 2013 that killed over 1,100 workers, they lobbied to get relief and compensation for the families of the dead and injured workers. These young scholars take to the streets with the workers to protest unfair labor practices, they analyze their actions within a theoretical framework, and they engage a new generation of young students and local people in their activism. In their work on factory labor, these anthropologists have avoided the donor-dependent model of the NGOs to keep their ideological integrity.

Another example of an alternative space for activism is the Center for Bangladesh Studies (cbs.org). This organization is a coalition of junior scholar-activists who are creating a digital archive on Bangladesh. They do not take NGO or donor funds, and instead solicit small sums of private donations. They have a symbolic donation box to showcase their autonomy. They are using social media to circulate knowledge. These are emergent para-sites of alternative discourses around state and market liberalization, but they still remain isolated sites of knowledge and activism.

Conclusion

This chapter has shown that the state is marked by historical contingencies that nurtured early onset market liberalization. The military state and Western donors were equally invested in creating an NGO sphere that would take on the work of development in the rural economy. With the embrace of the women's empowerment model in the 1970s, feminists and women's groups also joined in the NGO movement to improve Bangladeshi women's economic and social roles. This collusion between the state and NGO sphere also dictated the terms of the debates of market reforms and how they affected women's roles. What was addressed within the NGO sphere was how women could benefit from participating in the market and in democracy, rather than questioning what kinds of interests and policies these institutions were serving. More important, this long immersion in market liberalization in a military state that stifled oppositional voices, coupled with the NGO form resulted in the creation of a space where the questioning of women's empowerment models, most notably microfinance in Bangladesh, became an impossibility.

A class-based leftist feminist lens helps us to analyze how women get inserted into the market as objects for increasing profits, and not as subjects who are defined by working and voting. It also helps us to better locate the class-based politics of the people who represent poor women in public fora. A critical feminist politics of anti-neoliberalism and market reforms—whether it comes from *thotkatha*, CBS, Activist Anthropology, or elsewhere—will begin to disarticulate women from the market and engage with alternate ways of organizing resources and human capital. The silencing of critique that I have analyzed here is due to a discursive formation that is hegemonic in Bangladesh, and it does not imply that feminists in Bangladesh are unable to critique neoliberalism. Instead, it suggests that those voices (and they do exist) cannot be heard in the sphere dominated by a free-market ideology. Silence in speech is not an absence or a lack. Silence is the excavation of knowledge from hidden spaces, from kitchens across villages in Bangladesh where critiques of market reforms are in incubation. From silence we can uncover new modes of context-specific feminist inquiries to analyze women's locations in and out of the market economy and the neoliberal state.

NOTES

Acknowledgments: My sincere thanks to Leela Fernandes and Farida Khan for their thoughtful comments and help in improving this chapter. Thanks are also due to two anonymous reviewers of an earlier version of this essay. Thanks also to the members of the symposium "Feminists Rethink the Neoliberal State" at the University of Michigan, Ann Arbor.

1 BRAC was originally named the Bangladesh Rural Advancement Community when it was formed in 1972). It is now referred to simply as BRAC with no reference anymore to its original name.

2 "The First World Conference on Women was held in Mexico City, 1975 that focused on gender equality, elimination of gender discrimination, participation of women in development, and increased contribution by women towards strengthening world peace." www.worldbank.org. Accessed June 17, 2016.

3 There are certain limitations to the framing of this article. I have not studied the vernacular publications, such as newspaper opinion pieces, for feminist critiques of the free market reforms policies. For a future project, it would be good to examine the vernacular dailies for women's writings on the state and market economy. My focus here is on local Bangladeshi scholars, and not diasporans or westerners writing on these issues. In writing this essay I have met with and interviewed feminist scholars, NGO leaders, left activists and students. I have also drawn from my long-term research in Bangladesh.

4 Liberal feminism has developed different strands of thought. I have focused on the role of the individual as the agent of change in liberal feminist thought.

5 UBINIG is the abbreviation of its Bengali name, Unnayan Bikalper Nitinirdharoni Gobeshona. In English it means Policy Research for Development Alternative.

6 Author's interview with Anu Muhammad on December 27, 2015.

7 Based on author's research among women who belong to the pietist movement known as Tabligh-i-Ja'maat in Bangladesh.

8 Author's interview with Najma Akhter, September 11, 2014.

9 Author's interview with Farida Khan, June 14, 2016.

10 Author's interview with Firdaus Azim, December 22, 2016.

11 Kissinger was referring to the scale of corruption in Sheikh Mujib's Bangladesh, that is, the more aid you give, the more it disappears.

REFERENCES

Ahasan, Abu, and Katy Gardner. 2016. "Dispossession by Development: Corporations, Elites and NGOs in Bangladesh." *South Asia Multidisciplinary Academic Journal* 13.

Alamgir, Rohini, and Afroza Chaity. 2017. "Child Marriage Restraint Act to Practice no Restraint." *Dhaka Tribune*, February 28. www.dhakatribune.com/bangladesh/law-rights/2017/02/28/child-marriage-restraint-act. Accessed May 22, 2017.

Alvi, Hamzi. 1972. "The State in Post-Colonial Societies: Pakistan and Bangladesh." *New Left Review* 1, no. 74: 1–10.

Bajaj, Vikas. 2011. "Luster Dims for Public Microlender." *New York Times*, May 11. http://query.nytimes.com/gst/fullpage.html?res=9F03E4DF113AF932A25756C0A96 79D8B63. Accessed May 22, 2017.

Barry, Ellen. 2015. "Bangladesh Killings Send Chilling Message to Secular Bloggers." *New York Times*, March 30. www.nytimes.com/2015/03/31/world/asia/suspects-held-in-hacking-death-of-bangladeshi-blogger.html. Accessed May 22, 2017.

Bateman, Milford, and Kate Maclean. 2017. *Seduced and Betrayed: Exposing the Contemporary Microfinance Phenomenon*. New Mexico: SAR Press.

Bdnews24. 2010. "Yunus Siphoned Tk. 7b. Aid for the Poor." December 1. bdnews24. com/bangladesh/2010/12/01/exclusiveyunus-siphoned-tk-7bn-aid-for-poor. Accessed May 15, 2016.

Bernal, Victoria, and Inderpal Grewal, eds. 2014. "The NGO Form: Feminist Struggles, States, and Neoliberalism." In *Theorizing NGOs: States, Feminisms, and Neoliberalism*, 1–18. Durham, NC: Duke University Press.

British Broadcasting Service. 2010. "Grameen: Norway Gives All Clear to Bangladesh Bank." December 8. www.bbc.com/news/world-south-asia-119479. Accessed May 22, 2017.

Chowdhury, Zafrullah. 1995. *The Politics of Essential Drugs: The Making of a Successful Health Strategy-Lessons from Bangladesh*. London: Zed Book.

Economist. 2007. "The Minus-Two Solution." September 6. www.economist.com/node/9769010. Accessed June 14, 2016.

Faaland, Just, and J. R. Parkinson. 1974. *Bangladesh: A Test Case of Development*. Boulder, CO: Westview Press.

Famularo, Julia. 2015. "China-Russia NGO Crackdown." *Diplomat*, February 23. www.thediplomat.com. Accessed January 7, 2017.

Feldman, Shelley. 2010. "Paradoxes of Institutionalization: The Depoliticization of Bangladeshi NGOs." *Development in Practice* 13, no. 1: 5–26.

Fernando, Jude. 2011. *The Political Economy of NGOs: State Formation in Sri Lanka and Bangladesh*. London: Pluto Press.

Gilmore, Ruth Wilson. 2009. "In the Shadow of the Shadow State." In *Navigating Neoliberalism in the Academy, Non-Profits and Beyond*, ed. Soniya Munshi and Craig Willse. http://sfonline.barnard.edu/navigating-neoliberalism-in-the-academy-nonprofits-and-beyond/ruth-wilson-gilmore-in-the-shadow-of-the-shadow-state. Accessed June 5, 2017.

Guhathakurta, Meghna. 2015. *Agrarian Change in Bangladesh and its Implications for the Marginal Farmers: Issues, Debates, Challenges.* Dhaka: Research Initiatives in Bangladesh (RIB) Publications.

Gunewardena, Nandini, and Mark Schuller. 2008. *Capitalizing on Catastrophe: Neoliberal Strategies in Disaster Reconstruction.* Lanham, MD: AltaMira Press.

Hashemi, Syed, Sidney Schuller, and Anne Riley. 1996. "Rural Credit Programs and Women's Empowerment in Bangladesh." *World Development* 24, no. 4: 635–53.

"*Interim Report of the Grameen Bank Commission.*" 2013. Ministry of Finance, Government of Bangladesh, Dhaka. February 9. www.mof.gov.bd. Accessed May 1, 2017.

Jaggar, Alison. 1983. *Feminist Politics and Human Nature.* Totowa, NJ: Rowman and Allanfield.

Kabeer, Naila. 2005. "Gender Equality and Women's Empowerment: A Critical Analysis of the Third Millennium Development Goal." *Gender and Development* (special issue, *Millenium Development Goals*) 3, no. 1: 13–24.

Karim, Lamia. 2011. *Microfinance and Its Discontents: Women in Debt in Bangladesh.* Minneapolis: University of Minnesota Press.

Karim, Lamia. 2016. "Resistance and Its Pitfalls: Analyzing NGO and Civil Society Politics in Bangladesh." In *Sage Hand Book on Resistance,* ed. David Courpasson and Steve Vallas, 461–75. London: Sage.

Keck, Margaret, and Kathryn Sikkink. 1998. *Activists beyond Borders: Advocacy Networks in International Politics.* Ithaca, NY: Cornell University Press.

Lang, Sabine. 1997. The NGO-ization of Feminism." In *Transitions, Environments, Translations: Feminism in International Politics,* ed. Joan W. Scott, Cora Kaplan, and Cora Keats, 101–20. New York: Routledge.

Liton, Shakawat and Rashidul Hasan. 2011. "Caretaker System Abolished." *Daily Star,* July 1. www.thedailystar.net. Accessed June 14, 2016.

Mayoux, Linda. 1999. "Questioning Virtual Spirals: Microfinance and Women's Empowerment in Africa." *Journal of International Development* 11, no. 7: 957–84.

———. 2002. "Women's Empowerment and Participation in Micro-finance: Evidence, Issues and Ways Forward." www.researchgate.net. Accessed May 22, 2017.

Muhammad, Anu. 1998. *Bangladesher unnayan sangkot abong NGO model* (Bangladesh's development crisis and NGO model). Dhaka, Bangladesh: Prochinta Prokashoni.

Nazneen, Sohela, Maheen Sultan, and Naomi Hossain. 2010. "National Discourses on Women's Empowerment in Bangladesh: Enabling or Constraining Women's Choices?" *Development* 53, no. 2: 239–46.

Odhikar. 2009. "141 Killed by Law Enforcement in 11 Months." December 11. www.extrajudicialkilling.info. Accessed January 7, 2017.

Paprocki, Kasia. 2017. "Moral and Other Economies: Nijera Kori and Its Alternatives to Microcredit." In *Seduced and Betrayed: Exposing the Contemporary Phenomenon of Microfinance,* ed. Bateman Milford and Kate Maclean. New Mexico: SAR Press.

Prothom Alo. 2014. "Bangladesh Advances in Human Development," July 24. http://en.prothom-alo.com/bangladesh/news/51218/Bangladesh-advances-in-human-development. Accessed June 2, 2016.

Quadir, Fahimul. 2000. "The Political Economy of Pro-Market Reforms in Bangladesh: Regime Consolidation through Economic Liberalization?" *Contemporary South Asia* 2 (July): 197–212.

Rahman, Aminur. 2001. *Women and Microcredit in Rural Bangladesh: Anthropological Study of the Rhetoric and Realities of Grameen Bank Lending.* Boulder, CO: Westview Press.

Raynor, Janet, and Kate Wesson. 2006. "The Girls' Stipend Program in Bangladesh." *Journal of Education for International Development* 2, no. 2 (July): 1–10.

Riaz, Ali. 2016. *Bangladesh: A Political History Since Independence.* London: I. B. Taurus.

Rita-Ramos, Alcida. 1994. "The Hyperreal India." *Critique of Anthropology*, June 14, 153–71.

Ronneberger, Klaus. 2008. "Henri Lefebvre and the Urban Everyday Life: In Search of the Possible." In *Space Difference, Everyday Life*, ed. Kanishka Goonewardena, Stefan Kipfer, Richard Milgrom, and Christian Schmid, 134–46. New York: Routledge.

Sabur, Seuty. 2013a. "The Enemy of My Enemy Is My Friend." *Alal-o-Dulal*, May 2. https://alalodulal.org/2013/05/02/farida-akhter. Accessed June 16, 2016.

———. 2013b. "Did 'NGO-ization' Deradicalize the Women's Movement?" March 28, 2013. http://alalodulal.org/2013/05/28/ngoization. Accessed June 5, 2017.

Sassen, Saskia. 1996. *Sovereignty in an Age of Globalization.* New York: Columbia University Press.

Sharma, Aradhana, and Akhil Gupta. 2006. "Introduction: Rethinking Theories of the State in an Age of Globalization." In *The Anthropology of the State: A Reader*, ed. Aradhana Sharma and Akhil Gupta, 1–42. Malden, MA: Blackwell.

Srivathsan, A. 2013. "Muhammad Yunus Knew Seeking Political Office in Bangladesh Would Receive 'Bruising Response'." *Hindu*, June 6. http://www.thehindu.com/news/the-india-cables/Muhammad-Yunus-knew-seeking-to-   enter-politics-in-Bangladesh-would-receive-lsquobruising-response/article12060966.ece. Accessed May 22, 2017.

Wolch, Jennifer. 1990. *The Shadow State: Government and Voluntary Sector in Transition.* New York: Foundation Center.

World Bank Report. 1996. *Pursuing Common Goals.* Dhaka, Bangladesh: World Bank Publications.

———. 2014. *Four Decades of Partnership: The World Bank in Bangladesh.* Washington, DC: World Bank Online Publications. www.worldbank.org.

Zohir, Sajjad. 2004. "NGO Sector in Bangladesh: An Overview." *Economic and Political Weekly*, September 4, 4109–13.

Zohir, Sajjad, and Imran Matin. 2004. "Wider Impacts of Microfinance Institutions: Issues and Concepts." *Journal of International Development* 16: 301–30.

5

An Improvising State

Market Reforms, Neoliberal Governmentality, Gender, and Caste in Gujarat, India

DOLLY DAFTARY

Introduction

On a warm morning in July 2007, during a spell of fieldwork at Dahod town in Gujarat, western India, where I had returned to the district headquarters after a stretch of village-level fieldwork in Limkheda block (the block is the subdistrict administrative level), a chance encounter with the deputy director of the District Rural Development Agency (DRDA) resulted in an invitation to join his team for a meeting with elected leaders in Jhalod block. The opportunity to observe bureaucrats' interactions with the leaders of panchayats (elected local rural bodies) would be invaluable in understanding the bureaucrats' new relationship with these new centers of decentralized governance for enacting development. The nature of such local village organizations has changed dramatically since the 1990s when India accelerated its policies of economic liberalization. In 1994, closely on the heels of liberalization, the Indian state enacted Panchayati Raj Institutions, and the government devolved the power and resources for development and local governance to panchayats. Such local processes of state-making where bureaucrats negotiate power and authority with elected leaders in enacting economic change provide a key window into the nature of state practices and power in post-liberalization India.

The meeting was held at the Block Development Office in Jhalod, and decentralized governance forced bureaucrats to move outside familiar environments and into spaces controlled by subordinate actors. Upon reaching the Block Development Office, Pradeep, the deputy director, his assistant, and I moved to a quieter part of the office complex, where Pradeep began the meeting in an airy room, with forty elected leaders in attendance. Pradeep represented the District Rural Development Agency, the highest development agency at the district, the substate administrative level. Pradeep's objective was to inform sarpanches about the Backward Regions Grant Fund, a new program aimed at plugging infrastructure gaps in the country's poorest districts. Pradeep had traversed the administrative distance from Dahod to Jhalod—from district to block—to meet sarpanches to gain their cooperation in fulfilling the state's development objectives. This was extremely significant and indexed a repositioning of the relationship between the state and development agents such as sarpanches. The relationship had switched from development agents traveling to government offices to get an audience with bureaucrats to bureaucrats moving to the unfamiliar terrain of block-level offices to seek the cooperation of elected leaders. At a larger level, this indexes the restructuring of India's rural development bureaucracy in the twenty-first century and bureaucrats' growing reliance on nonstate actors to implement development policies. Periodic meetings with village-level elected leaders had become an integral part of development policy administration in the wake of the post-liberalization state's downsizing and shift of development implementation to nonbureaucratic and nontechnocratic local actors.

This vignette points to transformations in the nature of the state in India, visible in the downsizing of the development bureaucracy and the devolution of governance to local leaders and organizations. This chapter examines this restructuring of the state through the case of watershed development, the Indian state's largest development intervention for semi-arid areas. I focus on a case study of *Hariyali* ("Greenery"), the Indian state's largest developmental policy program initiated in 2003 for resource-poor rural areas characterized by "watersheds"—uplands descending to valleys where rainwater drains—in Dahod district in Gujarat, India's poster state of pro-market reforms.[1] Gujarat is publicly depicted as a model of the success of India's market reforms. India's globally high-profile prime minister won the 2014 national election partly by deploying the "Gujarat Model of Development" as a national blueprint, characterized by the veneration of market-driven growth and privileging entrepreneurial identities.

In a period of market reforms that has shifted state ideology from intervening for human well-being to linking the poor to markets to improve their well-being, Hariyali has switched from ecological regeneration and labor-intensive technologies to natural resource extraction and capital intensification in rain-fed agriculture (Daftary 2014b). This includes delivering microcredit largely to women's "self-help" groups for the purchase of capital for cash-crop production. With the downsizing of the rural bureaucracy, implementation has been delegated to contract workers appointed by large local NGOs. Following decentralization and the delegation of development to local elected representatives, contract workers have partnered with elected leaders to deliver inputs and training to communities.

This essay illuminates emergent features of state-led policies of liberalization in India, not taking "neoliberalization" as given or self-evident, but as a process that consists of reworking the state's boundaries with the market and civil society (specifically nongovernmental organizations [NGOs]), and involves the marketization of the state itself. Through an analysis of changes in state-led development practices and politics related to NGOs, contract workers, and elected leaders, I examine four features of the marketization of the state. First, I analyze the ascendance of market rationalities in government-owned rural banks. Established with the goal of financial inclusion, these banks have now switched to profit-generation. Second, I discuss the rise of contracting and subcontracting to NGOs, that is, the use of market mechanisms by the post-liberalization state's shrinking rural development bureaucracy. Third, I analyze the state's devolution of policy implementation to local elected leaders,[2] also rooted in the government's shrinkage in rural areas. Fourth, through an intensive study of self-help groups, I discuss the deployment of self-governance techniques, specifically notation and inscription technologies to bring about self-regulating development subjects, consistent with the new state's emphasis on "less government," and necessary in the context of its downsizing. While these changes reveal new relationships between the state and nonstate entities, these mutations emerge from transformations within the state itself.

In my analysis, I draw upon the state-in-society analytical approach, which emphasizes that the state is not an entity that stands above society but is influenced by social, economic, and political forces that leave their impression upon the state (Gupta 1998; Migdal 1994; Sivaramakrishnan 1996). Economic liberalization has led to pressures to shrink government and facilitate the expansion of private capital and markets (Kohli 2012). The dimensions of neoliberal reforms that I focus on include an ideology centered on market expansion, the valorization of contracts (Harvey 2005), and state restructuring, including downsizing the public sector (Fernandes 2000). Such reforms are associated with the ascendance of the ideology, tropes, and practices of markets becoming principles governing governmental entities (Daftary 2014a).

I also draw upon Michel Foucault's work on governmentality as the "conduct of conduct" (Foucault 2008), or the (state's) regulation of how the individual should regulate herself, to elaborate upon the mechanisms that an attenuated state uses to regulate both the agents and subjects of development. Hardt and Negri (2000) yield the insight that "late" capitalism is marked by the amplification of the state's dispersion of regulation to the social sphere. Individuals internalize regulation so that the state governs more by governing less. The result is the creation of circumstances that lead people to regulate themselves by means of inscription technologies, defined as practices of writing and documenting in order to measure productivity. The state deploys quasi-legal and legal texts that mandate the recording of development agents' and subjects' actions across levels—at the village, the "block" which is a cluster of villages, and the district which is the substate administrative level, and spheres—within the community, civil society and the state itself. By producing constant scrutiny of the self among development subjects and contingently employed development agents, this performs the function of surveillance. It thus divests the state from the responsibility for both supervising its workers and building the capacity of rural subjects.

Women are both the sites upon which such state practices of neoliberal development are enacted (as development subjects—those upon whom development is focused, and who are expected to transform and modernize in idealized ways through their participation in development) and agents for the enactment of state agendas (as development workers). The inherently unequal rules of neoliberal development that involve intensive surveillance and self-regulation affect women in distinctive ways. It may be no coincidence that microcredit, which demands punitively high financial discipline, has emerged as a key rural devel-

opment strategy in India for two categories of development subjects—
women and people with disabilities.[3] It is symptomatic of the deepening
inequality characterized by neoliberalism that the development strategy
that embodies the most exacting self-governance techniques is extended
to the most vulnerable social groups. Women appear to form the logi-
cal site of action for the state to craft disciplined and "useful" (Foucault
1997) bodies to undertake production for an exchange economy, made
possible by the discipline imposed by the imperative of repaying microcredit loans. Women had already become targets of both international
and state developmental policies and organizations, who emphasized
women's groups as agents for community change, women's leadership as
promoting participatory decision-making processes, and women's literacy as an instrument for family well-being. Microcredit builds upon the
infrastructure created by the commonplace acceptance of these models
among development practitioners. On the other side of the development
enterprise, women are now a growing part of the contracted workforce
that implements development. A downsized, attenuated state has become more feminized. Women's employment in the state is expanding,
in precarious terms, at the same time that the state itself is weakening,
with neoliberalism reproducing patterns of gender inequality.

My analysis is based on fieldwork that was conducted from August
2006 to January 2008 and was grounded in Dahod in eastern Gujarat,
which shares borders with the states of Rajasthan and Madhya Pradesh.
I analyzed circulars, policy guidelines, technical reports, and press re-
leases; and I conducted interviews and participant observation with the
DRDA, its partner-NGO and contractual workers. During a long-term
stay in Mahipura village in Limkheda block, I observed self-help group
(SHG) meetings and panchayat meetings, read panchayat records and
SHGs' registers. I also interviewed ten village leaders, three panchayat
leaders, ten SHG leaders, and thirty-three SHG members. India's marginal drylands are inhabited by its marginalized social groups—"lower"
cultivator castes, called Kolis in Gujarat, and tribes called Adivasis,
regarded as subordinate groups by caste Hindu society. Mahipura is
dominated by Kolis who regard themselves as hierarchically superior
to Adivasis, and Adivasis are in a minority in the community.[4] Gender interacts with caste in shaping the nature of development policies
designed for specific populations of "lower" castes and tribes, and the

particular groups within them—specifically women—who are intensive targets. Microcredit was delivered largely to women's groups mostly made up of Kolis and a few Adivasis.

Neoliberal Development and Gendered State Restructuring

Watershed development represents the attempt to incorporate remote rural areas into global circuits of commodity production, and microcredit forms a fecund ground for the creation of disciplined labor necessary for high-value commodity production. Hariyali is situated within this emphasis of post-liberalization agricultural policy on value-generation through commodity production (Chandrasekhar and Ghosh 2002). This includes the cultivation of "high-value" crops (Taylor 2011) such as milk, flowers, fruits, medicinal plants, and spices through disciplined and flexible labor, a quality seen as being better met by women (Singh 2002). Cash-crop production increases cultivators' dependence on commercial inputs, and watershed development delivers microcredit by means of the Swarnajayanti Gram Swarozgar Yojana (henceforth SGSY) to enable cultivators to purchase cash inputs. The dramatic growth of microcredit in India itself is linked to reforms in the financial sector that have transformed the goals of state-owned banks from financial inclusion to profit maximization (Ghosh 2012). A state-sponsored microfinance program, SGSY is based on the self-help approach wherein borrowers—mostly women—form self-help groups (SHGs). Members themselves monitor and sanction one another to ensure loan repayment and financial discipline.

Hariyali is administered by the Department of Land Resources of the central state's Ministry of Rural Development. The policy is jointly administered by the DRDA and an NGO, which appoints contract workers who implement the policy in local communities. At every block, which is a cluster of twenty to thirty villages, contract workers form watershed development teams, which are gendered entities that deliver input and training to communities in their respective blocks. Each team comprises an agronomist who is responsible for introducing high-value crops to cultivators, a civil engineer responsible for water harvesting and irrigation works, and a social development specialist who facilitates the delivery of microcredit. While watershed development guidelines mandate women's inclusion in watershed development teams, the regional state's guidelines foreclose the possibilities opened by this by mandating that the social development team member be a woman. Guidelines from the government of Gujarat's Commissionerate of Rural Development[5] to district rural development agencies specify that the social development team member "mandatorily" (*farajiyat*) be a woman (GOG 2003). Women are sequestered into the labor-intensive, underfunded arena of "social development," while the resource-rich arenas of agronomy, livestock development, civil engineering, and irrigation engineering remain, in practice, male domains. The microcredit portfolio is implicitly feminized in formulation and explicitly in implementation. Microcredit contract workers control the smallest proportion of financial resources allocated to each watershed development team, while being assigned the messy and conflict-ridden task of crafting and assisting self-help groups. Higher professional qualifications are required of women workers charged with microcredit than agronomists and civil engineers. While microcredit experts had to have a master's degree, only a bachelor's degree was required of agronomists and engineers. In this way, the regional state in Gujarat reproduces a patriarchal state in local contexts.

The feminization of the state's workforce, visible in the mandatory inclusion of women in watershed development teams, has occurred within the context of the growing precarity of the state itself. The actors to whom the attenuated state has devolved development are disproportionately contracted women development workers employed on contingent and precarious terms. Policy guidelines mandate the inclusion of women in the contracted workforce, which is tellingly marked by precarity, vulnerability, wage erosion, and growing pressures of self-monitoring and accountability. State policies of market liberalization are deployed in unique and new ways among women from marginalized groups, including subordinated castes and tribes. Feminization is visible not only in the case of contract workers but also within the rural bureaucracy itself, specifically the lowest-level bureaucratic representatives in the community: panchayat secretaries. The panchayat secretary manages land records and collects taxes. Since at least 2006, the panchayat secretary's salary has been lowered and a new five-year "probation" period introduced for new recruits. No benefits or pension contributions are made during the probation. This has precipitated a shift in the gender profile of new panchayat secretaries, with a disproportionate share being women.[6] The growing visibility of women in government is concomitant with an accelerating contingency of government employment and its wage erosion. Women's employment in ground-level government positions has expanded on a massive scale at the same time these positions have shifted from being permanent to contractual, have been stripped of benefits, and have had their salaries decline in real terms. The advancement of women's formal-sector employment at the same time that work conditions in the formal sector are made more vulnerable illuminates the ways in which inequalities produced by neoliberal policies intertwine with gender and caste inequality.

The celebration of women's economic agency while rendering their economic sphere increasingly unstable reveals the state's "gender selectivity" (Jessop 2007)—the simultaneous transformation *and* reproduction of asymmetries between men and women. The logic of neoliberalism operates through simultaneous processes of state feminization and state attenuation. This is visible in greater employment for women in development but on contingent terms, expansion of women's economic agency through microcredit but with the specter of financial punishment, and women's inclusion as government functionaries but their positions become contractual.

Profit-Oriented Rationalities in State-Owned Rural Banks

The ascendance of microcredit as a development intervention has occurred in the context of a particular set of financial reforms in India. Economic reforms have deepened a policy emphasis on the economic performance of state-owned banks in India (Kochar 2011). Policy texts articulate the imperative that state-owned banks generate financial returns (see GOI 2007). The logic of profit-making among government-owned banks is evident in changes in their lending practices to the poor. Their lending costs are higher, they deliver larger loans to well-endowed borrowers, they have divested from borrowers' capacity-building, and now emphasize repeated loans for profit-making at the expense of the debt repayment capacity of borrowers. Government-sponsored microcredit interventions, little studied in the microcredit landscape, need to be viewed in light of the movement of state-owned capital to new geographies in search of value. Whether driven by the need to stay afloat in the face of banking privatization and growing competition from private sector banks or the need to take advantage of their own dominance in rural areas, combined with support from the government machinery to capture rural financial markets, government-owned banks are now guided by the principle of profit among the rural poor. The imperative to earn higher returns has led government-owned banks to scale back from building the capacity of SHGs, reduce subsidies, and embark on larger loans to those who are financially well endowed. The morphing of the rationalities of state-owned banks signifies a vital change in their relationship with rural borrowers, from economic empowerment to profit maximization and from financial inclusion to preferential selection (Daftary 2014a). State-owned banks' practices reveal a substantive shift in development policy and denote its market-driven turn.

While capacity-building was a core objective of earlier microcredit programs and included emphasis on literacy, financial education, building group skills, sharing information on resources, and linking SHGs to government schemes and NGOs, this function has now been hollowed out. SHG leaders, rather than bank staff or NGOs assisting banks, now perform critical banking functions. SHG leaders are mandated to maintain individual members' and the group's records, estimate individual and group savings, calculate monthly deposits, enumerate loan repayment and interest rates, and travel to the bank to conduct transactions. SHG leaders have to sanction deviant members, conduct group meetings, and collect information on schemes. The burden of governance has been imposed on SHGs while banks have been freed of these responsibilities. Later in the essay, I discuss how the devolution of critical banking functions to SHG leaders strengthens existing power relations in the locality.

The rise of profit rationalities in state-owned agencies is one aspect of the marketization of the state; another is downsized state agencies' use of market mechanisms, specifically contracts, to carry out their work. Next, I discuss an attenuated rural bureaucracy's recruitment of NGOs and contingent workers on the basis of short-term contracts to enact development, and elaborate on how contracting raises questions about the fragility of the boundary between the state and market.

Contracting for Development

With the decline of the post-liberalization state as an employment provider and the downsizing of government agencies, government departments have initiated the use of contract workers, a market mechanism that was previously a characteristic of private sector liberalization (Fernandes 2000). A shrunken rural development bureaucracy has outsourced the administration of watershed development to a "lead NGO," who in turn works as a subcontractor to hire contingent workers who form the largest share of Hariyali's workforce. Contracting is both an instrument to transform the internal organization of the state by downsizing departments and cutting the labor force, and a symptom of state transformation in that it reveals the state's adoption of everyday market practices.

Contracts govern the relationship between the DRDA and lead NGO. The lead NGO is recruited on a two-year contract and denoted a "service provider" (GOG 2004), and treated as a "vendor of goods and services on the basis of a contract" (Gordenker and Weiss 1997). This contractual model has characterized the relationship between multilateral organizations and the NGOs that have "outsourced" their work during global privatization since the 1990s. The lead NGO is assigned participatory rural appraisals, recruitment and training of contract workers, and field evaluations. Policy guidelines stipulate that "only that NGO which has implemented 30 or more watershed development projects or crafted 100 or more SHGs, has a turnover in excess of 3,000,000 rupees the previous year, and at least five field staff working in the district" (GOG 2004) may become a lead NGO. State choice privileges large-scale NGOs with infrastructure and a technocratic vision akin to the state. In Dahod, the lead NGO during 2004–6 was Sadguru, an NGO established by the textile corporation Mafatlal and possessor of the largest headquarters among NGOs in Dahod. The lead NGO during 2006–8 was Gramin Vikas Trust, a government-owned NGO that extends hybrid seeds, fertilizer, and improved livestock breeds to the well-endowed, privileging technical intervention over social transformation. During 2008–10, the lead NGO was Mahatma Gandhi Pratishthan, which overwhelmingly executes government schemes.

The lead NGO works as a subcontractor through which the DRDA recruits contract workers. The director of the Development Support Center, an NGO headquartered in Ahmedabad, Gujarat's commercial capital and NGO hub, told me, dismissing the lead NGO as simply a recruiting agent: "The lead NGO's primary job is recruitment—there are more than 15 NGOs [state-wide] simply paid to recruit and re-recruit [contract worker] candidates each year for *Hariyali*."[7] The lead NGO, not the DRDA, issues newspaper advertisements to hire workers, administers candidates' tests, and conducts interviews along with DRDA bureaucrats. Tellingly, according to the bureaucrats' mandate, "The advertisement should be issued not by DRDA but by lead-NGO. . . . the appointment letter should be signed and issued by NGO" (GOG 2005). Thus the lead NGO functions as an intermediary that legally distances the DRDA from contract workers. This safeguards against workers litigating the state to be treated as government employees with long-term security and benefits (see GOG 2005).

The selection of large, technocratic NGOs breaks down the boundary between the state, civil society, and the market. NGOs' performance of "services" as business vendors, and their work as subcontractors to recruit workers, dismantles the boundary between civil society and the market. The rise of civil society in the 1990s was celebrated for the possibilities it created to mobilize the state to be more inclusive and just (Chandhoke 1995; Fukuyama 2001). However, having NGOs serve as subcontractors of the state raises questions about civil society's capacity to maintain distance from the state, and challenges the upward distribution of development resources underway in market-driven development paradigms. Unlike the powerful transnational NGOs in Bangladesh that force the state to comply with international conventions (see Lamia Karim's essay in this volume), development NGOs in India's resource-poor rural regions have little bargaining power with the state. Recent scholarship on state transformation has remarked on the shift from government to "governance" comprising state and nonstate actors (Jessop 1997), but governance evokes a neutral field of power. The state's incorporation of technocratic NGOs under the guise of governance cloaks the distinctive neoliberal dimensions of the developmental state. By coopting civil society, the neoliberal state can become more pervasive while seeming more indiscernible.

The lead NGO's recruitment of contract workers is symptomatic of the retrenchment of public-sector employees and the deployment of market instruments like contracts to recruit personnel. The norm, "the shorter the term of market contracts the better" (Harvey 2005), is evident in the contracts of contingent workers. Contract workers are hired on twelve-month contracts. Labor contracting mirrors one trait of labor market restructuring in India since the 1990s—job security being linked to productivity (Fernandes 2000). Contracts stipulate tasks in terms of numerical targets, and productivity is measured by singular targets. Contract workers face a 35 percent higher goal for forming SHGs than NGOs that delivered microcredit through NGO-implemented interventions concomitantly with Hariyali. Contract workers are fractured from bureaucrats, and supervision structures between technocrats and contract workers are broken: contract workers sit in a separate, temporary location, apart from the technocrats, who are at the Block Development Office. Contract workers scarcely meet the technocrats, who meet only with the head of each watershed development team. Paradoxically, it is the weakening of intradepartmental relationships and the lack of an institutional identity for contract workers that creates the imperative to specify work targets for them. With bureaucrats withdrawing from monitoring, contract workers are mandated to monitor themselves through documentary practices, a theme that will recur in my discussion of development subjects.

Contract workers' wage payments are made contingent on timely updates to their time diaries and monthly reports (GOG 2003). Discipline, a function of supervision, is built-in by linking wages to the submission of activity reports. Workers' writings are used to evaluate, discipline, and regulate them, a practice that is mirrored in the governance of SHGs. Making individuals write down things, and the nature of the things they are made to write down, is itself a kind of government of development agents (Miller and Rose 2008a). Progress reports and time diaries signify an "audit culture" (Atkinson and Coffey 2004) wherein workers are increasingly made to self-supervise, a feature of neoliberal governmentality. The use of workers' documentation as a tool to monitor productivity makes writing a critical tool to display performance. Later in the essay, I show how documentation was tactically employed by powerful development subjects to exhibit "good governance" and appropriate development goods.

Power and Governance in the Locality

Decentralization may be the starkest feature of state transformation in India. It constitutes the devolution of power from the central state to regional states and local governments, particularly since 1994 to panchayats, the elected local bodies. Political devolution has come close on the heels of economic liberalization in India (Gupta and Sivaramakrishnan 2011). Decentralization signifies "state capacities being reorganized territorially and functionally on sub-national levels" (Jessop 1997). Panchayats allow the state to exercise power through finer conduits. Elected bodies are now assigned a key role in implementing development policy and reveal how a reorganized state provides low-cost development by mobilizing already existing organizations that are able to penetrate villages. Panchayat leaders called sarpanches implemented Hariyali (GOI 2003). The village watershed development committee is headed by the sarpanch, who is elected by the entire electorate of a panchayat, and includes a representative from among ward members who are elected from each electoral ward overlapping with hamlet boundaries. The committee includes a representative each from farmers' groups, SHGs, and user-groups of natural resources.

Consider the characteristics of sarpanches. Sarpanches are at once government representatives possessing legal authority, local leaders who can mobilize groups, and information brokers with intimate awareness of families' economic circumstances; all of this is critical for crafting viable self-help groups. SGSY guidelines underscore that implementers "talk with as many sarpanches as possible" and that elected bodies be "an integral part of" self-help groups' day-to-day functioning (GOI 2011). Sarpanches closed the gap between contract workers and communities. Elected leaders held village meetings to illuminate microcredit's advantage over informal moneylending. Sarpanches provided the infrastructure of village schools and panchayat halls for the contract workers and bank officers to meet people. Sarpanches facilitated "the organization of the self-organization of partnerships" (Jessop 1997) between banks and rural borrowers, recording the names of potential SHG members and having their photographs taken to fill bank forms. At the loan-making stage, sarpanches became cultural brokers for bank officers who traveled to communities to ascertain borrowers' repayment ability. Land records typically reflect undivided holdings, with several inheritors' names on a single title (Trivedi 1998). Sarpanches helped bank officers assess individual repayment capacity on the basis of their awareness of kin relationships and individual landholding. The release of loan monies required both the bank officer and sarpanch's signatures. In case debtors failed to pay their loans, creditors could rely on sarpanches to back them if they had to seize an asset.

At the same time, sarpanches are overburdened with service delivery without having commensurate resources or taxation powers. The devolution of fiscal resources from the central state to regional states is much higher than that from regional states to local governments (Kalirajan and Otsuka 2012). Sarpanches may therefore demand bribes from SHGs to arrange meetings with contract workers, attest to bank officers about debtors' financial stability, or connect groups to banks. An SHG's ability to muster the support of a sarpanch was vital for securing credit. Based on a study of five SHGs in Mahipura, I will discuss how the decentralization of microcredit's governance led to local leaders who shared reciprocity with the sarpanch becoming the central actors in setting up self-help groups. SHGs were formed by lineage leaders who had *governmental* capacities in the community. These leaders enforced norms, sanctioned violators, and mediated disputes. With banks divesting from capacity building and the rural bureaucracy downsizing, social networks based on local relationships of power began to manage the implementation of development policies.

In eastern Gujarat, social organization and settlement is based on the lineage—a kinship network whose members trace their descent from a common ancestor (Mosse et al. 2002). The lineage is the basis for identity, cooperation, and political mobilization. Every lineage is ruled by one or more leaders who arbitrate disputes among lineage members regarding property, marriage, and violence. Lineage leaders are better endowed than most households in their lineage, and wealth gives them the resources to sanction violators. Together, leaders of lineages comprise a network of dispute mediators called the *panch*. Disputants avoid going to the courts or police because the police may take bribes, and courts entail traveling to the district headquarters and facing delays from a backlog of cases (Krishna 2002). Disputants instead rely on the *panch*, which involves two or more lineage leaders hearing disputing parties' accounts and delivering a verdict. The sarpanch is regarded as a village-wide dispute mediator who intervenes in serious cases like murder. Lineage leaders and the sarpanch share reciprocity, wherein leaders count on the sarpanch to mediate serious disputes, and the sarpanch relies on the lineage leader's support to back his judgments in larger disputes. Lineage leadership is founded in rules of village exogamy and male land inheritance, and women are excluded from the *panch*, with their interests poorly represented in disputes. Given that informal institutions strongly shape formal institutions of local governance, both the idea and practice of women's leadership in panchayats, despite one-third representation of women being mandated, is strongly resisted, perhaps the most by male political publics involved in the panchayat and *panch*. In every election, seats of ward members and the sarpanch are reserved by rotation for women candidates across the block (and in "tribal" districts, for Adivasis within this category). Male candidates prop up women from their families as stand-ins to meet formal requirements; while campaigning, strategizing, and if elected, participating as full and legitimate panchayat members themselves.[8] However, there are exceptions to this rule, and formal legislation and changing social norms have led to the rise of a small number of women who are panchayat leaders in their own right.[9]

The sarpanch usually collaborates with lineage leaders to deliver development because lineage leaders may retaliate by rejecting the sarpanch's judgment in a particular case, by re-opening an old case saying there was a miscarriage of justice, or by withdrawing electoral support (Daftary 2010). Consider the case of a conflict between the people and their sarpanch in Sukhdi, Garbada block, over use of the village pond. In 2005, the sarpanch unilaterally leased the village pond (used by households to provide drinking water for livestock and for surface irrigation) to a private entrepreneur for fish-farming. Sukhdi's lineage leaders led a massive protest against the quasi-privatization of the pond, convening a village assembly on the banks of the pond itself. Leaders exercised their juridical power to convene a public meeting in a collective space while rejecting the official space of the panchayat. The sarpanch was mandated to attend this *panch* as the accused party. Lineage leaders ruled that the pond was a communal resource over which the panchayat held no property rights, and produced village-wide collective action of watering livestock at, and drawing water for irrigation from the pond, effectively destroying the fish farm.

Lineage leaders are also development agents who rally resources from the sarpanch in return for their lineages' votes in panchayat elections because they influence lineage members' voting behavior. Lineage leaders contest, and often win, elections themselves as ward members. The leaders of Mahipura's largest lineages, Patels, Barias, and Chauhans, all Kolis, secured the most self-help groups based on their numerical and economic dominance in the community. With the backdrop of governance being devolved to formal and informal local institutions, the panchayat and *panch*, and their actors—specifically the sarpanch and lineage leaders—crafted self-help groups. The delivery of microcredit was structured by patriarchal and casteist institutions of local governance. Women's access to microcredit was contingent on their networks with male lineage leaders, and on patriarchal notions of citizenship rooted in rules of male land inheritance and village exogamy. Like women, Adivasis in Koli-dominated Mahipura held no position of informal leadership, were not represented in the *panch*, and were largely excluded from microcredit. While 43 percent of all Kolis gained membership in a self-help group, only 12 percent of Adivasis did.

The handing over of microcredit delivery to panchayats gave considerable influence to lineage leaders.[10] With a limited state delegating microcredit to contracted workers, authoritative lineage leaders commanded self-help groups based on their power to sanction, their link with the panchayat, and their wealth. As one SHG member explained, "There's no one else capable of making people pay, no one else who can impose the rules." Consider these lineage leaders' profiles. Shankar, the Chauhan lineage leader, was a development agent, cash-crop farmer, and sarpanch from 2002–6. Paaru, a Baria lineage leader, was a first-time ward member in 2007 and a cash-crop farmer. Veera, a Patel lineage leader, was a longtime ward member and development agent who traveled to government offices. Bharat, a younger Patel lineage leader, was a development agent, vote broker and cash-crop farmer who contested the 2007 panchayat election for a ward-member seat. I wish to show that lineage leaders took the place vacated by government agencies. During

May 2003 to June 2006, Mahipura formed eight SHGs covering eighty households. But by August 2007 only five survived, those led by lineage leaders who held authority (*hoddo*) and deduced the law (*kaaydo*), that is, performed *governmental* functions in the community. Lineage leaders could act upon members' "will and circumstances" (Miller and Rose 2008b) and ensure that members deposited their monies on time. Particularly when profit-based microcredit has squeezed borrowers by raising the collateral saving period from twelve to eighteen months, lineage leaders could meet a member's shortfall with the promise of being recompensed when her cash flow improved. Lineage leaders met the travel costs involved in the new and extended banking, amounting to some 180 rupees over eighteen months, equivalent to six months of individual savings. Wealth provided lineage leaders resources for sanctioning and meeting the transaction costs of profit-based microcredit. Table 5.1 delineates lineage leaders' assets, specifically livestock, wells, and irrigation motors, the bases of accumulation in dryland western India. Each leader's assets are compared to the average for his lineage, indicated in parentheses.[11]

TABLE 5.1. Lineage leaders' assets compared to the average for their lineage (in parentheses)

Lineage leader	Wells owned	Motor rights	Per capita livestock
Shankar	2 perennial (1 late-winter)	1 (0.31)	1.77 (1.04)
Paaru	1 perennial (1 mid-winter)	0.33 (0.42)	1.12 (1.08)
Bharat	3 perennial (1 late-winter)	2 (0.55)	2.67 (1.28)
Veera	1 perennial (1 late-winter)	1 (0.55)	1 (1.28)

Source: Household surveys conducted by the author in 2007.

Lineage leaders could best meet SHGs' external transaction costs, which needed cooperation from panchayat actors. Lineage leaders could constrain the sarpanch to hand over loan monies because they influence votes and jointly control dispute resolution. The panchayat secretary prepares the affidavits that borrowers have to submit to banks to get loans, and is seen as one of the most extractive state representatives in rural India (Gupta 2005). But the secretary has to cooperate with lineage leaders who are ward members. In order to advance to borrowing, self-help groups are evaluated by the contract worker for cohesion, procedural regularity, and financial soundness (GOI 2011). For this, the contract worker observes group meetings and examines its records. Lineage leaders travel to Limkheda's Block Development Office, where contract workers are situated, to grasp performance evaluation criteria. Proactive leaders use contract workers' field visits to demonstrate the commitment of their groups to microcredit.

Although lineage leaders met transactions costs for groups, they also fashioned the boundaries of inclusion in these groups. Leaders reported that the internal costs of managing their groups were more onerous than the costs incurred in transacting with banks, and attempted to reduce their costs. In eastern Gujarat, houses are set amid their fields and settlement is scattered. There are significant distances between dwellings, which increases the costs of conducting meetings. Therefore, lineage leaders included kin living in proximity, which were usually closer kin, and better-off neighbors. Moreover, leaders handpicked educated kin as the scribes of the group.

Lineage leaders did the work that government representatives, bank staff, and NGO workers once did in communities: they organized self-help groups and linked groups to external actors. Lineage leaders were made to expend their own resources to do the state's work in the aftermath of the state hollowing out its ground-level institutions. This signifies a major feature of the new state—shifting the costs of development on resource-poor communities and divesting the work of development to community actors. The state's divestment to community leaders indexes both the diminishment of ground-level governmental workers in rural India, and the imposition of costs of governance on new unpaid "development workers" in the community. The exclusive reliance on informal institutions also has implications for power, in that it reinforces hierarchies of gender and caste in the locality rather than provides a countervailing external governmental institution to challenge these forces.

While one mechanism the restructured state in India uses to enact development policies is to tacitly divest their administration to informal institutions, another is the use of inscription technologies for development subjects to regulate themselves. This is another mode by which costs are transferred to the beneficiaries of development policies. The use of inscription technologies is predicated on educational attainment and information literacy. Hierarchies of caste and gender shape access to education and information. Consider that the literacy rate for Dahod district is just 47 percent.[12] Furthermore, male literacy is 56 percent while female literacy is 38 percent. New technologies intersect with existing structures to reinforce social hierarchies. The next section discusses how powerful Koli scribes and lineage leaders employed inscription technologies to materialize an account of "good governance" of their self-help group in order to appropriate loans.

Inscription Technologies and the Production of Self-Regulation

Self-help groups are mandated to record the minutiae of their activities and transactions, and a group's evaluation is contingent on this. Inscription technologies have emerged as a critical feature of governance in the post-liberalization period in India. Inscriptive technologies comprise the mandatory documentation of processes and activities by development subjects and development workers. With banks delegating calculative and record-keeping functions to SHGs, leaders have to be able to calculate and notate financial and procedural elements of microfinance. Technologies of notation constitute a diffuse mechanism of rule to classify and act upon SHGs. Group leaders experience "constant metrological scrutiny" (von Schnitzler 2008)—they are required to note beginning and ending monthly balances, individual and group savings, interest earned, loan payments per member per year and till date, and individual and group loan compound interest.[13] These inscriptive mechanisms engender a "govern" *mentality*, a habitus of self-observation and self-recording. It is significant that the "group" rather than the community has become a new unit of acting on development subjects since the 1990s (Li 2007), during a time when large central states have been broken up into "decentralized," "local" governments—both consist of the atomization of political entities. While watershed development operates through groups on the ground—user groups of natural resources, farmer groups, irrigator groups, and (women's) self-help groups— the burden of self-governance is imposed only on self-help groups. Watershed development teams deliver inputs directly to individuals within user groups, farmer groups, and irrigator groups. But women (and people with disabilities) in self-help groups are subjected to self-monitoring and self-surveillance in order to receive benefits, and bear disproportionate costs of calculating, transacting, and managing groups, that is, carrying out the work of development agents themselves. Neoliberal governmentality reveals the imposition of greater burdens on the marginalized in ways that further sideline vulnerable individuals. This section discusses the implications of the state's deployment of inscriptive self-regulation for the distributional consequences of microcredit.

When a group is formed, the contract worker delivers the group's account book, minutes book, and group bank passbook, and lists all the members in the group register. A self-help group may have ten to twenty members, who deposit an equal sum ranging from thirty to fifty rupees over twelve months. Members then mandatorily draw their savings, which are denoted as an "internal loan," and repay these monies over six months. Internal loan repayment demonstrates financial discipline and the borrowers' commitment to repaying. On the basis of observing meetings and written accounts, the contract worker then rates a group "weak," "average," or "good" (GOI 2011). A ranking of "good" allows a group to advance unconditionally to taking loans. The delivery of an array of textual devices including the group register, bank passbook, and individual passbooks activates a timeline, the endpoint of which is a perfectly legible chronicle of group discipline at the end of eighteen months. SHGs are evaluated on the basis of meetings' regularity, member attendance, minutes, periodicity of savings, accounting, and successful repayment of internal loans.

With banks' withdrawal from empowerment, the tasks of recording minutes and calculating financial transactions fall on the president and secretary of the self-help group. Governmentality, or "the diffusion of self-regulatory modes of governance. . . . beyond the bounds of the state" (Sharma 2006) informs the institutionalization of inscriptive practices by the state. Inscriptive technologies regulate borrowers from a distance and render groups comparable, facilitating the selection of viable borrowers across scores of SHGs. Just as Block Development Officers evaluate and discipline contract workers based on their activity reports and biweekly dairies, SHGs are appraised on the basis of their monthly and annual notations. Mandatory inscriptions do the work of managing both SHG members and contract workers.

With SHGs having to subject themselves to computation, the development actors' ability to calculate, compute, and notate is critical for getting loans. Mahipura's lineage leaders appointed those individuals as paper leaders who could compute and elegantly deploy the lexicon of microcredit. Lineage leaders and scribes of the first loan-taking group in Mahipura materialized an account of "good governance" of their group to secure, and appropriate loans. Shankar, Mahipura's Chauhan lineage leader, formed Gayatri, a group comprising persons with disabilities. The group comprised three Chauhans, two Barias, and a Patel, all upper-caste Kolis, both men and women, in 2003. Gayatri had the most elaborate record of all SHGs in Mahipura. I gained access to its documents from Babu, the group's secretary. SGSY guidelines prescribe that groups "should devise a code of conduct" (GOI 2011). Gayatri was the only self-help group to list by-laws, demonstrating the codification of rules. The group identified its leaders' responsibilities as building solidarity, convening meetings, recording their proceedings, accounting, and presenting accounts "to anyone who asked to see them."[14] This aligned with SGSY directives to "develop financial management norms" (GOI 2011). The records revealed that members agreed on a date, time, and location for meetings and delegated the authority to conduct bank transactions to the group president. Members purportedly resolved to donate a rupee every month for stationery expenses and affirmed to meet periodically and deposit cash punctually. The group was an exemplar of SGSY directives to "be able to draw up an agenda for each meeting and take up discussions as per the agenda" (GOI 2011). Gayatri came across as a group with intent and democratic governance.

At a later stage, the group deliberated on securing a collective loan for a "productive purpose." Fissures in this chronicle appeared after one year. Minutes of the thirteenth meeting indicated that the Chauhan president and secretary, the only literate members and both kin of the panchayat leader, reassured the others that henceforth they would report on the bank transaction they conducted on behalf of the group. This clarification appeared to be in response to members' protest, suggesting prior malpractices by the leaders. However, at the subsequent meeting in July 2006, the group's non-Chauhans were obliterated from its roster and ten new Chauhans from the panchayat leader's lineage were added. The minutes stated that the Barias and Patels had been delinquent with their contributions and were expelled. At the crucial eighteenth meeting when the contract worker would evaluate the group, the expelled members were miraculously re-admitted. Group leaders appear to have attempted to reverse their irregularities in the face of outside scrutiny. With the non-Chauhans restored in the group, the group announced a decision to take a tractor loan "for the landowners to earn an income above their subsistence needs by growing crops for the market."[15] Members ostensibly acquiesced to this first and hefty loan being taken by a certain Gela Chauhan.

As Gayatri was one of Mahipura's few SHGs to acquire capital during the course of my fieldwork, I was able to see how capital was used once it arrived, and what its downstream distributional consequences were. I had been struck by the sight of a spanking-new Mahindra tractor, Mahipura's first, in the sarpanch Shankar's homestead during my early days in the village. Shankar had explained that he bought it with a bank loan accompanied by a subsidy. A triangulation of Shankar's account with Gayatri's records and interviews with Gayatri's members who sardonically called the tractor the "SHG tractor" (*juthnu* tractor) revealed that the machine was bought with the SHG's loan. The loan-taker Gela Chauhan was Shankar's father. Babu, Gayatri's secretary, displayed Gayatri's register to me one late summer afternoon. Babu disclosed that he used to write the minutes at the sarpanch's house.[16] Babu and Shankar shared reciprocity and Shankar, then sarpanch, channeled development goods to Babu, his kin, in return for Babu engineering Gayatri's records. Shankar had made Babu and Sunita, his cousin Ram's wife, the secretary and president, respectively, of the SHG. While both Babu and Sunita were literate, gender shaped control over the SHG. Shankar connived with Babu to manipulate the SHG's records and turned a blind eye when Babu siphoned group members' monies amounting to some eight hundred Indian rupees. However, Shankar promised Sunita and Ram that he would help them get a livestock loan.

The broader goal of this vignette is to illustrate that discursive practices are not just neutral written texts but are performative practices, that is, they materialize a certain reality (Barad 2007). Inscriptions serve as instruments that set certain processes into motion and bring about material effects. Notation is not an empty act of recording but is fraught with the politics of those who inscribe as well as those who deploy inscription technologies for regulation. Hierarchies of caste, gender, and class intersect with the project of a "limited state" to shape the effects of inscription technologies. Inscription technologies may obfuscate ground-level realities when they are decentralized and countervailing institutions of monitoring that once existed are eliminated. In the DRDA and the Bank of Baroda's records, Gayatri was likely classified as a successful group that had taken a viable loan. However, loans were appropriated by the skilled use of inscription technologies, enabled by the market-driven turn of state-sponsored microfinance that has obliterated meso-level institutions between communities and banks, and divested the work of banking to SHGs themselves.

Conclusion

This essay has used an analysis of development in India's resource-poor rural regions to examine the nature of state transformation. A scrutiny of development in rural Gujarat, the flagship state of pro-market reforms in India, reveals the marketization of the state. The rationale of state-owned banks shifting to profiting from "the fortune at the bottom of the pyramid" (Prahalad 2009) reveals a breakdown of the boundary between the state and market. Across the developing world, market-driven strategies like microcredit have ascended when the postcolonial socialist state has withered. In this context, the rural and urban poor are meeting their subsistence needs through borrowing. Both private and state-led microfinance schemes are meeting with success at a time when households are turning to borrowing to meet needs of social reproduction (Taylor 2011). This essay discussed how state-led processes are spurring market incorporation in remote rural India through microcredit. Further attention needs to focus on how policies, governmental mechanisms, and incentives are producing a dramatic transformation of social relations in rural India, as well as resource-poor communities in the global south and elsewhere.

While the profit-driven turn of government-owned banks is one feature of the postreform state, another is its internal transformation organizationally and its pervasive recourse to labor contracting. Globally, the employment-generating state has diminished, safety nets have frayed, and work has become contingent. The scaling back of government employment in rural India is particularly harsh because of the acute paucity of formal employment in rural geographies. The diminution of the government is embodied by a "shadow state" in Bangladesh (Karim, this volume), and in India, by a downsized bureaucracy and its temporary workers and contract NGOs. New government jobs, although witnessing the rise of female employment, are seeing women employed on more precarious terms and earning lower wages than men. Neoliberal governmentality finds a companion in the patriarchal state. Women's economic agency is celebrated at the same time that new segments of work opening to them are marked by contingency and instability. Furthermore, neoliberal development strategies like microcredit that attempt to craft disciplined bodies for entrepreneurial production are targeted at female development subjects, a theme Karim discusses in the case of garment sector workers in Bangladesh.

Contracting emanates from the market-based state's anxieties about the efficiency of government. While contracting diminishes anxieties concerning efficiency, it heightens anxieties concerning the possibility of labor litigation by disaffected workers. Contract work creates the paradox of the state enforcing strong rules to secure productivity from workers who are employed on weak terms. With governmental downsizing, inscription technologies demanded at periodic junctures are emerging as key instruments for controlling contract workers. Notation technologies function as governmental devices of a retrenched state that imposes self-governance on its workers.

This essay contributes to our understanding of the nature and practices of the neoliberal state through a multiscalar account. While neoliberal governmentality is conceived of as a dismantling of the state, the neoliberal state may be more pervasive while being more invisible in the guise of state-civil society partnership and democratic decentralization. I characterize the new state as an improvising state, constantly departing from precedent and certainty, and provisionally doing the work of government and administering social life. One feature of improvisation is state *nonintervention* or the creation of an ungoverned space in the locality. Here local forms of power step in to fill the chasm created by state withdrawal. The new state's assemblage includes formal and informal leaders who enforce norms, mediate disputes, and deliver services. Further study is needed into how new modes of governance are shaping political identities and practices.

NOTES

1 Gujarat has historically been one of India's most pro-market states (Sinha 2003, 2005). It embarked in 1995 on a particularly market-driven path under the rule of the Hindu nationalist Bharatiya Janata Party (Sud 2012).

2 Elected local leaders are actors in political society, the realm that arises from civil society and consists of all organizations and actors concerned with capturing state power (Cohen and Arato 1992).

3 Microcredit as a development intervention is vested in narratives of empowerment (e.g., Rankin 2001; Sharma 2008) that construct marginalized populations, including the poor, women, and people with disabilities (e.g., Chaudhry 2011), as objects of economic transformation. In the case of disability, the focus on multiplied and intersecting marginalities heightens the legitimacy of the "empowerment" narrative. For example, in the southern Indian state of Andhra Pradesh, the World Bank funded self-help groups (*sanghams*) of marginalized people, chief among them people with disabilities, through a structural adjustment loan.

4 I also conducted household surveys (N=123) focused on subsistence production, education, market participation, participation in village organizations, migration, and wealth. A list of all households was built from Mahipura's voters' list. A household was defined as a unit that had a common kitchen. Data were entered in SPSS Version 17.0 and statistical analysis was conducted in SAS Version 9.1.

5 Commissionerate is the term used by the government agency.

6 Participant observation of meetings of the Block Development Officer with female panchayat secretaries at the Block Development Office, Limkheda, on November 23, 2006.

7 Interview in Ahmedabad on March 9, 2007

8 From the mid-2000s onward, partly as a result of mobilization by women panchayat leaders and civil society groups mobilizing for greater political representation of women, male panchayat members who rule by proxy are careful not to represent themselves as panchayat representatives in public speeches, but to state that they are assisting the female household member who is the nominal panchayat candidate/incumbent.

9 The institutionalization of women's representation in panchayats and changing norms has also led to girls and young adult women aspiring to political careers by way of the panchayat system.

10 Kohli has argued that panchayats are less effective local governments designed after the diminution of centralized states.

11 Well ownership (table 5.1, column 1) was defined as household rights to wells that are owned or inherited jointly with kin. Wells were categorized as perennial, late-winter, and mid-winter wells. Perennial wells hold water all year and allow three to four sowings. Late-winter wells dry up in March and enable two to three sowings. Mid-winter wells dry up by January and allow one or two sowings. Wells

have to be used with motors that pump water to fields through pipes. Motors (column 2) may be shared like wells. A household with exclusive ownership of a diesel or electric motor was allocated full rights (represented as "1"). A motor shared by two households led to each being assigned 0.5 rights, and so on. Livestock (column 3) are a critical form of wealth because they can be sold for cash in case of drought without having to sell or mortgage land. Livestock wealth was measured in terms of per capita livestock per household. Bulls were assigned a weight of 1.25 because of their centrality in plowing. Milk cattle had a weight of 1, calves 0.5, and goats 0.25. The total number of each livestock type was multiplied by its weight, and this figure was added across types to measure total endowment. Per capita livestock was measured by dividing each household's livestock by the number of household members using the adult equivalent scale, which is often calibrated based on nutritional requirements for individuals by age and gender. Following Deaton and Muellbauer (1980), I assigned a weight of 0.2 to children aged 0–6, 0.3 to those aged 7–12, 0.5 to those aged 13–18, and 1.0 to those 18 and older. This formula was used to convert the number of individuals in the household to the adult equivalent by multiplying the total members in each age category by the category's weight and adding the figures across age groups. This figure was used to divide household livestock to obtain per capita values.

12 According to the 2011 census.

13 Reading of registers distributed to self-help groups by Dahod's lead NGO in 2007.

14 Gayatri self-help group register

15 Ibid.

16 Interview with Babu on March 21, 2007 at his home.

REFERENCES

Atkinson, Paul, and Amanda Coffey. 2004. "Analysing Documentary Realities." In *Qualitative Research: Theory, Methods and Practice*, ed. D. Silverman, 56–75. London: Sage.

Barad, Karen. 2007. *Meeting the Universe Halfway: Quantum Physics and the Entanglement of Matter and Meaning*. Durham, NC: Duke University Press.

Bateman, Milford. 2010. *Why Doesn't Microfinance Work?* London: Zed Books.

Chandhoke, Neera. 1995. *State and Civil Society: Explorations in Political Theory*. New Delhi: Sage.

Chandrasekhar, C. P., and Jayati Ghosh. 2002. *The Market That Failed: A Decade of Neoliberal Economic Reforms in India*. New Delhi: Manohar.

Chaudhry, Vandana. 2011. "Disability and the Neoliberal Indian State: The Perils of Community Participation." *Research in Social Science and Disability* 6: 265–81.

Cohen, Jean, and Andrew Arato. 1992. *Civil Society and Political Theory*. Cambridge, MA: MIT Press.

Daftary, Dolly. 2010. "Elected Leaders, Community and Development: Evidence on Distribution and Agency from a Case in India." *Journal of Development Studies* 46: 1692–707.

———. 2014a. "Development in an Era of Economic Reform in India." *Development and Change* 45: 710–31.

———. 2014b. "Watershed Development and Neoliberalism in India's Drylands." *Journal of International Development* 26: 999–1010.

Deaton, Angus, and John Muellbauer. 1980. *Economics and Consumer Behavior*. Cambridge: Cambridge University Press.

Fernandes, Leela. 2000. "Restructuring the New Middle Class in Liberalizing India." *Comparative Studies of South Asia, Africa and the Middle East* 20: 88–104.

Foucault, Michel. 1997. "Technologies of the Self." In *Ethics: Subjectivity and Truth*, ed. Paul Rabinow, 223–52. New York: New Press.

———. 2008. *The Birth of Biopolitics: Lectures at the College de France, 1978–1979*. Basingstoke: Palgrave Macmillan.

Fukuyama, Francis. 2001. "Social Capital, Civil Society and Development." *Third World Quarterly* 22: 7–20.

Ghosh, Jayati. 2012. "Microfinance and the Challenge of Financial Inclusion for Development." Paper presented at the Annual Conference of the Central Bank of Argentina, October 1–2, Buenos Aires.

Gordenker, Leon, and Thomas G. Weiss. 1997. "Devolving Responsibilities: A Framework for Analysing NGOs and Services." *Third World Quarterly* 18: 443–43.

GOG (Government of Gujarat). 2003. "Letter from the Commissioner of Rural Development, Government of Gujarat, Regarding the Employment and Wages of Watershed Development Team Members, Dated 25th September 2003." Gandhinagar: Government of Gujarat.

———. 2004. "The Use of NGOs for Community Development and Training in the Hariyali Watershed Development Program. Gandhinagar: Government of Gujarat.

———. 2005. "Letter from the Commissioner Secretary, Department of Rural Development to Directors of District Rural Development Agencies, No. Crd/Vnk/1599(12)/315–39, Dated 13th January 2005." Gandhinagar: Government of Gujarat.

GOI (Government of India). 2003. "Guidelines for the Watershed Development Program 'Hariyali.'" New Delhi.

———. 2007. "Report of the Expert Group on Agricultural Indebtedness." New Delhi: Government of India.

———. 2011. "SGSY Guidelines." New Delhi: Government of India.

Gupta, Akhil. 1998. *Postcolonial Developments: Agriculture in the Making of Modern India*. Durham, NC: Duke University Press.

———. 2005. "Narratives of Corruption: Anthropological and Fictional Accounts of the Indian State." *Ethnography* 6: 5–34.

Gupta, Akhil, and Kalyanakrishnan Sivaramakrishnan. 2011. "Introduction: The State in India after Liberalization." In *The State in India after Liberalization: Interdisciplinary Perspectives*, ed. Akhil Gupta and Kalyanakrishnan Sivaramakrishnan, 1–27. New York: Routledge.

Hardt, Michael, and Antonio Negri. 2000. *Empire*. Cambridge, MA: Harvard University Press.

Harvey, David. 2005. *A Brief History of Neoliberalism*. New York: Oxford University Press.

Jessop, Bob. 1997. "Capitalism and Its Future: Remarks on Regulation, Government and Governance." *Review of International Political Economy* 4: 561–81.

———. 2007. *State Power: A Strategic-Relational Approach*. Cambridge, MA: Polity.

Kalirajan, Kaliappa, and Keijiro Otsuka. 2012. "Fiscal Decentralization and Development Outcomes in India: An Exploratory Analysis." *World Development* 40: 1511–21.

Kochar, Anjini. 2011. "The Distributive Consequences of Social Banking: A Microempirical Analysis of the Indian Experience." *Economic Development and Cultural Change* 59: 251–80.

Kohli, Atul. 2012. *Poverty Amid Plenty in the New India*. Cambridge: Cambridge University Press.

Krishna, Anirudh. 2002. *Active Social Capital: Tracing the Roots of Development and Democracy*. New York: Columbia University Press.

Li, Tania Murray. 2007. *The Will to Improve: Governmentality, Development, and the Practice of Politics*. Durham, NC: Duke University Press.

Migdal, Joel S. 1994. "The State in Society: An Approach to Struggles for Domination." In *State Power and Social Forces: Domination and Transformation in the Third World*, ed. Joel S. Migdal, Atul Kohli, and Vivienne Shue, 7–34. Cambridge: Cambridge University Press.

Miller, Peter, and Nikolas Rose. 2008a. *Governing the Present: Administering Economic, Social and Personal Life*. Cornwall: Polity.

———. 2008b. "Introduction: Governing Economic and Social Life." In *Governing the Present: Administering Economic, Social and Personal Life*, ed. Peter Miller and Nikolas Rose, 1–25. Cornwall: Polity.

Mosse, David, Sanjeev Gupta, Mona Mehta, Vidya Shah, Julia Rees, and KRIBP Project Team. 2002. "Brokered Livelihoods: Debt, Labour Migration and Development in Tribal Western India." *Journal of Development Studies* 38: 59–88.

Prahalad, Coimbatore Krishnarao. 2009. *The Fortune at the Bottom of the Pyramid: Eradicating Poverty through Profits*. Upper Saddle River, NJ: Wharton.

Rankin, Katherine. 2001. "Governing Development: Neoliberalism, Microcredit, and Rational Economic Woman." *Economy and Society* 30: 18–37.

Sharma, Aradhana. 2006. "Crossbreeding Institutions, Breeding Struggle: Women's Empowerment, Neoliberal Governmentality, and State (Re)Formation in India." *Cultural Anthropology* 21: 60–95.

———. 2008. *Logics of Empowerment: Development, Gender, and Governance in Neoliberal India*. Minneapolis: University of Minnesota Press.

Singh, S. 2002. "Contracting Out Solutions: Political Economy of Contract Farming in the Indian Punjab." *World Development* 30, no. 9: 1621–38.

Sinha, Aseema. 2003. "Rethinking the Developmental State Model: Divided Leviathan and Subnational Comparisons in India." *Comparative Politics* 35: 459–76.

———. 2005. *The Regional Roots of Developmental Politics in India: A Divided Leviathan*. Bloomington: Indiana University Press.

Sivaramakrishnan, Kalyanakrishnan. 1996. "Forests, Politics and Governance in Bengal, India, 1794–1994." Doctoral thesis, Department of Anthropology, Yale University.

Sud, Nikita. 2012. *Liberalization, Hindu Nationalism, and the State: A Biography of Gujarat.* New Delhi: Oxford University Press.

Taylor, Marcus. 2011. "'Freedom from Poverty Is Not for Free': Rural Development and the Microfinance Crisis in Andhra Pradesh, India." *Journal of Agrarian Change* 11: 484–504.

Trivedi, Harshad. 1998. "Tribal Land in Gujarat." In *Tribal Situation in India: Issues in Development with Special Reference to Western India,* ed. Vidyut Joshi, 151–74. New Delhi: Rawat Publications.

von Schnitzler, Antina. 2008. "Citizenship Prepaid: Water, Calculability, and Techno-Politics in South Africa." *Journal of Southern African Studies* 34: 899–917.

6

The Broken Windows of Rosa Ramos

Neoliberal Policing Regimes of Imminent Violability

CHRISTINA HEATHERTON

THE BROKEN WINDOW OF ROSA RAMOS

Chelsea, Massachusetts 1991

Rosa Ramos could spread her palm
at the faucet for hours
without cold water
ever hissing hot,
while the mice darted
like runaway convicts
from a hole in the kitchen floor.

The landlord was a spy,
clicking his key in the door unheard
to haunt the living room,
peeking for the thrill of young skin,
a pasty dead-faced man still hungry.

Her husband was dead.
She knew this
from *El Vocero* newspaper,
the picture of his grinning face
sprayed with the black sauce of blood,
a bullet-feast.
Rosa shows his driver's license,
a widow's identification,
with the laminated plastic
cracking across his eyes,
so that he watches her
through a broken window.

> She leaves the office
> rehearsing with the lawyer
> new words in English
> for the landlord:
> *Get out. Get out. Get out.*
> —Martín Espada

Nuyorican poet Martín Espada penned "The Broken Window of Rosa Ramos" in 1991.[1] At the time, Espada was working as a supervisor of Su Clínica Legal, a legal services program for low-income, Spanish-speaking, mainly immigrant tenants in Chelsea, Massachusetts, just outside of Boston. In this "tough little town, a gateway city, a city of immigrants," as Espada recounted, most residents were squeezed into dense neighborhoods, one-third of the population compressed into ten blocks of cramped housing. Espada and his associates worked on housing issues. They fought evictions, sought court orders to exterminate rats and roaches, and forced landlords to fix heating during winters. In 1991, the year of the poem, the town was placed in receivership, the first time a state government had taken such measures against a U.S. municipality since the Great Depression, a measure toward fiscal austerity that would soon be replicated in other cities throughout the country.[2]

Rosa Ramos was a pseudonym for a recently widowed Puerto Rican client of Espada's, a woman trapped in space. She is depicted attempting to escape the cold, the vermin, and the unwanted incursions of her landlord. Her physical environment is a porous testament to her vulnerability: holes in the kitchen floor, broken windows, and a door that won't stay locked. She is exposed, and the poem heaves with the threat of violence against her. The fictional Ramos was one of many women in Espada's office who hailed not only from Puerto Rico but also from the Dominican Republic, Guatemala, El Salvador, Nicaragua, and to a lesser degree, Vietnam and Cambodia. These were captives of occupation, refugees of U.S.-backed wars, women whose lives overlay the imagined divides between "home" and "abroad."[3]

In 1992, a neoliberal administration in Puerto Rico campaigned to improve the "quality of life" of Puerto Ricans through a new policy of *mano dura contra el crimen* (a firm hand against crime). In practice, *mano dura* authorized a series of militarized policing measures waged in coordination with the National Guard against poor and working-class residents of public housing projects and barrios. The subsequent onslaught of checkpoints, sweeps, brutality, and campaigns of intimidation, as well as a dramatic uptick in homicides, left many on the island wondering whose "quality of life" was actually being improved. By locating disorder in the bodies of the poor, *mano dura* refashioned space and disciplined subjects suitable for the privatization of public housing and new regimes of neoliberal accumulation. As American Studies scholar Marisol Lebrón recounts, Puerto Rican officials had "turned to policing in an effort to maintain 'order' and manage populations rendered redundant." Such policing measures complimented the broader restructuring of the Puerto Rican economy.[4]

But the violence of *mano dura* was not imposed by an isolated regime. It sprouted from practices implemented in the crowded neighborhoods of Chelsea, Massachusetts, and the broader Boston area during the 1980s and 1990s. It permeated cities throughout the contiguous United States and seeped insidiously around the world through a multitude of broken windows. *Mano dura* was one example of a policing philosophy called the "broken windows theory." This theory asserted that when police stopped small petty crimes such as graffiti or loitering—often called "quality of life" offenses—they could prevent more serious violent crimes from occurring. By endowing police with the expanded discretion to control and moderate individual behavior, the implementation of this doctrine vastly broadened the capacities of police both nationally and globally, from New York, to Johannesburg, San Juan, and beyond.[5]

Broken windows policing, this chapter argues, is a key mechanism through which the social volatility, necessary for neoliberal regimes of accumulation, is maintained. Indeed, broken windows policing has flourished within and also has furthered the volatile economic context of neoliberalism. As a specific regime of capital accumulation, neoliberalism is characterized by a contradictory temporality: the immediacy of the present (short-term investments) and the potential of unrealized futures (circulations of fictitious capital and speculative investments). This disjuncture generates ceaseless social and spatial instability. The dictates of the neoliberal political economy constantly fall out of alignment with the collective needs and desires of the people whose labors, rents, consumption, and compliance enable it to function. Neoliberalism therefore requires a method of regulation that can discipline bodies and reconfigure space at the pace of capital's needs. Broken windows policing is that mobile practice: a portable logic capable of reconfiguring space in the name of regulating disorder. It builds on and expands already existing race, class, and gendered exclusions, renovates them and intensifies them toward new ends. In an era of mass incarceration, this doctrine has transformed people into the walking warrants of neoliberal cities.[6]

The presiding social logic of neoliberalism, as other essays in this volume explain, does not imply a dismantling of government but rather constitutes a specific and strategic technique of governing. As the co-author of the broken windows theory, James Q. Wilson has similarly suggested, broken windows policing is better understood as a type of *broken windows government*. Accordingly, broken windows must be regarded beyond the realm of policing procedure and be understood in its capacity to abet local regimes of accumulation and to reinforce governing functions of the reconfigured neoliberal state. This chapter argues that broken windows policing has emerged as the social regulating mechanism used by cities and local states to discipline bodies, refashion public space, and render cities suitable for regimes of neoliberal capital accumulation. It is a predictive model of policing appropriate for an era of speculative capital.[7]

At the time of this writing, the United States is experiencing the most dramatic denunciation of broken windows policing since the practice first came to prominence. High-profile police killings of people of color and Native people such as Michael Brown, Rekiya Boyd, Loreal Tsingine, and Alex Nieto, alongside the filmed executions of Eric Garner, Walter Scott, Tamir Rice, and others, have provoked sustained and growing outrage. As mass protests from Ferguson and Baltimore have been met with armored weapons, tanks, and tear gas, much attention has focused on the militarization of the police. While doubtlessly disturbing, most of these deaths required no unusual authorization of force: Eric Garner was strangled to death, Tanisha Anderson was slammed on the pavement, and Laquan McDonald was shot by officers. In addition, Officer Daniel

Holzclaw required no armored tanks when he stalked and raped several Black women during routine traffic stops. Protests have broadened the critique of police violence, not only condemning people's deaths in police custody but also questioning how people have been forced to live under the current policing regime. As feminists confronting the neoliberal state, we are charged to think specifically about the conditions authorizing these developments (Baker et al. 2015; Larimer 2016; Serna 2015; Shaffer 2015; Welborn 2013).

Drawing from Espada's "The Broken Window of Rosa Ramos" (1994), this chapter proposes the concept of *imminent violability* as an analytic through which vulnerability might be comprehended within the racial, spatial, and ultimately gendered dimensions of neoliberal securitization. Though the poem is not about policing, it captures multiple aspects not customarily associated with broken windows policing such as the exclusions of propertied citizenship, the gendered violence of poverty, and the transcendence of imperial violence beyond the borders of nation-states. The poem also condenses the experience of violation as a looming threat. Fear, especially fear of impending bodily harm, is not an existential state nor a "subpolitical emotion" but a condition produced through specific shifts in the political economy. By thinking within and across scales, from the regulation of bodies and behavior to the refashioning of spaces for global capital, the chapter argues that *imminent violability* can serve as a radical feminist critique linking racism, capital accumulation, and the increasingly commonplace vulnerability to state violence most keenly experienced by poor and working-class communities of color across the United States and beyond.[8]

Broken Windows Policing

"The unchecked panhandler is, in effect, the first broken window."
—James Q. Wilson and George Kelling

Discretion, the capacity of police officers to interpret various situations and make decisions about how to best enforce law, is now a mainstay of policing procedure. Legal scholars brought renewed attention to the issue in the late 1960s and early 1970s during urban uprisings and

urban renewal redevelopment projects of the period. "Order maintenance policing," the practice of aggressively enforcing laws against petty
crimes, is an outgrowth of those debates. It is the formal name for what
has come to be known as broken windows policing. The term "broken
windows" was popularized by a 1982 article in the *Atlantic* magazine by
political scientist James Q. Wilson and criminologist George Kelling:
"Broken Windows: The Police and Neighborhood Safety." The article
touted the success of a Newark, New Jersey, pilot program funded by
the Police Foundation where Kelling was research director. The broken windows theory was subsequently promoted by conservative social
scientists and most vigorously by the Manhattan Institute, a right-wing
think tank, of which Kelling was, and continues to be, a fellow.[9]

Police have historically had a limited range of formal discretionary
powers, deployed through measures such as vagrancy laws, loitering
laws, Black codes, and other forms of banishment aimed at purported
sex workers. The concept of order maintenance policing expanded their
discretionary powers to stop, question, cite, or arrest any person they
deemed to be a source of disorder. By expanding police capacity from
response to preemption, broken windows policing came to constitute a
dramatic shift in the legal functioning of police. Praised as "a revolution
in American policing," it was quickly adopted by police departments
across the country.[10]

In their *Atlantic* article Kelling and Wilson concluded that the best
way for police to prevent major crimes was to maintain visible signs of
order in communities. The central metaphor describes an unaddressed
broken window in a neighborhood as signaling neglect and encouraging small crimes, which then lead to larger ones. Unchecked disorder—
graffiti, litter, panhandling, public urination, and the like—is presumed
to breed more grievous crimes such as rape, assault, and homicide. The
expansion of discretion, according to the theory, simply encourages officers to maintain spatial order. What constitutes "order" and for whom
is presumed to need no explanation.[11]

Broken windows draws upon earlier discursive practices that naturalized urban blight as a product of individual behavior rather than government policy of "organized abandonment."[12] Broken windows policing
dissimulates police power relations in a similar manner. The seemingly
innocuous transition from spatial metaphor to presumptive behavioral

assessment is replete with biologized geographic assumptions. Through the metaphor of broken windows, human action is aggregated and abstracted into its spatial effects. The landscape is presumed to visually communicate social control, or the lack thereof, like a patient bearing symptoms. Crime is naturalized into an external invading pathogen. Criminals are construed as exterior forces, singularly driven in their quest to infect spaces with ever-greater crimes. Accordingly, assailable space and its presumptive victims are metaphorized into organs or cells lacking proper immunity. This imagined ecology is highly local and also nonspecific: the pathology of spatialized disorder can be grafted onto the streets of any city at any time.[13]

In this scientific-seeming presentation, the police appear to possess unique expertise to diagnose and treat these symptoms in the landscape. But police are not doctors, landscapes are not diseased bodies, and crime is not a pathogen but a transgression of the law. Crimes change as laws change, and laws change, as geographer Ruth Wilson Gilmore notes, "depending on what, in a social order, counts as stability, and who, in a social order, needs to be controlled." *Crime, order,* and *safety* are unfixed contested terms whose definitions shift over time. A country where African slavery, Native genocide, racial segregation, eugenic sterilization, and the lobotomization of homosexuals were all legal practices should keep this truth at the fore. As the life of broken windows policing has shown, there is great danger in fixing notions of crime and order, just as there is great danger in basing policy on a metaphor.[14]

Rosa Ramos's Broken Windows

While broken windows policing is most often defined as a strategy that took root in New York City, the practice was deeply tied to the world of Rosa Ramos. As noted above, the term was coined in the *Atlantic* magazine, which was then based in Boston. It was Wilson and Kelling who tapped a young Boston police lieutenant named William Bratton to experiment with the theory as chief of the Massachusetts Bay Transit Police. Later, as superintendent of the Metropolitan District Commission Police, Bratton practiced the theory in patrols of poor sections of the Boston metropolitan area. (In his memoir *Turnaround*, Bratton describes Kelling and Wilson's theory as giving name to a practice that he had intuitively been enacting throughout his time patrolling Boston). Not just a renovated policing strategy, the practice facilitated local urban redevelopment. Bratton engaged in active partnership with planners and urban redevelopers in Boston through a public-private initiative called the Boston-Fenway Program, which he described as "one of the first community-policing initiatives in the nation." In this capacity, Bratton was charged with formally bridging the interests of capital and the state, deploying the police force to minimize signs of urban disorder in order to attract new capital investment to the city. Bratton was well suited for such a position: he had studied urban geography at Boston State College in 1971 where he, as he writes, began to "learn the importance of cities and how they develop."[15]

In 1990 Bratton was tapped to bring these tactics to New York City where he served as the city's transit police chief. Under the continued guidance of George Kelling, Bratton came to fame for targeting people who were jumping over subway turnstiles and sleeping on benches as signs of disorder. After increasing citations and arrests, Bratton and the Manhattan Institute declared the philosophy a success. Shortly after, he brought these practices back to Boston, becoming superintendent-in-chief of the Boston Police Department in 1992. That year he issued a plan of action, writing, "In city after city, where relatively few people were actually the victims of crime, it was fear of crime and of general social decline that drove middle class people from their homes in the urban centers to what they regarded as the safer havens of the suburbs." With such insights about policing and urban development, Bratton became commissioner of the Boston Police Department.[16]

New York mayor Rudolph Giuliani (also working with the Manhattan Institute) appointed Bratton as police commissioner in 1993. George Kelling again served as a consultant to the city on the implementation of broken windows policies. Under this new regime, police officers were ordered to target petty crimes, which might compromise the quality of life of New Yorkers with a policy of "zero tolerance." The question of whose quality of life was being preserved and whose was compromised was not long contemplated. A cruel new landscape was already emerging, with a growing number of people forced to sleep in public, panhandle, become "squeegee men" offering to clean car windows for change, engage in sex work, and otherwise occupy public space to reproduce their lives.

Rather than signs of social crisis, these actions became symbols of urban disorder, as Neil Smith has demonstrated. Police clamped down accordingly. In logging the vast numbers of citations issued and arrests made, the NYPD produced a massive new database to track and monitor bodies of impoverished New Yorkers. In extrapolating data where previous arrests occurred, police "predicted" where crimes might be committed next and deployed officers accordingly. Such practices naturalized the highly subjective practice of policing into a "denuded mathematical simulacra," as Josh Scannell notes. Through this CompStat model (short for computer statistics), Bratton claimed credit for migrating the logic of risk assessment from the financial sector to the realm of social control.[17]

The unfolding of broken windows policing in New York sanctioned a violent new intimacy between police and the people determined to be sources of disorder. A string of high-profile police murders included the killing of Anthony Baez, a Puerto Rican man killed in an illegal chokehold after the football he was tossing around with his brothers hit an officer's car in 1994. The same year Nicholas Heyward Jr., a young African American boy, was playing with friends in the stairwell of a housing project with clearly marked toy guns. Although Heyward shouted, "We're only playing, we're only playing," NYPD officers shot the thirteen-year-old in the stomach. A year later, Yong Xin Huang, a sixteen-year-old Chinese teenager was shot in a friend's driveway after officers saw him holding a pellet gun. Such murders exceeded plausibility for concerned New Yorkers, who were unconvinced that people at play constituted threatening disorder. Protests would mount in later years against brutal assaults such as the rape and torture of Haitian immigrant Abner Louima in a police station bathroom in 1997 and the 1999 assassination of Guinean immigrant Amadou Diallo, killed in front of his apartment in a hail of forty-one bullets while reaching for his wallet to show officers his ID.[18]

Broken windows gained its greatest legitimacy in the displacing brutality unleashed against homeless populations as well as very poor and working-class queer, trans, and gender-nonconforming communities of color. In places like Times Square and the Chelsea Piers, queer communities had created spaces of belonging constituting alternative kinship networks as well as survival economies. Through arrests, citations, surveillance, and less catalogued acts of brutality, these populations were displaced. Because these populations transgressed normative orders through their gender presentation, sexual preferences, labor and leisure activities, and sociality, the violent policing deployed against them was depicted as a legitimate restoration of order. As a result of these policing practices, both spaces were cleared for redevelopment: the new tourist-friendly Times Square became the proverbial proving ground of New York's "turnaround."[19]

Despite massive opposition organized by groups like the Malcolm X Grassroots Movement, the National Congress for Puerto Rican Rights, CAAV Organizing Asian Communities, and the Audre Lorde Project—all united in the Coalition Against Police Brutality—Bratton and Giuliani were credited with "cleaning up" New York City and making it safe for new investment. Broken windows policing was praised for producing a drastic drop in crime rates, and Bratton and Giuliani fought for bragging rights. Scholars refuted the purported correlation. They denounced the supposed effectiveness of broken windows, noting that the decline of New York City's crime rates coincided with broader national trends. Since many cities where broken windows policing had not been implemented had experienced similar "turnarounds," scholars invalidated the strategy's so-called success. Against these detractors, the Manhattan Institute nonetheless declared, "It works!"[20]

After working as a security consultant, Bratton was appointed chief of police in Los Angeles in 2002 on the basis of his "success" in New York City. There he inaugurated broken-windows-style measures, again appointing Kelling as a consultant, and enlisting the city to pay Kelling over half a million dollars in consulting fees. Bratton and Kelling ushered in some of the most pernicious versions of broken windows policing in the poorest areas of the city, as will be described shortly. Despite widespread organized outrage by groups like the Los Angeles Community Action Network, Youth Justice Coalition, and the Stop LA Spying Coalition, multiple media outlets touted Bratton's term as a success. In 2013 Bratton was reappointed as New York City's police commissioner, a full two decades since his first appointment in the position. In the intervening years, broken windows has been exported around the planet to cities like Johannesburg, Mexico City, Choloma, London, Dublin, Sao Paulo, Barcelona, Bremen, Oslo, Vienna, Stockholm, Caracas, and Rio de Janeiro, with Bratton serving as global security consultant, long after its early trial runs in Newark, New York, and Boston.[21] While Bratton did not originate broken windows policing, he brought the practice to prominence and claimed it as a victory of his own making. As a result, his name has become nearly synonymous with it, a point not lost on protestors who have challenged the validity of broken windows ever since Bratton's first term as NYPD police commissioner.

The Neoliberalism of Broken Windows

Broken windows policing operates in an aspirational future tense. By intervening against presumptive "disorder," it enables police to stop crimes that have not yet been committed. Officers become arbiters of an order to be realized, guardians against activity that could become criminal, and protectors of populations deemed to be the legitimate occupants of cities. This policing regime fortuitously aligns with the future-oriented set of neoliberal economic policies alongside which it arose.

The rise of broken windows policing should be understood within the shifting configurations of capital accumulation during the 1980s and 1990s. This period saw the advance of neoliberalization, a concept that refers to processes such as the imposition of economic policies promoting the free flow of capital unencumbered by state regulation; the reconfiguration of the state away from social service provision and toward the facilitation of finance-led accumulation regimes; the reorientation of state capacities toward punitive functions to manage surplus populations and repress opposition; and an ideological project rationalizing how these transformations are understood, experienced, and explained. The implementation of neoliberal economic policies has had distinct impacts on urban governance.[22]

In U.S. cities, urban governments adopted new social functions. No longer primary sites of social reproduction for productive labor forces, deindustrialized urban centers like Boston and New York were redeveloped into sites for local investment by global capital. In accordance, local urban and municipal governments reorganized their capacities, abolishing the vestiges of New Deal state investment in public infrastructure and social spending and redirecting public investment toward the facilitation of capital mobility. The burden of shrinking public services, including transportation, education, healthcare, mental health, food subsidies, public housing, and access to public space, has been borne by the poorest communities and keenly carried by poor and working-class women.[23]

To manage these transformations, U.S. cities also have vastly expanded their punitive state functions. The criminalization of the urban poor and the political crushing of left and labor opposition were necessary prerequisites for repurposing urban space into localized sites of investment. Police were conscripted to shore up investments and discipline bodies and behaviors in order to reshape the structures and function of cities. In these ways, broken windows policing has not only regulated behavior in space, it has also transformed the very space of its regulation.[24]

These transformations should be situated alongside the state restructuring practices and disciplinary mechanisms unleashed more drastically throughout the global south by structural adjustment. To receive loans, recipient countries have been required to reorganize their economies in the most suitable manner for repayment, creating new sites of investment for transnational finance capital. Most significantly, this has meant procuring cheap, exploitable, docile, unorganized, and more often feminized labor. Social programs have been slashed and privatized, becoming additional sites for investment. Poor and working-class women have also disproportionately subsidized the depleted social infrastructure with their own bodies and labor. Organized state abandonment has rendered feminized labor more easily exploitable and further enhanced specifically gendered vulnerabilities to violence and particularly state violence. These axes of vulnerability are, as Tithi Bhattacharya describes, "the braided chains of discipline that bind the most vulnerable sections of global labor." As the social reproductive functions of the state have been drained, new capacities of law and order have been enlarged. This has meant more police, more military, and more securitized investments. Under structural adjustment policies, the governing functions of states have also shifted from social provisions to the maintenance of social volatility.[25]

Just as former strongholds of leftist and anticolonial struggle were strangled by newly imposed debt regimes in the global south, in the United States former strongholds of organized labor were subject to the most punitive transformations. Leading organized sectors of the U.S.

working class were subject to mass firings, and their plants became early targets of offshoring. Such developments served as warnings to other segments of the class who dared to organize. Similarly, the period saw the overturning of many of the gains of the anticolonial, Black freedom struggles and the social movements of the 1960s and 1970s—a repression of the very memory of social equity. Absent leftist channels for political protest, rage sought new targets.[26]

The implementation of neoliberal policies required discursive practices to render people simultaneously less worthy of the state's shrunken largesse and more deserving of its expanded punitive capacities. Accordingly, this era saw a shift in sensibilities, whereby the debased conditions of poverty, homelessness, and unemployment, went from grievable to contemptible. As unemployment grew, wages continued to stagnate, poverty increased, social services eroded, incarceration rates skyrocketed throughout the 1980s and 1990s, and popular outrage was redirected toward racialized targets.[27]

Rising conservative reaction coalesced in this period, configuring immigrants, Black communities, welfare recipients, queer populations, and the homeless as the culprits of urban decline. As immigration increased, particularly as a result of globalization and U.S.-backed wars in Central America, nativist anger was stoked against "people coming to take American jobs." "Welfare queens," a racist and sexist moniker for imagined African American women supposedly getting rich on undeserved state subsidies, encapsulated the vengeance at the heart of neoliberal ideology. Such constructs incurred the wrath of people who felt their country was being stolen from them. While white working-class people were, and continue to be, the largest recipients of welfare and other forms of state aid, this zero-sum imaginary reconfigured social provisions as unearned racial theft. The neoliberal restructuring of the state, and the slashing of social services, was therefore popularly received, not with anger, but with visceral joy.[28]

Broken windows emerged amid the congealing of racist revenge driven politics. Popular rage was articulated with state transformations against social provisions and toward expansion of law and order. As George Kelling, quoted at length in Bratton's memoir, put it, "Crime prevention can be achieved only by vast social change . . . by restoring family values, primarily by eliminating welfare." In these ways, policing and prisons supplanted liberal state functions: social insecurity was re-inscribed as a way of life. In this distorted landscape, the public presence of poverty shifted from being seen as a symptom of social crisis to a sign of disorder. As Wilson and Kelling note, "The unchecked panhandler is, in effect, the first broken window." Through broken windows policing, the transformations of the neoliberal political economy was diverted into the body of blamed.[29]

Neoliberalism and the Crisis of U.S. Cities

If arrest is "the political art of individualizing disorder" as Allen Feldman suggests, then broken windows performs the art of individualizing capital's abandonment.[30] Through its metaphor, state retrenchment is naturalized as a spatial relation. Amid destructive cycles of deindustrialization, disinvestment, and redevelopment, broken windows policing has been presented as the legitimate and commonsensical practice of restoring order—or more mundanely, cleaning up trash. Broken windows policing therefore unwittingly offers a perfect metonym, albeit not according to its authors' intent. As deindustrialized cities have become veritable landscapes of broken windows—replete with abandoned factories, crumbling infrastructure, and derelict apartment buildings—policy makers, city planners, and police departments alike have utilized this logic to naturalize immiseration as a disease endemic to itself. Poverty has become reducible to its effects and regulated accordingly, a mystification as incredulous as it is callous.[31]

Broken windows do not represent signals of individualized disorder or failing but, rather, capital's production of landscapes of assault and abandonment populated by increasingly vulnerable people. The cleavages of the neoliberal city have only intensified already existing and heavily entrenched race and class divisions. In its logic, poverty, particularly racialized poverty, appears to have no origin. Alongside physical displacements and disinvestments, the era has seen a correlative epistemological displacement, where meaning has been offloaded into space. Broken windows, like other spatial euphemisms such as "ghetto" convey enormously racist meaning without the indelicacy of racist language. Segregation, which was previously codified in law, as legal scholar john a. powell argues, persists without Jim Crow legislation because "those practices are largely inscribed in geography." Speaking about places instead of people has deepened segregation from this period on through our purportedly postracial era.[32]

Broken windows, as many critics have described it, is less of a theory and more of a spatial metaphor. It inhabits the realm of the figurative, allowing its meaning to shift and stray. Accordingly, in their *Atlantic* article, Wilson and Kelling extol the subjective processes that gave people the *feeling* of security. They celebrate an early Newark pilot program that failed to alter crime rates but allowed residents "to feel more secure." Critical for them was the artifice of safety, what legal scholar Bernard Harcourt calls the "illusion of order." To accomplish this, Wilson and Kelling emphasized how broken windows could limit potentially uncomfortable interactions in public space with, for example, an "obstreperous teenager" or a "drunken panhandler," both of which they describe as being as "fear-inducing . . . as the prospect of meeting an actual robber." The equivalence is instructive. The expectation that police can protect people from their imagined fears implies that both protector and protected share the same imaginary, the same fears, and the same normative interpretations of order.[33]

In 1968 James Q. Wilson had offered an earlier iteration of his definition of order, described from the vantage point of a police officer: "A teenager hanging out on a street corner late at night, especially one dressed in an eccentric manner, a Negro wearing a 'conk rag' . . . girls in short skirts and boys in long hair parked in a flashy car talking loudly to friends on the curb, or interracial couples—all of these are seen by many police officers as persons displaying unconventional and improper behavior."[34] This earlier version of Kelling and Wilson's theory exposes the assumptions underlying their construction of disorder. This imaginary laid bare is extraordinarily significant—not because it reveals a secret racist, classist, heteronormative, and homophobic agenda within broken windows to which all practitioners ascribe, but because it challenges the presumed objectivity of the discretion upon which the theory's validity lies.

Discretion is not a value-free concept because space is not a neutral entity. Deep racist social divisions, such as histories of colonial removal, displacement, segregation, and restricted access to federal subsidies such as home loans and tax abatements, are already reified in the spatial organization of cities. Racism, in geographer Laura Pulido's pithy summary, is not a discrete act of animus but rather a sociospatial relation that is "both constitutive of the city and produced by it." Thus, the mechanisms by which police officers "define and seek to control the spaces they patrol" are predetermined. In his study of the Los Angeles Police Department (LAPD), geographer Steve Herbert observes how police assign different moral orders to different spaces of the city and then "patrol with that order in mind, and not the law." Police more often perceive poor and working-class communities of color as "unsafe" and "morally unclean," in contrast to wealthy areas of mostly white residents. The territoriality of policing—the spatialized normative orders determining police discretion—is deeply integrated within and reproductive of racist structures of domination. In these ways, broken windows policing reflects and reinforces the racist sociospatial order from which it springs.[35]

Nearly three decades of broken windows policing has borne the violence prefigured in James Q. Wilson's early spatial imaginary. As neoliberal policies have governed the redevelopment of U.S. cities, non-normative, politicized, racialized, native, immigrant, poor, and working-class communities have suffered disproportionate levels of dispossessions, displacements, evictions, policing, and incarceration as a result. Minimizing the threat of unwelcome encounters has unequivocally meant removing stigmatized people from urban space. In this respect, the metaphor of broken windows reveals as much as it conceals. It is impossible to fix broken windows. They cannot be repaired. They can only be replaced.[36]

Future Orders

Like broken windows policing, neoliberal ideology represents an ideal, not an accomplished fact. Theorists Neil Brenner and Nick Theodore draw attention to "actually existing neoliberalism" as a means of signaling the disjuncture between the "utopian" aspirations of neoliberal ideology and its actually existing forms. The neoliberal ideal takes place, they note, in "no place"—smooth interchangeably imagined spaces upon which market logic is uniformly projected. In practice, neoliberal policies are enacted in places that are distinct, uneven, and capable of generating dense decelerating friction. These are "striated" terrains, spaces where people labor, carve out lives, accrete histories, and organize forces of opposition. Neoliberal policies must therefore build upon and intensify inherited institutional frameworks in every distinct locality, city, or region. Only by re-entrenching already existing forms of difference—deepening class, race, gendered, religious, colonial divides—can neoliberalism produce the disciplinary regimes necessary to compel and coerce people to animate cities with their bodies, their labor, their presences, and their absences. In this way, neoliberal ideology orients itself toward the future while necessarily anchoring itself to the persistence of the state's foundational violence.[37]

There is great distance between what the neoliberal ideal imagines (the free movement of capital, a frictionless process of value realization, interchangeable spaces of accumulation) and what it actually encounters (developments held in abeyance; unrealized speculative value; projects rebuffed because of local law, custom, popular opposition, or legal barriers, etc.). This distance is critical to locating neoliberalism's violence. To reconcile the lived present with neoliberalism's aspirational future, great violence—along with the very threat of it—must be deployed to bridge the distance. In this way, neoliberal doctrine does not merely assert a future tense, imagining how things will be; it inhabits a subjunctive tense, declaring how things ought to be: a normative order, unrealizable in this present world. Broken windows policing can be understood as a key mechanism for instituting this order and deploying the socially regulating violence necessary to bridge this unbridgeable gap.[38]

Working hand in hand with neoliberal policies, broken windows policing helps to inscribe a normative order, first upon the movement of capital but necessarily and simultaneously upon the movement, productivity, desires, and behavior of people who inhabit those spaces. By reinforcing neoliberal accumulation schemes of volatility, broken windows policing produces extant states of imminent violability.[39]

Imminent Violability

Broken windows policing must be comprehended as a phenomenon of increased public expenditure for policing alongside a commensurate defunding of other social services. Such policing practices have soaked up the resources for social programs so that, in many cities, the police effectively function as counselors, teachers, sports coaches, and charity event and youth activity organizers as well as mental health facilitators, school disciplinarians, public housing managers, and guards against park trespassing. A recent report by the U.S. Department of Education found that 1.6 million public schoolchildren (kindergarten to twelfth grade) attend schools that employ at least one law enforcement officer but no school counselors. In some municipalities, the police also aggressively function as surrogate tax collectors or "revenue generators," as a Department of Justice investigation into the Ferguson, Missouri police department recently concluded. Policing has come to stand in as a catch-all solution. A recent audit by the Los Angeles City Administrative Office showed that of $100 million dollars spent to mitigate homelessness, $87 million went to police. When your only tool is a hammer, every problem looks like a nail: this is the crisis of neoliberal governance produced through broken windows policing.[40]

Recent high-profile police assaults have amplified these transformations. Akai Gurley and Freddie Gray both died at the hands of police who were patrolling public housing units; Tamir Rice, a twelve-year-old African American child, died at the hands of police patrolling a public park; Marlene Pinnock was brutally beaten by highway patrol officers regulating a freeway on-ramp; and Eric Garner was strangled to death on a public sidewalk for the sale of untaxed commodities. Beyond their spectacular violence, these incidents enable us to see how police not only regulate public space but produce and delimit particular spatialities of the "public." This production is critical to both the physical construction and the legitimation of neoliberalism.[41]

The uprisings in Ferguson after the killing of eighteen-year-old Michael Brown, and the subsequent Department of Justice (DOJ) report, also brought renewed attention to these aspects of broken windows policing. In 2013, the city of Ferguson issued the highest number of warrants in the state relative to the size of its municipality. Ferguson, home to just over 21,000 people, issued over 24,000 warrants in one year. This amounted to an average of three warrants per Ferguson household. The disproportionality resulted from vigilant policing around crimes of poverty, often traffic violations such as driving with a suspended license, expired registration, or without proof of insurance. When drivers did not or could not pay their traffic tickets and subsequently failed to show up for court dates, municipal courts transformed these unpaid tickets into warrants. In this period, more than 9,000 warrants were issued for missed court appearances or unpaid (or partially paid) fines. Given that fines and subsequent fees often constituted more than the amount of many residents' monthly income, it is not surprising that fees could not be paid in full. Adding insult to injury, those with outstanding warrants were also rendered ineligible for most forms of public assistance.[42]

The rising issuance of these warrants directly correlated to their increasing significance in city coffers. The DOJ report revealed that since 2011, city revenue from traffic fines increased dramatically, constituting 20 percent of the city's $12 million budget. Warrants also resulted from other crimes of poverty, what are often called "quality of life" violations. These "crimes" include minor victimless infractions such as fare-hopping on public transportation, playing loud music, trespassing, wearing "saggy pants," or even more mundanely, jaywalking (once suggested as the plausible pretext for Michael Brown's fatal encounter with the Ferguson police). So extreme is this routine surveillance and surreal and arbitrary criminalization, the DOJ study reported an incident where St. Louis police charged a man for making a false declaration: he had said his name was Mike while his ID read Michael.[43]

The situation in Ferguson is replicated throughout the country, particularly in the poorest regions, which are disproportionately Black, Native, and Latino/a. In her recent dissenting opinion in the case of *Utah vs. Streiff*, Supreme Court justice Sandra Sotomayor outlined the dread that permeates the lives of people of color where the constant threat of removal hangs over them. Policing crimes of poverty against people too poor to pay their tickets, court fees, or citations has made people and their bodies "subject to invasion," making them feel like "subject(s) of a carceral state, just waiting to be cataloged."[44] The evidence Sotomayor cites in her dissenting opinion includes a bewildering range of similar circumstances to Ferguson in cities from New Orleans to Newark. She notes that there are over 7.8 million outstanding warrants logged in state and federal government databases, "the vast majority of which appear to be for minor offenses." Such a conclusion is further substantiated by the situation in Skid Row, Los Angeles.[45]

Skid Row in downtown Los Angeles, the nation's capital of homelessness—which, like Ferguson, New Orleans, and Newark, is also mostly Black—has endured a similar degree of disproportional enforcement. Los Angeles, like many major U.S. cities, has reinvigorated efforts to "reclaim" its downtown. Downtown LA has witnessed rapid growth in the form of high-end business and residential developments, the creation of tourist- and consumer-friendly commercial zones, and increased transportation routes to what were previous no-go areas for tourists and wealthy residents. Property owners, responding to redevelopment in the area have employed the soft coercion of raised rents and depleted maintenance services to push low-income residents out.[46]

In September 2006, the mayor's office in conjunction with Chief William Bratton launched its form of broken windows policing called the Safer Cities Initiative (SCI) to "secure" the area with increased policing. While the entire city budget for homelessness that year was $5.7 million, SCI funneled $6.5 million into policing. One hundred and ten new officers poured into a fifty-square-block area, an "unprecedented" deployment of police officers commensurate to the area's size. According to a UCLA School of Law report, SCI saturated Skid Row with the highest sustained concentration of police officers anywhere in the world outside of Baghdad.[47]

This expansion of law enforcement presence has dramatically increased the amount of citations, arrests, and individuals imprisoned and otherwise lost in the system. In the first three years of SCI, the LAPD gave out more than 40,000 citations and made 28,000 arrests in a place home to fewer than 15,000 people. Skid Row officers issued citations over sixty times more often than in the rest of the city, even though Skid Row has a relatively low crime rate. As in Ferguson, citations were often for minor infractions, such as blocking the sidewalk, jaywalking, not crossing the street in time, trespassing, or loitering. Other minor infractions like sitting or sleeping on the sidewalk, in violation of Municipal Code 41.18(d), have been heavily criminalized. One woman has been arrested fifty-seven times, all for the same "crime" of being on the sidewalk at the exact same location, on the corner of Sixth and Towne Streets, where she made a home.[48]

As the late geographer Clyde Woods described it, criminalized behavior on Skid Row includes "walking too slow, walking too fast, eating, or standing"—in other words, simply existing in space where one was unwanted. The mundane "crime" of not being able to cross the street in time has resulted in thousands of arrests and incarceration. While the fine for such an infraction was \$159, this was over half of the \$221 most residents on Skid Row received from General Relief. Since most were unable to pay the fines and/or obtain legal representation, they faced subsequent arrest and jail time.[49]

Minor drug possession has rigorously been prosecuted as a "sales" crime, deeming people ineligible for drug treatment and sending to state prison. Police officers have also admitted to practicing "shifting," an outright movement of residents against their will to other parts of the city.[50] The disproportionate number of police officers has further enabled brutal displays of force, aimed less at addressing the "problems" of the area than establishing an order of brutality that sets an example for all those around. Residents describe their neighbors as being "disappeared," a term anthropologists of state violence use to name routine violations, torture, and abuse and also to describe the condition of being lost in anonymous public spaces—"hospitals and prisons but also morgues and the public cemetery."[51]

In places like Skid Row and Ferguson, people endure an ever-present vulnerability. For the specious crime of an unpaid traffic ticket or not crossing the street in time, people are made intensely vulnerable. They become, in essence, walking warrants (whether or not there are actually warrants out for their arrest): when SCI was first initiated, Skid Row residents drew straws among neighbors deciding who would have to leave the building in order to buy food or cigarettes; the likelihood of arrest was so great.[52]

Backed by statistical inevitability and emboldened by the distinct dictates of the regional political economy, police can reasonably treat any person they choose as an arrestable suspect. Once someone is stopped for minor infractions and their record is pulled up, an outstanding ticket they couldn't afford to pay the first time can become the pretext for their arrest on a subsequent stop. Impoverished residents of areas like Skid Row exist in a state of imminent violability, poised on the brink of uncertainty while police are endowed with arbitrary capacities to govern their existence.[53]

The stakes in theorizing broken windows policing in sites such as Skid Row and Ferguson are urgent and decidedly global. In cities worldwide, broken windows policing has become the social regulating mechanism of the neoliberal state at the urban scale.[54] Bratton and his collaborators have profitably exported these strategies to other police departments, foreign governments, and global security agencies, especially with the advent of counterterrorism policing. The deep success of broken windows policing in Los Angeles enabled the city to be the launching pad for a major post-9/11 Homeland Security counterterrorism initiative known as the National Suspicious Activity Reporting Initiative. This initiative involves the mass collection of data around "suspicious activity," defined as "observed behavior reasonably indicative of pre-operational planning of terrorism or other criminal activity." This pilot program involved the sharing and disseminating of intelligence among the federal, state, and local law enforcement agencies and aspired to connect campus, transit, rural police, and sheriffs' departments. The broader goal is to interlink such agencies across the country through fusion centers and information-sharing databases.[55]

It is essential to bear in mind that seemingly "new" models of counterterrorism policing have evolved from established models of domestic policing. In examining the mutation of practices from those used for Skid Row, it becomes clear how counterterrorism practices are fortified versions of already existing and legitimated forms of broken windows policing (which are themselves outgrowths of entrenched racist and colonial structures of domination). These forms of policing have been directly tied to the reorganization of space and the redirection of resources by capital—processes legitimated through racism. The intimate and seemingly micro-scale policing of a poor Black community and individual crimes of poverty in places like Skid Row are therefore central to an understanding of the flows of securitization on a global scale. In sum, the more broken windows appears to be a success, the more the features of U.S. policing and the spatial relations of neoliberal security will continue to spread as global phenomena.[56]

Conclusion

"Get out. Get out. Get out."
—Rosa Ramos

The political economy of the late twentieth century and early twenty-first century poses an existential question: will the metabolism of cities reproduce the lives of its inhabitants or will it wantonly and violently consume them? The answer is not foregone. As this chapter argues, imminent violability characterizes the looming threat of violence that hangs over poor and working-class communities in U.S. cities— particularly Black, Native, Latino/a, and immigrant populations, as well as queer, trans, and gender-nonconforming individuals (which are not mutually exclusive categories)—in cities where the state has been reconfigured and police have been conscripted to abet local regimes of accumulation. Groups like Black Lives Matter, Communities United for Police Reform, Los Angeles Community Action Network, The Red Nation, Critical Resistance, and the Coalition to End Broken Windows have organized against the mundane, everyday, intimate forms of policing that render lives imminently vulnerable and violable by calling for an end to broken windows policing.[57]

Recounted through the story of Rosa Ramos, we come to understand the multiple dimensions of broken windows policing: its intimate violence, its imperial dimensions, the collisions of poverty and racism, the perpetual states of surveillance, and the exacerbation of already existing vulnerabilities around race, class, and gender. Ramos's inability to secure her own body is proportionate to her lack of control over property. Simply put, someone else owns her key. We do not know the specifics of Ramos's situation, but we do know that poor and working-class women of color have faced the brunt of the neoliberal onslaught. In these ways, the fictive but not fictional story of Rosa Ramos offers us an opening to understand the production of insecurity more broadly. Under the logic of broken windows, the racialized poor are depicted as the source of their own social problems. But through the windows of Rosa Ramos, we see that another path is possible. The legitimacy of these logics can be challenged. Through Rosa's story, we can reject the social relations of imminent violability that it produces at all scales. With Rosa Ramos, we can learn to say, "Get out. Get out. Get out!"[58]

NOTES

1 "Nuyorican" refers to a person of Puerto Rican descent who hails from New York City.
2 Bash, Amato, and Sacks 2000; interview with Martín Espada by author and Jordan T. Camp, Sunday, May 31, 2015, full transcript unpublished; Luis Urrea, "On Standing at Neruda's Tomb: Interview with Martín Espada," *Poetry Foundation* (January 2007).

3 For U.S.-backed wars in Central America throughout the 1980s, see Grandin 2006.

4 Dinzey-Flores 2013; LeBrón 2016.

5 Vitale 2008; McArdle 2001a.

6 Aalbers 2015; Woods 2007; Harvey 2007.

7 Brown 2008; Bratton et al., 2004.

8 On fear, see Jeffries 2004, 251.

9 Sousa 2010; Bratton et al. 2004; Kelling 1999; Kelling and Coles 1996.

10 Harcourt 2001, 3–4; Stewart 1998; Thacher 2004; Beckett and Herbert 2009, 37–42.

11 Wilson and Kelling 1982; Bratton et al. 2004; Beckett 2016.

12 On organized abandonment, see Gilmore 2008, 31.

13 On urban blight, see Fullilove 2004.

14 On geographic assumptions and spatialized projections, see Herbert and Brown 2006; Gilmore 2007, 12.

15 Manhattan Institute, "George L. Kelling" biography page, 1998, www.manhattan-institute.org (accessed July 6, 2016); Bratton and Knobler 1998, 49; Seigel 2012.

16 Bratton 1992, 3; Bratton and Knobler 1998, 108–85.

17 Manhattan Institute, "George L. Kelling"; *Police Strategy No. 5: Reclaiming the Public Spaces of New York* (New York City Police Department, 1994); Smith 1998, 2–5; Hopper 2003; Scannell 2015.

18 McArdle 2001a and Hsiao 2001.

19 Hanhardt 2013; Delany 1999; Papayanis 2000.

20 Harcourt and Jens 2006; Camp and Heatherton, eds. 2016; Bratton et al. 2004.

21 Camp 2016, 136; Smith 2001; Herzing 2011; Bowling and Sheptycki 2011.

22 Gilmore 2007; Harvey 2005; George 1999.

23 Smith 2002; Harvey 1989; Pearce 1990.

24 Gilmore 2007; Vitale 2008; K. Mitchell 2010; Gottschalk 2015, 10–19.

25 Connell 2010, 25; Armstrong 2014, 178–87; Katz 2008, 15–29; Battacharya 2013–14; Fraser 2013.

26 Dan and Surkin 1998; Weir 2004; Camp 2016; Prashad 2003; Fraser 2009.

27 Hopper 2003.

28 Nadasen 2012; Marchevsky and Theoharis 2006; Lubiano 1992.

29 Smith 1996; Wilson and Kelling 1982; Bratton and Knobler 1998, 88.

30 Feldman 1991, 109; see Gilmore 2007, 235, for elaboration and analysis of this quote.

31 Herbert and Brown 2006.

32 powell 2007; quote from "Interview with john a. powell," edited transcript from *Race: The Power of an Illusion*, California Newsreel (2003); Herzing 2016, 267–78; on the question of the postracial, see Goldberg 2015.

33 Wilson and Kelling 1982; Harcourt 2001, 5–6, 16–17; George Kelling and Katherine Coles defend broken windows, defining order as "behavior that violates widely accepted standards and norms of behavior, and about which a broad consensus exists, in spite of racial, ethnic and class differences" (Kelling and Coles 1996, 4).

34 The passage from James Q. Wilson, *Varieties of Police Behavior* (Cambridge, MA: Harvard University Press, 1968), 40, is quoted in Harcourt 2001, 16.

35 Pulido 2000; Smith and Katz 1993; Lipsitz 2011; Herbert 1996, 572, 578.

36 Mitchell 2003; Willse 2015; Floyd 2009, 199–208; Fred Moten, "The Meaning of 'Broken Windows'" (talk presented at Eso Won Books, Los Angeles, June 23, 2005).

37 Brenner and Theodore 2002; Goonewardena and Kipfer 2006.

38 Brenner and Theodore 2002.

39 Hennessy 2000, 1–36; Joseph 2014.

40 Michael S. Scott, "Problem-Oriented Policing: Reflections on the First 20 Years," Office of Community-Oriented Policing Services, U.S. Department of Justice, October 2000; Gilmore 2007, 23; Gilmore and Gilmore 2016, 173–200; Harcourt 2001, 5–6; U.S. Department of Education, "First Look Report," Civil Rights Data Collection, 2013–14 data (issued June 7, 2016); Camp and Heatherton 2016, 141–50.

41 Gina Bellafante, "In New York Public Housing, Policing Broken Lights," *New York Times*, November 26, 2014; Joseph P. Williams, "Tamir Rice Shooting: Not Just a Tragedy," *U.S. News and World Report*, December 29, 2015; Serna, "No Criminal Charges.

42 Radley Balko, "How Municipalities in St. Louis County, Mo., Profit from Poverty," *Washington Post*, September 3, 2014; ArchCity Defenders, Municipal Courts white paper, 2014; Walter Johnson, "Ferguson's Fortune 500 Company," *Atlantic* (April 2015); George Lipsitz, "Ferguson as a Failure of the Humanities" (presentation, Department of African American Studies, Princeton University, May 1, 2015).

43 U.S. Department of Justice, Civil Rights Division, "Investigation of the Ferguson Police Department" (March 4, 2015); Balko, "How Municipalities Profit."

44 *Utah v. Strieff*, no. 14–1373 (U.S. June 20, 2016) (5–3) (Sotomayor, J. dissenting)

45 Ibid.

46 Gary Blasi, "Policing Our Way Out of Homelessness? The First Year of the Safer Cities Initiative on Skid Row," UCLA Fact Investigation Clinic (September 2007); Mitchell 2003, 20, 50; Sam Quinones, "Rent Hike May Force Novel Dome Village to Find a New Home," *Los Angeles Times*, December 25, 2005; Tom Slater, "The Downside of Upscale," *Los Angeles Times*, July 30, 2006; Cara DiMassa, "Area's Homeless Can't Find Shelter," *Los Angeles Times*, December 23, 2006; Evelyn Nieves, "Skid Row Makeover," *Salon*, August 8, 2006.

47 Gary Blasi and Forest Stuart, "Has the Safer Cities Initiative in Skid Row Reduced Serious Crime?" *UCLA School of Law Research Report* (September 2008): 1–2; Blasi, "Policing Our Way," 5; Wilson and Kelling 1982. For an analysis of the racial legacy of the theory, see Stewart 1998; Tami Abdollah, "Arrest Leads to Investigation," *Los Angeles Times*, June 7, 2007; editorial, "More Violence under 'Safer Cities' Initiative," *Community Connection* (December 2008–January 2009); editorial, "Abuse Continues under the Banner of 'Safer Cities,'" *Community Connection* (September–October 2008).

48 Blasi, "Policing Our Way," 32; Richard Winton and Cara Mia DiMassa, "Skid Row Cleanup Is Challenged," *Los Angeles Times*, March 3, 2007; Anat Rubin, "One Downtown but Two Sets of Rules?," *Daily Journal*, June 20, 2007.

49 Woods 2011; Blasi, *Policing Our Way.*

50 Duke Helfand, "Bratton Conceded Skid Row Migration," *Los Angeles Times*, October 3, 2007.

51 Anat Rubin, "Prosecutors Target Drugs on Skid Row," *Daily Journal*, January 29, 2007; Peter Y. Hong, "Defense Lawyers Protest Skid Row Drug Crackdown," *Los Angeles Times*, February 2, 2007; Tami Abdollah, "Arrest Leads to Investigation," *Los Angeles Times*, June 7, 2007; Scheper-Hughes 2004, 183; Camp and Heatherton 2016, 141–50.

52 Lipsitz 2016, 123–40.

53 My thinking about imminent violability owes much to Butler 2004; Brown 1995; and Kunzel 2008.

54 Camp and Heatherton, eds. 2016.

55 Jenna McLaughlin, "L.A. Activists Want to Bring Surveillance Conversation Down to Earth," *Intercept*, April 6, 2016; Camp and Heatherton 2012; Darwin Bond-Graham and Ali Winston, "Forget the NSA, the LAPD Spies on Millions of Innocent Folks," *LA Weekly*, February 27, 2014.

56 Of course, the spread of security measures is not unidirectional, from the United States outward, but it is beyond the scope of this particular essay to describe the multidirectional flows, particularly from colonial contexts, that come to inform the various policing practices domestically and amid the War on Terror.

57 Robin D. G. Kelley, "Why We Won't Wait," *Counterpunch*, November 25, 2014; Yi-hyun Jeong, "Witness to Fatal Winslow, Arizona, Shooting of Loreal Tsingine: 'He Shot Her Dead,'" *Arizona Republic*, April 8, 2016; Rebecca Solnit, "Death by Gentrification: The Killing That Shamed San Francisco," *Guardian*, March 21, 2016; Matthew Speiser, "Black Lives Matter Has a Plan to Radically Change America's Police," *Business Insider*, August 24, 2015; Ken Auletta, "Fixing Broken Windows," *New Yorker*, September 7, 2015.

58 Cohen, 2010–11.

BIBLIOGRAPHY

Aalbers, Manuel B. 2015. "The Potential for Financialization." *Dialogues in Human Geography* 5, no. 2: 214–19.

Armstrong, Elisabeth. 2014. *Gender and Neoliberalism: The All India Democratic Women's Association and Globalization Politics.* New York: Routledge.

Baker, Al, J. David Goodman, and Benjamin Mueller. 2015. "Beyond the Chokehold: The Path to Eric Garner's Death." *New York Times*, June 13.

Bash, Chadwick, Maria Amato, and Michele Sacks, 2000. "Chelsea, Massachusetts: A City Helps Its Diverse People Get Along." *Practitioner Perspectives* (January). U.S. Department of Justice—Bureau of Justice Assistance.

Battacharya, Tithi. 2013–14. "Explaining Gender Violence in the Neoliberal Era." *International Socialist Review* (Winter): 25–47.

Beckett, Katherine. 2016. "Uses and Abuses of Police Discretion: Toward Harm Reduction Policing." *Harvard Law and Policy Review* 10: 77–100.

Beckett, Katherine, and Steven Herbert. 2009. *Banished: The New Social Control in Urban America.* New York: Oxford University Press.

Bowling, Ben, and James Sheptycki. 2011. "Policing Globopolis." *Social Justice* 38½: 184–202.

Bratton, William. 1992. *Neighborhood Policing: A Plan of Action for the Boston Police Department.* Boston: Boston Police Department.

Bratton, William, with Peter Knobler. 1998. *The Turnaround: How America's Top Cop Reversed the Crime Epidemic.* New York: Random House.

Bratton, William, James Q. Wilson, George L. Kelling, Reverend Eugene Rivers, and Peter Cove. 2004. "This Works: Crime Prevention and the Future of Broken Windows Policing." *Manhattan Institute Civil Bulletin* 36 (April): 1–15.

Brenner, Neil, and Nik Theodore. 2002. "Cities and the Geographies of 'Actually Existing Neoliberalism.'" *Antipode*, 349–79.

Brown, Wendy. 1995. *States of Injury: Power and Freedom in Late Modernity.* Princeton, NJ: Princeton University Press.

———. 2008. "Neoliberalism and the End of Liberal Democracy." *Theory and Event* 7, no. 1: 1–21.

Butler, Judith. 2004. *Frames of War: When Is Life Grievable?* New York: Verso Books.

Camp, Jordan T. 2016. *Incarcerating the Crisis: Freedom Struggles and the Rise of the Neoliberal State.* Oakland: University of California Press.

Camp, Jordan T., and Christina Heatherton. 2012. "What You Need to Know about Special Order 11: An Interview with Hamid Khan." In Camp and Heatherton, eds. 2012, 74–78.

———. 2016. "Asset Stripping and Broken Windows Policing on LA's Skid Row: An Interview with Becky Dennison and Peter White." In Camp and Heatherton, eds. 2016, 141–50.

Camp, Jordan T., and Christina Heatherton, eds. 2012. *Freedom Now! Struggles for the Human Right to Housing in LA and Beyond.* Los Angeles: Freedom Now Books.

———. 2016. *Policing the Planet: Why the Policing Crisis Led to Black Lives Matter.* New York: Verso Books.

Cohen, Cathy. 2010–11. "Death and Rebirth of a Movement: Queering Critical Ethnic Studies." *Social Justice* 37, no. 4: 126–32.

Connell, Raewyn. 2010. "Understanding Neoliberalism." In *Neoliberalism and Everyday Life*, edited by Susan Braedley and Meg Luxton, 22–36. Montreal: McGill-Queen's University Press.

Delany, Samuel. 1999. *Times Square Red, Times Square Blue.* New York: New York University Press.

Dinzey-Flores, Zaire Zenit. 2013. *Locked In, Locked Out: Gated Communities in a Puerto Rican City.* Philadelphia: University of Pennsylvania Press.

Espada, Martín. 1994. "The Broken Window of Rosa Ramos." *City of Coughing and Dead Radiators.* New York: W. W. Norton.

Feldman, Allen. 1991. *Formations of Violence: The Narrative of the Body and Political Terror in Northern Ireland*. Chicago: University of Chicago Press.

Floyd, Kevin. 2009. *The Reification of Desire: Toward a Queer Marxism*. Minneapolis: University of Minnesota Press.

Fraser, Nancy. 2009. "Feminism, Capitalism, and the Cunning of History." *New Left Review* 56 (April): 97–117.

———. 2013. *Fortunes of Feminism: From State-Managed Capitalism to Neoliberal Crisis*. New York: Verso Books.

Fullilove, Mindy Thompson. 2004. *Root Shock: How Tearing Up City Neighborhoods Hurts America, and What We Can Do about It*. New York: Ballantine.

Georgakas, Dan, and Marvin Surkin. 1998. *Detroit, I Do Mind Dying: A Study in Urban Revolution*. Cambridge: South End.

George, Susan. 1999. "A Short History of Neoliberalism." Paper presented at the Conference on Economic Sovereignty in a Globalising World. Global Policy Forum, Bangkok, Thailand, March 24.

Gilmore, Ruth Wilson. 2007. *Golden Gulag: Prisons, Surplus, Crisis, and Opposition in Globalizing California*. Berkeley: University of California Press.

———. 2008. Forgotten Places and the Seeds of Grassroots Planning." In *Engaging Contradictions: Theory, Politics, and Methods of Activist Scholarship*. Berkeley: University of California Press.

Gilmore, Ruth Wilson, and Craig Gilmore. 2016. "Beyond Bratton." In Camp and Heatherton, eds. 2016, 173–200.

Goldberg, David Theo. 2015. *Are We All Postracial Yet?* Cambridge: Polity Press.

Goonewardena, Kanishka, and Stefan Kipfer. 2006. "Postcolonial Urbicide: New Imperialism, Global Cities and the Damned of the Earth." *New Formations* 59: 23–34.

Gottschalk, Marie. 2015. *Caught: The Prison State and the Lockdown of American Politics*. Princeton, NJ: Princeton University Press.

Grandin, Greg. 2006. *Empire's Workshop: Latin America, the United States, and the Rise of the New Imperialism*. New York: Metropolitan Books.

Hanhardt, Christina. 2013. *Safe Space: Gay Neighborhood History and the Politics of Violence*. Durham, NC: Duke University Press.

Harcourt, Bernard. 2001. *Illusions of Order: The False Promise of Broken Windows Policing*. Cambridge, MA: Harvard University Press.

Harcourt, Bernard E., and Ludwig Jens. 2006. "Broken Windows: New Evidence from New York City and a Five-City Social Experiment." *University of Chicago Law Review* 73, no. 1: 271–320.

Harvey, David. 1989. "From Managerialism to Entrepreneurialism: The Transformation in Urban Governance in Late Capitalism." *Geografiska Annaler. Series B, Human Geography* 71, no. 1: 3–17.

———. 2005. *A Brief History of Neoliberalism*. New York: Oxford University Press.

———. 2007. "Neoliberalism as Creative Destruction." *Annals of the American Academy of Political and Social Science* (March): 610.

Heatherton, Christina, ed. 2011. *Downtown Blues: A Skid Row Reader*. Los Angeles: Freedom Now Books.

Hennessy, Rosemary. 2000. *Profit and Pleasure: Sexual Identities in Late Capitalism*. New York: Routledge.

Herbert, Steve. 1996. "The Normative Ordering of Police Territoriality: Making and Marking Space with the Los Angeles Police Department." *Annals of the Association of American Geographers* 86, no. 3: 567–82.

Herbert, Steve, and Elizabeth Brown. 2006. "Conceptions of Space and Crime in the Punitive Neoliberal City." *Antipode* 38, no. 4: 755–77.

Herzing, Rachel. 2011. "Resisting the Bratton Brand: Lessons from the US." *Institute of Race Relations News*, August 24. www.irr.org.uk.

———. 2016. "The Magical Life of Broken Windows." In Camp and Heatherton, eds. 2016, 267–78.

Hopper, Kim. 2003. *Reckoning with Homelessness*. Ithaca, NY: Cornell University Press.

Hsiao, Andrew. 2001. "Mothers of Invention: The Families of Police-Brutality Victims and the Movement They've Built." In *Zero Tolerance: Quality of Life and the New Police Brutality in New York City*, edited by Andrea McArdle and Tanya Erzen, 179–95. New York: New York University Press.

Jeffries, Fiona. 2014. "Reappropriating the City of Fear." *Space and Culture* 17, no. 3: 251.

Jeffries, Robin C. 2004. *Fear: The History of a Political Idea*. Oxford: Oxford University Press.

Joseph, Miranda. 2014. *Debt to Society: Accounting for Life under Capitalism*. Minneapolis: University of Minnesota Press.

Katz, Cindi. 2008. "Bad Elements: Katrina and the Scoured Landscape of Social Reproduction." *Gender, Place and Culture* 15, no. 1: 15–29.

Kelling, George L. 1999. "'Broken Windows' and Police Discretion." U.S. Department of Justice, Office of Justice Programs.

Kelling, George L., and Catherine M. Coles. 1996. *Fixing Broken Windows: Restoring Order and Reducing Crime in Our Communities*. New York: Free Press.

Kunzel, Regina. 2008. *Criminal Intimacy: Prison and the Uneven History of Modern American Sexuality*. Chicago: University of Chicago Press.

Larimer, Sarah. 2016. "Disgraced Ex-Cop Daniel Holtzclaw Sentenced to 263 Years for On-Duty Rapes, Sexual Assaults." *Washington Post*, January 22.

LeBrón, Marisol. 2016. "Mano Dura Contra El Crimen and Premature Death in Puerto Rico." In Camp and Heatherton, eds. 2016, 95–108.

Lipsitz, George. 2011. *How Racism Takes Place*. Philadelphia: Temple University Press.

———. 2016. "Policing Place and Taxing Time on Skid Row." In Camp and Heatherton, eds. 2016, 123–40.

Lubiano, Wahneema. 1992. "Black Ladies, Welfare Queens, and State Minstrels: Ideological War by Narrative Means." In *Race-ing Justice, En-gendering Power: Essays on Anita Hill, Clarence Thomas, and the Construction of Social Reality*, edited by Toni Morrison, 290–322. New York: Pantheon.

Marchevsky, Alejandra, and Jeanne Theoharis. 2006. *Not Working: Latina Immigrants, Low-Wage Jobs, and the Failure of Welfare Reform*. New York: New York University Press.

McArdle, Andrea. 2001a. "Introduction." In McArdle and Erzen 2001, 1–18.

———. 2001b. "Turnstile Jumpers and Broken Windows: Policing Disorder in New York City." In McArdle and Erzen 2001, 19–49.

McArdle, Andrea, and Tanya Erzen, eds. 2001. *Zero Tolerance: Quality of Life and the New Police Brutality in New York City*. New York: New York University Press.

Mitchell, Don. 2003. *The Right to the City: Social Justice and the Fight for Public Space*. New York: Guilford Press.

Mitchell, Katharyne. 2010. "Ungoverned Space: Global Security and the Geopolitics of Broken Windows." *Political Geography* 29, no. 5: 289–97.

Nadasen, Premilla. 2012. *Rethinking the Welfare Rights Movement*. New York: Routledge, 2012.

Papayanis, Marilyn Adler. 2000. "Sex and the Revanchist City: Zoning Out Pornography in New York." *Environment and Planning D: Society and Space* 18 (June): 341–53.

Pearce, Diana. 1990. "Welfare Is Not for Women: Why the War on Poverty Cannot Conquer the Feminization of Poverty." In *Women, the State, and Welfare*, edited by Linda Gordon, 265–79. Madison: University of Wisconsin Press.

powell, john a. 2007. "Structural Racism and Spatial Jim Crow." In *The Black Metropolis in the Twenty-First Century: Race, Power, and the Politics of Place*, edited by Robert Bullard, 41–65. Lanham, MD: Rowman and Littlefield.

Prashad, Vijay. 2003. *Keeping Up with the Dow Joneses: Debt, Prison, Workfare*. Boston: South End Press.

Pulido, Laura. 2000. "Rethinking Environmental Racism: White Privilege and Urban Development in Southern California." *Annals of the Association of American Geographers* 90, no. 1: 12–40.

Scannell, Josh. 2015. "What Can an Algorithm Do?" *Dis Magazine*. http://dismagazine.com/discussion/72975/josh-scannell-what-can-an-algorithm-do. Accessed June 7, 2017.

Scheper-Hughes, Nancy. 2004. "Bodies, Death, and Silence." In Scheper-Hughes and Bourgois 2004, 183.

Scheper-Hughes, Nancy, and Philippe Bourgois, eds. 2004. *Violence in War and Peace: An Anthology*. Malden, MA: Blackwell.

Seigel, Micol. 2012. "William Bratton in the Other LA." In *Beyond Walls and Cages: Prisons, Borders and Global Crisis*, edited by Jenna M. Loyd, Matt Mitchelson, and Andrew Burridge, 115–28. Athens: University of Georgia Press.

Serna, Joseph. 2015. "No Criminal Charges for CHP Officer Seen Punching Woman in Video." *Los Angeles Times*, December 3.

Shaffer, Cory. 2015. "Tanisha Anderson Was Restrained in Prone Position; Death Ruled Homicide." *Cleveland Plain Dealer*, January 2.

Smith, Neil. 1996. *New Urban Frontier: Gentrification and the Revanchist City*. New York: Routledge, 1996.

———. 1998. "Giuliani Time: The Revanchist 1990s." *Social Text* 57, no. 3: 1–20.

———. 2001. "Global Social Cleansing: Postliberal Revanchism and the Export of Zero Tolerance." *Social Justice* 28, no. 3 (Fall): 68–74.

———. 2002. "New Globalism, New Urbanism: Gentrification as Global Urban Strategy." In *Spaces of Neoliberalism: Urban Restructuring in North America and Western Europe*, edited by Neil Brenner and Nik Theodore, 80–103. Malden, MA: Blackwell.

Smith, Neil, and Cindi Katz. 1993. "Grounding Metaphor: Towards a Spatialized Politics." In *Place and the Politics of Identity*, edited by Michael Keith and Steve Pile, 66–81. London: Routledge.

Sousa, William H. 2010. "Paying Attention to Minor Offenses: Order Maintenance Policing in Practice." *Police Practice and Research* 11, no. 1 (February): 45–59.

Stewart, Gary. 1998. "Black Codes and Broken Windows: The Legacy of Racial Hegemony in Anti-Gang Civil Injunctions." *Yale Law Journal* 107, no. 7 (May 1998): 2249–80.

Thacher, David. 2004. "Order Maintenance Reconsidered: Moving beyond Strong Causal Reasoning." *Journal of Criminal Law and Criminology* 94, no. 2: 381–414.

Urrea, Luis. 2007 "On Standing at Neruda's Tomb: Interview with Martín Espada," *Poetry Foundation* (January). https://www.poetryfoundation.org/features/articles/detail/68844. Accessed June 5, 2017.

Vitale, Alex. 2008. *City of Disorder: How the Quality of Life Campaign Transformed New York Politics*. New York: New York University Press.

Weir, Stan. 2004. *Singlejack Solidarity*. Minneapolis: University of Minnesota Press, 2004.

Welborn, Larry. 2013. "Kelly Thomas Case: Officers Ordered to Trial." *Orange County Register* January 18.

Willse, Craig. 2015. *The Value of Homelessness: Managing Surplus Life in the United States*. Minneapolis: University of Minnesota Press.

Wilson, James Q., and George L. Kelling. 1982. "Broken Windows: The Police and Neighborhood Safety." *Atlantic Monthly* (March): 29–38.

Woods, Clyde. 2007. "Sittin' on Top of the World: The Challenges of Blues and Hip Hop Geography." In *Black Geographies and the Politics of Place*, edited by Katherine McKittrick and Clyde Woods, 46–81. Cambridge, MA: South End Press.

———. 2011. "Traps, Skid Row, and Katrina." In Camp and Heatherton 2011, 50–55.

7

After Neoliberalism?

Resignifying Economy, Nation, and Family in Ecuador

AMY LIND

Introduction

Latin America provides a distinctive perspective on debates on policies of neoliberalism. As a region, Latin America was the first to declare default on its loans (Mexico being the first country to do so), the first to undergo structural adjustment measures, and the first to experience severe economic crisis and neoliberal restructuring. With the highest per capita inequality rates in the world in the 1980s and 1990s, the foreign debt crisis only exacerbated this level of stratification. Given this, it is no surprise that the region has also been the first to propose such widespread responses to "the long neoliberal night" that so many experienced firsthand during this time period. In response to widespread discontent with global financial institutions and national neoliberal elites, beginning in the late 1990s and continuing throughout the 2000s, governments across the region have been democratically elected on the basis of their anti-neoliberal and/or socialist platforms. In this chapter, I address the purported shift *away* from neoliberalism in Latin America toward the socialist or "post-neoliberal" experiments we are witnessing in two-thirds of the region in the 2000s.[1] I present my analysis through a detailed look at Ecuador's post-neoliberal experiment. Many of the chapters in this volume address the meaning, making, and unfolding of neoliberalism in various geopolitical contexts. Ecuador provides a unique case for analyzing the attempt of a nation-state that has sought to break from neoliberal policies and forge an alternative path.

Ecuadorian President Rafael Correa (2007–17) was elected to challenge the global neoliberal hegemony, specifically through his Citizen

Revolution, which has aimed to broaden citizen rights, increase access to state resources, and redistribute income. Ecuador, like other nations in Latin America, had experienced the long-term negative consequences of neoliberal policies. Ecuador's inequality rate in 1999, for example, was the highest in the world. Correa's Citizen Revolution specifically sought to break from this trajectory. Terms such as "post-neoliberal" and, to a lesser extent, "decolonization" have become commonplace in policy, legal, and everyday conversations, as the state and many Ecuadorians have worked to create "another world" beyond neoliberalism. From a decolonial feminist standpoint, and central to this discussion, everyday life, including familial and intimate arrangements, has been restructured and/or resignified alongside the broader shifts taking place. How, for example, might a move away from neoliberalism contribute not only to class-based economic redistribution but also to a restructuring of familial and intimate arrangements such that a new set of relationships among citizens and the post-neoliberal state become possible? Put slightly differently, if new kinds of post-neoliberal subjectivities are formed, what implications does this have for redistributive projects? And likewise, to the extent that post-neoliberal redistributive projects take on an anti-normative, decolonizing stance (arguably so), what are the potential implications of a more transgressive redistributive project for all people, and not just the traditional, class-based heteronormative "family" that has been the classic recipient, protagonist, and/or cultural foundation of socialist revolutions and of capitalist markets? Finally, to what extent does the move to resignify the nation, economy, and family represent a significant shift away from a neoliberal, toward a postcapitalist or decolonial, future?

In this chapter, I address these questions in the context of Ecuador's Citizen Revolution. I argue, on the one hand, that the Citizen Revolution has led to innovative resignifications of citizenship, broadly defined, which potentially link citizens, via the resignified family and household, to the state's redistributive project in more effective and equitable ways. In so doing, these resignifications provide openings to reimagine new kinds of post-neoliberal political subjectivities, including innovative forms of "family" and intimate arrangements. However, despite these discursive and institutional innovations, I demonstrate that contradictions abound, and I argue that ultimately much needs to be addressed to truly remake the nation in a way that surpasses neoliberal, market-based logics of citizenship and the economy; that leads to more sustainable forms of daily life and democratic practices; and that allows for broader conceptions of family, intimacy, and subjectivity. At the center of my analysis is an understanding of how heteronormativity is central to the governance of nations, economic redistribution, and the making of political subjectivities. Through this analysis, I illustrate that post-neoliberalism does not connote a complete break with a neoliberal past. Rather, post-neoliberalism represents a partial break, a rupture, a challenge to global neoliberal hegemonies. This partial break has occurred in part because the neoliberal state was never unified but rather fragmented and messy. Some state actors and spaces supported neoliberal policies whereas others did not, thus creating transgressive possibilities for social change despite the broader neoliberal hegemony, as I demonstrate below.

Gender, Heteronormativity, Coloniality, and (Post)Neoliberal States

Until very recently, scholars have paid scant attention to how heteronormativity has been central to various forms of colonial and postcolonial governance.[2] By "heteronormativity," I am referring to "institutions, structures and practices that normalize dominant forms of heterosexuality as universal and moral righteous" (Bedford 2009; Berlant and Warner 1998), and to the privileging of dominant forms of heterosexuality over all others. Heteronormativity necessarily relies on naturalized gender binaries and an understanding of "the family" as a "normal" and "natural" way of life. As in other studies of political economy, heteronormativity is seen as secondary, often conflated with discussions of sex and thus trivialized, naturalized, and left unexamined. This is true about the scholarship on the state, governance, social movements, and the economy in Ecuador, which is largely heteronormative in its scope. Yet clearly emergent historical and contemporary research on colonial states and logics points in another direction. For example, as in many other countries, sex-related laws were set up in newly independent Ecuador in 1822 precisely to regulate reproduction across race and class, especially among indigenous and mestizo/a populations, and to set up a division between good and bad, pure and polluted, healthy and unhealthy, legal and criminal forms of behavior often based on a colonialist cultural understanding of respectability and private versus public. Key areas where such state regulation occurred were in relation to miscegenation and segregation laws and prostitution and homosexuality laws. During the colonial period (1544–1822),[3] state laws banned indigenous-mestizo/a marriage and spatially segregated indigenous populations from Spanish settlers. These laws were based on European ideas of race, purity, and honor, whereby white Spanish women were thought to be in need of protection and indigenous women were seen as lacking morals and at times being sexually loose. Laws criminalizing homosexuality (specifically, sodomy) and prostitution were institutionalized during the colonial period, reflecting then-predominant European values concerning race, class, gender, and sexuality. Indigenous women were subjected to these laws and also to sexual violence by Spanish men, as documented in indigenous leaders' accounts of the time period (Lavrin 2010). Forced labor practices such as the Spanish *encomienda* system, which forced indigenous inhabitants to work for Spanish settlers under exploitative and sometimes enslaved conditions, operated in tangent with these laws to secure the hegemony of colonial rulers. In these ways, both social and biological reproduction, including intimate and sexual relations, have been central to state governance, not secondary to it.

Heteronormativity thus limited and shaped opportunities not only for non-normative individuals and households as we discuss them now, but also those of heterosexual families that transgressed "respectable" racial, spatial, or class boundaries. Sex was always already in the state and produced through various forms of governance. The criminalization of homosexuality, prostitution, and cross-racial marriage worked hand-in-hand to construct the ideal citizen as being of Spanish or mestizo/a origin, middle- to upper-class, urban, and heterosexual (Clark 2012; Prieto 2004); this ideal citizen prototype remains under contestation today. As Steven Seidman observes, "regimes of heteronormativity not only regulate the homosexual but control heterosexual practices by creating a moral hierarchy of good and bad sexual citizens. . . . It is not just the homosexual that is defiled, but specific sexual practices such as pleasure driven sex, multiple partner sex, or sex outside quasi-marital intimacy" (2001, 322). In this sense, heteronormativity shapes and limits heterosexual citizens' opportunities, desires, and forms of expression as much as nonheterosexuals. States themselves are "constituted as heterosexual bodies" and have "heterosexual imperatives that constitute citizens" (Bedford 2009, xxi; Phelan 2000, 432). Following this line of thought, how the family is defined in political and economic discourse greatly affects how nations distribute their resources, define their borders, and provide for and protect members of their national communities (Luibhéid 2002; Yuval-Davis 1997). From the colonial period to the present, the state's role in regulating intimate relations—be it through miscegenation laws or seemingly benign contemporary family planning practices—is based not only on conceptions of race, class and gender, but also on patriarchal, European notions of heterosexuality as an institution, what some refer to as heteropatriarchy (Smith 2006). Combined, these conceptions allow us to better understand how binary, colonial notions of gender and sexuality, alongside taxonomies of ethnicity and race, are embedded in neoliberal cultural formations, economic doctrine, and global political hegemonies.

Perhaps ironically, as heteronormativity has remained "invisible" in many accounts of political economy, reproductive heterosexuality has simultaneously been made hyper-visible in contemporary development discourse, given the obsession with linking procreation and the nuclear, heterosexual family to the survival and health of national economies, and to the modernization of poor countries. Referred to by some as "reprocentrism," or the privileging of heteronormative reproduction over all other familial/intimate arrangements (Mortimer-Sandilands and Erickson 2010), the implicit or explicit family/economic development linkage has contributed in numerous powerful ways to shaping discussions on macroeconomic policy, labor reform, the social costs of structural adjustment, climate change, poverty, and human survival. Heteronormative reproduction, which is rooted in biogenetic, racialized definitions of the family, is seen as the foundation of nations and as a modernizing force that, if done "appropriately," will lead to the progress of nations, be they capitalist or socialist (Hartmann 1995; Parr 2012, chap. 3). The "reproductive imperative" in development frameworks (Stürgeon 2010), in which normative notions of femininity and masculinity are reinforced and even celebrated, pervades post-neoliberal discourse as well. In particular, like neoliberal leaders, post-neoliberal state leaders have appealed to women in their roles as mothers and wives to garner their support in heteronormative social reproduction. This is evident in Correa's public call on Mother's Day for women to support the Citizen Revolution and in his claim that the "revolution has a woman's face" (Lind 2012).[4] Such heteronormative battle cries call for an otherwise untouched capitalist paradigm of economic modernization based on resource extraction and economic growth, which links heterosexual reproduction to the sustainability of nature and the success of development. And, as feminist and queer studies scholars have pointed out, the developmentalist paradigm is enmeshed in cultural values concerning "the family," in which not only the ideal heterosexual, nuclear, Western-style family but also the particular homonormative conceptions of "gay" and "lesbian" are increasingly a visible part of sexual modernization and modernity and are themselves linked to developmentalist notions of visibility, rights, and empowerment (Horn 2010; Lind, 2010; Lind and Share 2003). These notions "travel" across borders and through transnational discursive and institutional networks in multiple ways. Actors within post-neoliberal states are no less inclined to "modernize" sexuality along the lines of respectability than are actors within neoliberal states. For example, an Ecuadorian feminist activist stated, "Right now in Ecuador it is easier to talk about homosexuality than water," referring both to the ongoing protests concerning the right to water and other natural resources, led by indigenous communities, and the increased visibility and acceptance of lesbian, gay, bisexual, transgender, and intersex (LGBTI) individuals and issues (Coba 2012). In this imaginary, LGBTI individuals are linked to progress, whiteness, urban centers, and class respectability; water, in contrast, is linked to a lack of "development," racialized indigeneity, rural areas, and poverty. Interestingly, this followed the appointment of Ecuador's first "out" lesbian in a ministerial position: Carina Vance was appointed minister of health in January 2012.[5] During the same time period, a national march for indigenous rights, including a march for water, took place on March 8, 2012. Thus sexual politics and regimes of heteronormativity are central to seemingly benign macroeconomic development planning and state (and civil society practices)—be they in capitalist or socialist, or neoliberal or post-neoliberal, contexts—and are inherently racialized and classed from the start. Just as I am arguing that scholars cannot understand the material effects of redistribution without recognizing regimes of heteronormativity, scholars cannot discuss sexual politics without also accounting for how other categories of social recognition are understood and manifested in a given geopolitical, cultural, and legal context.[6]

Heteronormativity is central to post-neoliberal forms of governance as well, as evidenced by ongoing struggles concerning women's and sexual rights in "new Left" contexts in Latin America.[7] By "post-neoliberal," I am not implying that neoliberal policies no longer exist but, rather, that they have lost their "quasi-hegemonic position," as new forms of collective action and articulations of economic and social policy have gained salience (Fernandes 2007; Grimson and Kessler 2005). Post-neoliberal forms of governance in Ecuador and throughout Latin America have proposed socialist and/or hybrid development approaches that take into account noncapitalist economies, forms of exchange, and notions of economic well-being. Governments have created new south-south trade alliances (e.g., ALBA) as a counterproposal to the World Trade Organization and global financial hegemonies.[8] Governments have challenged liberal conceptions of gender and race, including through critiques of "multicultural neoliberalism" and individualist legal traditions (Postero 2007). Yet it is important, I argue, that post-neoliberalism does not connote a complete break with a neoliberal past. Rather, post-neoliberalism represents a partial break, a rupture, a challenge to global neoliberal hegemonies (Fernandes 2007; Goodale and Postero 2013; Grimson and Kessler 2005). Post-neoliberal forms of governance in and of themselves still operate through neoliberal market-based logics to varying degrees. Like other "posts-" (e.g., poststructuralism, postmodernism), post-neoliberalism represents something that comes *after* the decidedly neoliberal period; something in the making to create the possibility of "another world." Some argue that Correa's anti-neoliberal stance, like that of other new Left leaders, "should not be confused with anti-capitalist politics" (Hart-Landsberg 2009, quoted in Becker 2011, 104).[9] Yet there are some important differences between neoliberal and post-neoliberal forms of governance with regard to family norms, perhaps most obviously as found in the 2008 Constitution and in the Correa administration's *buen vivir (in Spanish)* or *sumac kawsay* (in Quichua) agenda, terms now used widely to connote his economic alternative to neoliberalism.

In contrast to neoliberal notions of development, which privilege the free market over all else, the concept of *buen vivir* is about seeking a more "balanced relation between the state, the market and society in harmony with nature" (Deere 2010, 2). Importantly, the notion of *buen vivir* "constitutes a critique of the concept of development and economic growth as the motor force of development" (2). In theory, it privileges solidarity over competition, and sustainability over economic growth. In the 2008 Constitution, *buen vivir* appears as a set of principles to guide the economy and as a series of rights and social, economic, and environmental guarantees, including the right to water and sufficient access to food; to a wholesome environment that is ecologically balanced; to information; to culture, science, and education; to housing and a safe environment; to health; and to work and social security (Deere 2010; Republic of Ecuador 2008).

In theory, the concept of *buen vivir* arguably opens up space to consider feminist concerns and potentially challenge heteronormativity. Magdalena Leon (2009) has argued that by putting human life center stage, the concept of *buen vivir* provides an opening to discuss the centrality of human reproduction—"all those unpaid activities generally carried out by women to reproduce the labor force on a daily and generational basis" (Deere 2010, 3). This provides an opening for reimagining and operationalizing state policies concerning caring labor that remains largely "invisible" in capitalist development frameworks; as such, the *buen vivir* framework potentially challenges heteronormativity. Nonetheless, contradictions abound. As Deere points out in her study of asset ownership and *buen vivir*, "the care economy usually gets short shrift" in discussions of development (3), even in the current context. Correa's claim that the revolution has a "woman's face" is not insinuating that women are autonomous subjects; rather, in many ways his discourse reinforces and prolongs the neoliberal discourse of the family, in which (especially poor) women are targeted as recipients of development assistance in their roles as mothers and caretakers, *and* also are seen as key facilitators of development insofar as they provide unpaid and cheap labor to the economy.

Whereas women in neoliberal discourse are viewed as contributing unpaid and cheap labor to an increasingly privatized economy, women in presumed post-neoliberal discourse are viewed as contributing to the caring economy as part of a postcapitalist ethic of solidarity. And whereas in the neoliberal development mantra women have been told to "work harder" (Bedford 2009), in Ecuador's post-neoliberal framework women are now being told to "care more" and "work harder" for the revolution. In both scenarios, women are viewed as absorbers of economic change and as the "subjects of others" (Guchín 2010). That is, they are seen through a maternalist lens, as linked to the family and not as autonomous subjects, a common observation made in contexts of male-dominated nationalist struggles (Gutiérrez-Chong 2007).[10] One way this occurs is through a maternalist discourse of economic development found in both neoliberal and post-neoliberal agendas. Reprocentric notions of "vulnerability" and "respectability" are implicit or explicit parts of state laws and policies addressing redistribution, just as in earlier struggles for/against neoliberal restructuring; indeed, these notions continue to inform post-neoliberal development logic, as I illustrate below.

Ecuador's Citizen Revolution (2007–Present)

A U.S.-trained economist, former professor at the Quito-based Latin American Faculty of Social Sciences (Facultad Latinoamericana de Ciencias Sociales, or FLACSO-Ecuador), and self-defined socialist, Rafael Correa and the Alianza PAIS (Country Alliance) coalition won the 2006 presidential elections with 56 percent of the popular vote. In his campaign, he promised a "citizen revolution" that would work to reject neoliberalism as a social, economic, and political model and construct a new anti-imperialist path for Ecuador. Soon after taking office, Correa called for a referendum to decide whether to convene a Constituent Assembly. The referendum passed by a huge margin, with 82 percent voting in its favor, and the Constituent Assembly convened to begin the work of drafting the new Constitution in November 2007. The Constitution was passed by national referendum and took effect in July 2008. In 2012, Correa was re-elected in a landslide victory. In 2016, Correa's former vice president, Lenin Moreno (2017–present), won the presidential election, carrying on the Citizen Revolution under his leadership.

Ecuador's Citizen Revolution has been institutionalized through two key frameworks: the 2008 Constitution and the 2009–13 and 2013–17

National Plan of Well-Being (Plan Nacional del Buen Vivir, formerly known as the National Development Plan). Combined, these two sets of policies and laws create a foundation for understanding the country's shift away from neoliberalism and toward increased state sovereignty vis-à-vis the global north. Centrally involved in this process is a resignification of the family, as well as the nation and economy.

To begin, Ecuador's 2008 Constitution contains several important innovations. It affirms the country as a "plurinational" state, one that respects and affirms the identities and autonomy of the diverse groups within it; it affirms the importance of grounding the economy in a notion of *sumak kawsay/buen vivir* or living well; and it recognizes legally enforceable ecosystem rights, the first constitution in the world to do so. Although it has received less attention then some of the other important features in the 2008 Constitution, the new Constitution also resignifies the family, shifting from a singular notion of the family rooted in a legal definition of biological kinship or sanguine relations to one based on a notion of *la familia diversa*, the family in its diverse forms, rooted in "alternative logics" to that of traditional kinship. Such a move creates possibilities for extending state recognition to non-normative families, including transnational migrant,[11] communal, same-sex, and other non-normative forms of kinship (Lind and Keating 2013).

When the Constituent Assembly passed the Constitution in July 2008, Ecuador's president Rafael Correa described it as heralding Ecuador's move away from global neoliberal hegemony and toward its "second independence" (Peralta 2008). The notion of the necessity of a second struggle against colonialism—one that challenges and restructures the racialized social, political, and economic power relations imposed or exacerbated by colonization yet preserved in postcolonial regimes, or what Anibal Quijano (2000) calls the "coloniality of power," is central to decolonial theory and politics. According to Nelson Maldonado-Torres, decolonization refers "to a confrontation with the racial, gender, and sexual hierarchies that were put in place or strengthened by European modernity as it colonized and enslaved populations throughout the planet" (2007, 261). Indeed, although Ecuador achieved its national independence in 1822, ending three hundred years of Spanish colonial rule, post-independence life in Ecuador has been marked by the continuity of deeply entrenched inequitable power relations, in which indigenous communities, women, the poor, sexual dissidents, and others have faced political exclusion, social marginalization, and economic exploitation and deprivation. Internationally, Ecuador has been subject to global economic and political hierarchies that have served to sediment inequitable power relations domestically as well. For example, even though Ecuador's 1998 Constitution went some way in recognizing the rights of indigenous groups and Afro-Ecuadorians, women, and LGBTI groups, it did so largely through a neoliberal multicultural logic that helped to create acceptable, responsible citizens (Postero 2007), constrained in part by the state's reliance on—yet also heeding—World Bank and IMF structural adjustment guidelines (Lind 2013). Observing the 1998 Constitution, Catherine Walsh notes that "the fact that these constitutional recognitions . . . [were] in accordance with the directives and policies of multilateral organizations (most specifically the World Bank) . . . suggests that the intention [was to] open the path for the neoliberal project of structural readjustment" (2009, 69). Although the 1998 Constitution provided new forms of legal recognition to historically marginalized groups, as part of this process these forms of recognition were not linked to the state's neoliberal redistributive agenda (it's important to remember that neoliberalism is also a form of redistribution; Lind 2013).[12] Given the impossibility of questioning the neoliberal redistributive agenda amid structural adjustment measures, the politics of recognition prevailed and, paradoxically, a historically record high number of policies and laws were passed that affirmed the rights of women and in many ways led to the neoliberalization of struggles for women's rights and of feminisms (Lind 2005, 2013; also see Prügl 2014).

The 2008 Constitution radically reinterpreted state-society relations, institutional structures, and legal subjectivities. It linked legally recognized marginalized groups to the state's redistributive project, in part by integrating these groups into various sections of the Constitution, including, to some extent, its economic guidelines. At least on paper it attempted to link struggles for recognition to those for redistribution, and it was the legal basis for what Rafael Correa called the refounding of the state and political constitution. It included a resignification of several concepts, including state, plurinationalism, family, and development (*buen vivir/sumac kawsay* or living well/well-being).

The first article drafted by the Constituent Assembly was momentous; taking up the question of the nature of the state itself, the Assembly redefined Ecuador as a plurination, that is, a state that respects, affirms, and enables the autonomy of the multiple groups within it. The article reads as follows: "Article 1. Ecuador is a constitutional State of rights and justice, a social, democratic, sovereign, independent, unitary, intercultural, plurinational and secular State" (Republic of Ecuador 2008). The recognition and affirmation of plurinationalism as both a descriptive and normative concept had been a central demand of indigenous groups in Latin America since the early 1990s. Although the call for plurinationalism came primarily from indigenous groups in Ecuador, Assembly member and indigenous leader Mónica Chuji stressed that the concept of plurinationalism should be applied widely: "In Ecuador, the concept of plurinationalism has been proposed by the indigenous movement to challenge the racism, exclusion, and violence that has characterized the relationship of the modern nation-state with indigenous peoples, but plurinationalism can also generate conditions of possibility for the state recognition for gender diversity, for example. . . . Plurinationalism is not only a concept having to do with ethnicity, it is a concept that opens the social contract to multiple differences, be they differences of ethnicity, or of gender, or of culture, or of age, etc." (Chuji 2008, n.p.).

This innovative understanding of the notion of plurinationalism, as discussed in the Constituent Assembly, must be understood in relation to the new legal definition of the family. Migrants' rights advocates, feminist, and LGBTI advocates in particular worked within the Constituent Assembly to redefine the family, with the idea of shifting from a singular, traditional conception of family rooted in biological kinship and/or marital relations to one based on a notion of the family in its "diverse forms." Article 67 of the Constitution affirms the following: "Article 67. The family in its diverse forms is recognized. The State shall protect it as the fundamental core of society and shall guarantee conditions that integrally favor the achievement of its goals. They shall be comprised of legal or common-law ties and shall be based on the equality of rights and the opportunities of their members." Elizabeth Vásquez, an assistant to Constituent Assembly member Tania Hermida and one of the principal activists involved in the struggle for resignifying the family, explains that this approach was informed by a "transfeminist" politics that sought to "profoundly question male privilege from an alliance that aimed to challenge social and legal institutions such as the family" (2009, 100). In this approach, the "trans" in the term "transfeminism" implies a break not only with the traditional gender/sex system but also with other forms of normativities based on race, ethnicity, class, and geopolitical location. One of the advantages of the transfeminist approach, Vásquez writes, is that "the legalization of the notion of family diversity does not conflict with the notion of common law marriage, but includes it as one more manifestation of diversity. In contrast, struggling only for common law marriages excludes struggles for a more broad conception of a diversity of families" (101).

In many ways, this intersectional approach to redefining the family is grounded in historical struggles to challenge the postcolonial state. Historically, colonial patriarchal state laws concerning marriage reflected colonial mestizo interests, often in deep tension with indigenous understandings of family and marriage, which tended to emphasize a communal logic, valuing community over the individual. Indigenous women lost access to inheritance and land due to European patriarchal laws granting fathers and sons inheritance and land rights. Indigenous rights activists have thus challenged marriage by the state for a long time. Transfeminist activists drew from and benefitted from this long-standing, multidimensional critique of the state as they constructed their intersectional approach to redefining the family. In addition to affirming the concept of the diverse family, the 2008 Constitution addresses communal rights, at least on paper, by protecting the land, territory, rights, identities, and economic, political, and cultural practices of indigenous communities. Article 84 of the Constitution preserves ownership of communal/ancestral lands; guarantees preconsultation on any development plans on indigenous-owned lands; and provides protection of indigenous traditions. Indigenous women have emphasized the importance of paying attention to ways that both patriarchal state ideologies and masculinist indigenous movement ideologies rendered invisible and disadvantaged indigenous women, both historically and in the present (Clark 2012; Prieto 2004, 2013).

It was argued as well that individuals or couples can potentially use these new definitions to expand the form of common-law marriage to extend legal recognition and benefits to same-sex couples and to extend state benefits to non-normative households. Finally, this approach to the resignification of the family links with struggles for migrant rights and the need to attend to the familial issues faced by transnational families, households, and kinship networks. During the Constitutional Assembly, fifty-eight articles were introduced that addressed migration (Herrera 2008). Article 40 of the 2008 Constitution guarantees that the state will provide assistance to migrant families, whether they live abroad or in Ecuador, avers that no person shall be considered illegal because of his or her migratory status, and guarantees protection to "transnational families." ·

Finally, the 2008 Constitution redefined the state's role in directing the economy, recentralizing state functions and overturning more than two decades of neoliberal reforms aimed at privatization, economic liberalization, state retrenchment, and decentralization. At the center of the Constitution's definition of the economy and economic planning is the notion of *buen vivir* development. According to the Constitution (as mentioned in several articles and sections) and importantly to the National Plan of Well-Being, *buen vivir* development aims to redefine the economy as rooted in solidarity rather than merely competition, and as privileging sustainability over economic growth. It calls for the creation of a "solidarity economy" in which collective well-being, redistribution, use values, and human needs prevail over market-based ideologies and needs. Redistribution is brought (back) more closely into state control, including the state's control over profits from extractive industries (especially oil). The National Plans of Well-Being (2009–13 and 2013–17) even more explicitly operationalize these definitions and goals. For example, the 2009–13 plan established twelve goals that encompass endogenous development, including a solidarity economy, recognition of unpaid labor (including reproductive/caring labor), cultural diversity, viewing nature as constitutive of and intrinsically valuable as social life, and environmental sustainability.[13] In the constitution and the plans, sustainability is defined to include "human and nonhuman life." Broadly speaking, *buen vivir* development draws upon "indigenous border thinking," and from the antiglobalization movement and Latin American decolonial thought, "making it one of the first nation-state endorsements of non-western approaches" (Radcliffe 2015). Most concretely, the state's *buen vivir* agenda resulted from "new assemblages of social movements leading to new agendas in development, citizenship and rights" (Goodale and Postero 2013, 263; Radcliffe 2015). Combined, these resignifications potentially yield "another world" after neoliberalism, yet in practice there is a great disjuncture between discourse and practice, as I illustrate below.

The Potential and Pitfalls of the Citizen Revolution

To some extent, the Correa administration successfully redirected the economy and redistributed resources. Like other left-wing and center-left governments in the region, especially in countries such as Bolivia and Venezuela where more radical projects have taken place, income inequality and poverty rates have been significantly reduced. For example, poverty levels dropped from 37.5 percent in 2007 to 25 percent in 2014, and extreme poverty rates dropped from 17 percent to 8 percent. Inequality rates were reduced from .55 to .48, three times more than the regional average between 2007 and 2012 (SENPLADES 2014; World Bank 2014). Between 2007 and 2012, the Correa administration spent more than three times as much on social spending than did the three previous governments combined. Between 2008 and 2016, the state spent more than US$16 billion in social spending, including on its conditional cash transfer program, the Bono de Desarrollo Humano, or Human Development Bond, which in 2013 had a budget of just over US$1 billion and through March of that year had 1,901,088 registered beneficiaries (Economía de Ecuador 2014). Coverage provided through universal healthcare has been extended to include new benefits based on the 2008 Constitution, and Ecuadorians living abroad also have newly acquired access to healthcare and citizen benefits provided by Ecuadorian embassies and consulates. State planners and policy makers are working on several projects aimed at reaching caring laborers and nontraditional families. Ecuador ratified the International Labour Organization (ILO) Domestic Workers Convention in 2011, making it only the eleventh country in the world to do so.

Innovative attempts have been made to understand non-normative households and families as well. For example, the state census bureau administered the first-ever national LGBTI census survey of over 2,500 individuals from ten cities or provinces in Ecuador, with the aim of assessing employment, experiences with poverty and violence, and the living and social conditions of self-identified LGBTI individuals (INEC 2013). Largely as a result of these successful economic and social reforms, coupled with the state's work toward expanding citizen access to state resources and improving income distribution, public opinion polls continue to demonstrate strong support for Correa.

Correa himself has also taken a strong stance against U.S. imperialism. For example, in 2009 his administration opted not to renew the U.S. lease of the Eloy Alfaro Air Base in Manta, Ecuador, effectively ending the U.S. presence at its military base. In 2012 the Correa administration offered asylum to WikiLeaks founder Julian Assange after the United States sought his extradition (Assange has been holed up in the Ecuadorian Embassy in London for more than two years). Correa has also threatened to not pay back the foreign debt and has placed tighter controls on multinational corporations that operate in Ecuador, including most notably those that work in extractive and mining industries (in 2011, the Ecuadorian court found Chevron guilty of polluting the Amazon region, which is historically unprecedented). Since 2007, as the Constitution has been operationalized, judicial, criminal justice, health, planning, media, and other state sectors have gradually institutionalized the reforms, a process due in part to Correa's and Alianza PAIS's control of these sectors. Having received his PhD in economics at the University of Illinois, Correa is politically savvy in challenging U.S. and global hegemonic institutions. As a populist leader with authoritarian tendencies, he has effectively recentralized control over key sectors such as the media, higher education, and natural resources.

Despite the economic successes, these reforms have taken place with costs. To begin, recentralization efforts have involved an attempt to manage social movements and knowledge about marginalized populations through a top-down approach reminiscent of earlier socialist eras in the region and steeped in colonialist logic. Just as earlier colonial and postcolonial governments have attempted to acquire knowledge about and thus control historically marginalized sectors (e.g., indigenous, Afro-Ecuadorian, *montubio*, women, LGBTI), so too has the Correa administration utilized classificatory schemes to "know" and classify Ecuadorian populations in accordance with the Citizen Revolution's scientific understanding of difference and modernity (Appadurai 1993).

Almost from the start the organized indigenous movement, which is comprised of multiple indigenous confederations representing communities across the country, has held great contempt for the government. The Correa administration alienated the indigenous movement through its support of extractive development (in primarily indigenous territories), which is typically done with no "prior consultation" with local communities. The Constitution itself affirms support for extractive development and, unlike the Bolivian Constitution, does not guarantee "prior consultation." Similarly, Correa's policies have largely splintered the organized feminist movement, and women's rights (especially reproductive rights) have been under attack, especially since 2014, when Correa appointed Mónica Hernández, a pro-life administrator with Opus Dei ties, as director of the National Interagency Strategy for Family Planning and Prevention of Teen Pregnancies (Estrategia Nacional Interseccional de Planificación Familiar y Prevención del Embarazo de Adolescentes, or ENIPLA), the state's primary agency focused on family planning. The 2008 Constitution called for the creation of five permanent commissions that represent each of the five legally defined marginalized groups: women; elderly, youth and adolescents; nationalities and originary *pueblos* (especially indigenous and Afro-Ecuadorian); people with disabilities; and migrants. It was not until May 2014, more than six years after the commissions were approved in the new Constitution, that the National Assembly finally approved the equal opportunity law needed to establish the permanent commissions. During that time, the former National Women's Council (Consejo Nacional de las Mujeres, or CONAMU) was dismantled and designated as a "transition commission," receiving relatively little institutional support or funds, until 2014. Correa himself is a devout Catholic and opposes abortion and homosexuality (pro-LGBTI reforms have been passed due to his advisors and to the support of his coalition party, in spite of his personal beliefs [see Lind and Keating 2013]). Thus while the post-neoliberal state has utilized transgressive notions of family, nation, and economy, in practice the reality of state restructuring is messy, partial, and incomplete, and best understood by examining the workings of spaces within the state, rather than as a unified state or Citizen Revolution.

This contradictory nature of the state is evident in more recent attempts of the Correa administration to centralize power and engage in practices that counteract the transgressive policies of the post-neoliberal state. Particularly during the final years of his presidency, the Correa administration increasingly repressed expressions of dissent to maintain its control of the state, citizenry, and oil development, particularly in media and higher education sectors. One of the Correa administration's first institutional reforms was to centralize control of the media, and it has also appointed new directors of leading universities. In 2016, two of Ecuador's leading graduate institutions, Quito-based FLACSO and the Universidad Andina Simón Bolívar, were both under threat of losing their state funding as a result of disagreements with the government (Puente and Bravo 2016). The government continues to attack women's rights and to view women's and LGBTI rights activism that challenges gender and sexual norms as threatening to national sovereignty. In this scenario, class continues to be the ultimate signifier in the Citizen Revolution, as evidenced by the state's reluctance to fully embrace indigenous, feminist, LGBTI, and other social movements as part of the revolution and as evidenced in its prioritization of redirecting the economy and recentralizing the state. Throughout these changes, the heteropatriarchal roots of the revolution continue intact, despite the various instances of post-neoliberal ruptures, moments or spaces within the state (Lind 2012). While family norms have been resignified, they have also been renormalized—again, as heteronormative—in a post-neoliberal context. This has occurred through political discourse supporting traditional "family values," through the president's explicit attack on what he calls imported "gender ideologies," including ideas about gender being taught in university gender studies programs, and through anti-abortion, pro-life rhetoric at state-based ENIPLA. The progressive implications of the resignified family are caught in a loophole and stalled, despite legal and policy language to the contrary. We have yet to see meaningful shifts in cultural formations, daily life, and political subjectivities as a result of these resignifications.

Likewise, much of this depends upon how long the Citizen Revolution and/or the challenge to neoliberalism lasts in Ecuador's longer-term political process. Correa suggested revising the Constitution to extend presidential term limits to three, rather than two, full terms, although ultimately he was unsuccessful in revising the Constitution.[14] He thus had to necessarily step down as president after his second full term ended. In 2017, candidate Lenin Moreno, former vice president under Correa and Alianza País, became president, carrying on the legacy of the Citizen Revolution. In this context, women's rights continue to be a highly contested terrain and if we are to learn from other New Left contexts, post-neoliberal forms of governance do not necessarily lead to more progressive views on reproductive and sexual rights (Ewig 2012); rather, we have witnessed sometimes unexpected alliances of religious morality and socialist modernization doctrine alongside the more hopeful instances of moving away from neoliberal practices and rationalities, thereby solidifying heteropatriarchal norms in new language.

Conclusion

So, what comes "after" neoliberalism? I argue that Ecuador's Citizen Revolution gives us an opportunity to imagine this possibility, albeit with limitations. For a small Latin American state to challenge the global neoliberal hegemony, in part by challenging U.S. imperialism and global financial institutions such as the World Bank and the IMF), this is significant. Through the 2008 Constitution and the government's National Plans of Well-Being, the state has introduced notions of *buen vivir*, resignifying development as something beyond capitalism, or post-capitalist, and expanding redistribution to benefit the poorest sectors. And importantly, the state has resignified the family, thereby leading in practice to a potentially broader notion of family, household, and citizenship. We have already witnessed this, for example, among transnational households, where Ecuadorian family members living outside the country now have increased access to state resources overseas, and in the legalization of same-sex domestic partnerships. This broader notion of citizenship potentially links these new political subjectivities to the state's post-neoliberal redistributive project, thereby benefitting marginalized groups not only in terms of legal recognition but also in terms of access to economic redistribution. In these ways, the state has arguably moved away from neoliberalism and "decolonized" Western, colonial notions of gender, race, and sexuality, potentially challenging reprocentric heteronormativity as well, at least on paper.

Yet, as I have demonstrated, there are drawbacks and contradictions. Ultimately, the state—itself a legacy of colonization—maintains colonial, heteronormative modernization narratives of progress and citizenship, albeit in new legal and institutional forms. For starters, while the state addresses noncapitalist forms of labor and utilizes an anticapitalist discourse, it continues to rely on capitalist (including extractive) development, and on a notion of modernization that privileges capital over human life. Arturo Escobar (2010) considers this kind of New Left an "alternative modernization" project rather than a break with Western, colonialist modernization logic, similar to what we have observed of other socialist projects around the world. This kind of alternative modernization challenges global hegemonic institutions to some extent, yet ultimately the Ecuadorian state remains bound by its reliance on oil development and by its foreign debt obligations and the conditions that go along with that debt. The traditional family remains the foundation of this alternative modernization discourse, even in its "diverse" form. In the quest for new institutional arrangements and subjectivities "after" neoliberalism, projects such as the Citizen Revolution are interesting and bold proposals yet lack the vision, sometimes the political will, and certainly the full political and economic ability, to make that world possible.

NOTES

1 Venezuela was the first country to shift to the Left, as part of the "pink tide," with the democratic election of Hugo Chávez in 1998 (1999–2013, followed by Nicolás Maduro, 2013–). Since then, other countries that have shifted to the Left include Chile (2000–10 and 2014–), Brazil (2003–10, 2011–16), Argentina (2003–15), Dominican Republic (2004–), Uruguay (2005–), Bolivia (2006–), Honduras (2006–9), Ecuador (2007–), Nicaragua (2007), Guatemala (2008–12), Paraguay (2008–12), El Salvador (2009–), Peru (2011–16), and Costa Rica (2014–).

2 Portions of this section are based on Lind 2012, 539–42.

3 The Spanish first invaded this region in 1534, with notable indigenous resistance. The territory officially became part of the Spanish viceroyalty in 1544.

4 In the so-called New Left, Venezuelan President Hugo Chávez (1999–2013) has been perhaps the most successful in mobilizing women in their roles as mothers through his Cuban-style, community-based *misiones*, which rely on women's volunteer labor to manage healthcare and other community needs in poor neighborhoods (Lind 2010).

5 She resigned from this position in November 2015.

6 This certainly applies as much to the north as to the south. By "sexual politics," I am referring to the terrain in which contemporary actors struggle for the right to self-determination as sexual beings, to freedom of sexual and gender expression,

and to control one's own body. It includes but is not limited to the "rights, obligations, recognitions and respect around those most intimate spheres of life—who to live with, how to raise children, how to handle one's body, how to relate as a gendered being, how to be an erotic person" (Plummer 2001, 238; also see Cabral/Grinspan and Viturro 2006). This terrain thus extends far beyond the legal, formal, or public, and includes political-cultural struggles over what constitutes citizenship, economy, and national belonging; how axes of personal/intimate life are structured, including along racial, class, gender, and geopolitical lines; and who "counts" as a citizen in the first place. It also exemplifies how and why body politics such as abortion and homosexuality tend to take central place in national (and global) political discussions, yet are simultaneously viewed as "private" issues.

7 To date, thirteen countries in the region have voted in officials who espouse anti-neoliberal ideals.

8 ALBA, the Alianza Bolivariana para los Pueblos de Nuestra América, was created by Venezuela and Cuba in 2004 as an alternative to the U.S.-proposed Free Trade Area of the Americas (FTAA or ALCA in Spanish), with the goal of promoting economic integration among Latin American nations. There are nine member countries; Ecuador joined in 2009. UNASUR, the Union de Naciones Suramericanas, is an intergovernmental union combining two South American regional trade organizations: MERCOSUR (the Southern Community Market) and CAN, the Andean Community of Nations. Its institutional headquarters are based in Quito, Ecuador.

9 See Hart-Landsberg, Martin. 2009. "Learning from ALBA and the Bank of the South: Challenges and Possibilities." *Monthly Review* 61, no. 4. https://monthlyreview.org/2009/09/01/learning-from-alba-and-the-bank-of-the-south-challenges-and-possibilities. Accessed May 31, 2017. Some characterize Correa's approach as nationalist and Keynesian rather than Marxist (see Becker 2011).

10 Here I am drawing from the gender and development literature on women and neoliberal restructuring, which provides an understanding of how poor women in particular have served as "shock absorbers" for broader economic restructuring processes, including trade liberalization, privatization, and state retrenchment measures, in which the burden of social reproduction is shifted to poor families and especially to poor women (Benería and Feldman 1992).

11 Approximately two million Ecuadorians have migrated to Spain, Italy, and elsewhere since 2000, the peak year of the country's regulatory financial crisis, in which twenty of the country's leading banks collapsed, and the year in which the economy was "dollarized." Ecuador's total population is about fourteen million.

12 By this I wish to highlight that neoliberal economic approaches have redistributive goals just like more explicitly framed socialist redistributive economic frameworks, even if supporters of neoliberal agendas do not explicitly use the term "redistribution." For countries bound by World Bank and IMF-sponsored structural adjustment policies due to their foreign debt, they are allowed to spend

only a small percentage of their GDP on social welfare initiatives. In a post-neoliberal context, drawing from Marxian theories of redistribution, there tends to be more explicit focus on state social spending for social welfare initiatives, and on improving income among the poorest sectors, as needed mechanisms to address inequality.

13 Quote from Alberto Acosta, "El buen vivir para la construcción de las alternativas." In *Entre el quiebre y la realidad: Constitución 2008*, ed. Alberto Acosta, 27–37. Quito: Abya Yala (cited in Radcliffe 2015, 314).

14 Currently, presidents are allowed to complete up to two full terms in office before being required to step down. The proposed legislation would allow presidents to complete three full terms in office. Interestingly, because Correa began his term halfway through a regular term (2007–9) and completed his first full term in 2009–13, he is now already in what people typically consider his "third" term (2013–17). Thus, if his legislation passes, he'll be eligible to run for a "fourth" term, although the legal language states that a president would be allowed to complete three full terms, not including extraordinary circumstances.

REFERENCES

Appadurai, Arjun. 1993. "Number in the Colonial Imagination." In *Orientalism and the Postcolonial Predicament: Perspectives on South Asia*, ed. Carol Breckenridge and Peter Van der Veer, 314–40. Philadelphia: University of Pennsylvania Press.

Becker, Marc. 2011. *¡Pachakutik! Indigenous Movements and Electoral Politics in Ecuador*. Lanham, MD: Rowman and Littlefield.

Bedford, Kate. 2009. *Developing Partnerships: Gender, Sexuality, and the Reformed World Bank*. Minneapolis: University of Minnesota Press.

Benería, Lourdes, and Shelley Feldman, eds. 1992. *Unequal Burden: Economic Crises, Persistent Poverty, and Women's Work*. Boulder, CO: Westview Press.

Berlant, Lauren, and Michael Warner. 1998. "Sex in Public." *Critical Inquiry*, 547–66.

Cabral, Mauro (A. I. Grinspan) and Paula Viturro. 2006. "(Trans)Sexual Citizenship in Contemporary Argentina." In *Transgender Rights*, ed. Paisley Currah, Richard M. Yuang, and Shannon Price Minter, 262–73. Minneapolis: University of Minnesota Press.

Chuji, Mónica. 2008. "Diez conceptos básicos sobre Plurinacionalidad e Interculturalidad." September 4. *ALAInet*. http://www.alainet.org/es/active/23366. Accessed June 1, 2017.

Clark, Kimberly. 2012. *Gender, State and Medicine in Highland Ecuador: Modernizing Women, Modernizing the State*. Pittsburgh: University of Pittsburgh Press.

Coba, Lisset. 2012. Activist, Asamblea Mujeres Populares Diversas. Personal interview, Quito, Ecuador, February 16.

Deere, Carmen Diana. 2010. "Asset Ownership and 'El Buen Vivir' in Ecuador: Towards A Gendered Analysis." Paper presented at the Latin American Studies Association International Congress, Toronto, October 6–9.

Economia de Ecuador. 2014. Bono de Desarrollo Humano. www.credito.com.ec/econo-mia/bono-de-desarrollo-humano-2014. Accessed October 17, 2014.

Escobar, Arturo. 2010. "Latin America at a Crossroads." *Cultural Studies* 24, no. 1: 1–65.

Ewig, Christina, ed. 2012. "Pinking the Latin American Left." *Politics and Gender*, Critical Perspectives special issue 8, no. 2.

Fernandes, Sujatha. 2007. "Everyday Wars of Position: Media, Social Movements, and the State in Chávez's Venezuela." Paper presented at the annual meeting of the Latin American Studies Association, Montreal, September 3–7.

Goodale, Mark, and Nancy Postero, eds. 2013. *Neoliberalism, Interrupted: Social Change and Contested Governance in Latin America*. Stanford, CA: Stanford University Press.

Grimson, Alejandro, and Gabriel Kessler. 2005. *On Argentina and the Southern Cone: Neoliberalism and National Imaginations*. New York: Routledge.

Guchín, Mónica. 2010. *El estado ecuatoriano y las mujeres: ¿nuevos sujetos de la Revolución Ciudadana?* Master's thesis, FLACSO-Ecuador, Quito.

Gutiérrez-Chong, Natividad. 2007. *Women, Ethnicity and Nationalisms in Latin America*. London: Ashgate.

Hart-Landsberg, Martin. 2009. "Learning from ALBA and the Bank of the South: Challenges and Possibilities." *Monthly Review* 61, no. 4. https://monthlyreview.org/2009/09/01/learning-from-alba-and-the-bank-of-the-south-challenges-and-possibilities. Accessed May 31, 2017.

Hartmann, Betsy. 1995. *Reproductive Rights and Wrongs: The Global Politics of Population Control*. New York: South End Press.

Herrera, Gioconda. 2008. "States, Work and Social Reproduction through the Lens of Migrant Experience: Ecuadorian Domestic Workers in Madrid." In *Beyond States and Markets: The Challenges of Social Reproduction*, ed. Isabella Bakker and Rachel Silvey, 93–107. London: Routledge.

Horn, Maja. 2010. "Queer Dominican Moves: In the Interstices of Colonial Legacies and Global Impulses." In *Development, Sexual Rights and Global Governance*, ed. Amy Lind, 169–81. New York: Routledge.

INEC (Institute Nacional de Estadistica y Censos). 2013. GLBTI Survey. Quito: Instituto Nacional de Estadística y Censos. www.inec.gob.ec. Accessed October 17, 2014.

Lavrin, Asunción. 2010. "Sexuality in Colonial Spanish America." In *The Handbook of Latin American History*, ed. José Moya, 132–52. Oxford: Oxford University Press.

León, Magdalena. 2009. "Cambiar la economía para cambiar la vida: Desafíos de una economía para la vida." In *El Buen Vivir: una vía para el desarrollo*, ed. Alberto Acosta and Esperanza Martínez, 63–74. Quito: Abya Yala.

Lind, Amy. 2005. *Gendered Paradoxes: Women's Movements, State Restructuring and Global Development in Ecuador*. University Park: Pennsylvania State University Press.

———. 2010. "Introduction: Development, Global Governance, and Sexual Subjectivities." In *Development, Global Governance and Sexual Rights*, ed. Amy Lind, 1–20. New York: Routledge.

———. 2012. "'Revolution with a Woman's Face'? Family Norms, Constitutional Reform, and the Politics of Redistribution in Post/Neoliberal Ecuador." *Rethinking Marxism* 24, no. 4: 536–55.

———. 2013. "Sexual Politics and Constitutional Reform in Ecuador: From Neoliberalism to the *Buen Vivir*." In *Global Homophobia: States, Movements, and the Politics of Oppression*, ed. Meredith L. Weiss and Michael J. Bosia, 127–48. Urbana-Champaign: University of Illinois Press.

Lind, Amy, and Christine Keating. 2013. "Navigating the Left Turn: Sexual Justice and the Citizen Revolution in Ecuador." *International Feminist Journal of Politics* 15, no. 4: 515–33.

Lind, Amy, and Jessica Share. 2003. "Queering Development: Institutionalized Heterosexuality in Development Theory, Practice and Politics in Latin America." In *Feminist Futures: Re-Imagining Women, Culture and Development*, ed. Kum-Kum Bhavnani et al., 55–73. London: Zed Books.

Luibhéid, Eithne. 2002. *Entry Denied: Controlling Sexuality at the Border*. Minneapolis: University of Minnesota Press.

Maldonado-Torres, Nelson. 2007. "On the Coloniality of Being." *Cultural Studies* 21, no. 2/3 (March/May): 261.

Mortimer-Sandilands, Catriona, and Bruce Erickson, eds. 2010. "Introduction: A Genealogy of Queer Ecologies." In *Queer Ecologies: Sex, Nature, Politics, Desire*, 1–47. Bloomington: Indiana University Press.

Parr, Adrian. 2012. *The Wrath of Capital*. New York: Columbia University Press.

Peralta, José. 2008. "La nueva constitución fue entregada por la Asamblea Constituyente." July 25. www.www.asambleaconstituyente.gov.ec. Accessed September 30, 2013.

Phelan, Shane. 2000. "Queer Liberalism?" *American Political Science Review* 94, no. 2: 431–37.

Plummer, Ken. 2001. "The Square of Intimate Citizenship: Some Preliminary Proposals." *Citizenship Studies* 5, no. 3: 237–53.

Postero, Nancy. 2007. *Now We Are Citizens: Indigenous Politics in Postmulticultural Bolivia*. Stanford, CA: Stanford University Press.

Prieto, Mercedes. 2004. *Liberalismo y temor: Imaginando los sujetos indígenas en el Ecuador postcolonial, 1895–1950*. Quito: FLACSO/Abya-Yala.

———. 2013. "Indigenous Women in Latin America: Building a Research Agenda from the South." Unpublished paper.

Prügl, Elisabeth. 2014. "Neoliberalising Feminism." *Political Economy Review* 20, no. 4: 614–31.

Puente, Diego, and Diego Bravo. 2016. "La Flacso y la Universidad Andina marchan hasta la SENESCYT." *El Comercio*, July 15. www.elcomercio.com. Accessed July 21, 2016.

Quijano, Anibal. 2000. "Coloniality of Power, Eurocentrism, and Latin America." *Nepantla: Views from the South* 1, no. 3: 533–80.

Radcliffe, Sarah. 2015. *The Dilemma of Difference: Postcolonial Development and Social Exclusion in Ecuador*. Durham, NC: Duke University Press.

Republic of Ecuador. 2008. "Asamblea Constituyente." Political Database of the Americas. http://pdba.georgetown.edu/Constitutions/Ecuador/ecuador08.html. Accessed June 1, 2017.

SENPLADES. 2014. "Ecuador celebra logros alcanzados en la ruta hacía la erradicación de pobreza." Secretaría Nacional de Planificación y Desarrollo. www.planificacion. gob.ec. Accessed October 17, 2014.

Seidman, Steven. 2001. "From Identity to Queer Politics: Shifts in Normative Heterosexuality and the Meaning of Citizenship." Citizenship Studies 5, no. 3: 321–28.

Smith, Andrea. 2006. "Heteropatriarchy and the Three Pillars of White Supremacy." In Incite! Women of Color against Violence, The Color of Violence: The Incite! Anthology, 66–73. Boston: South End Press.

Stürgeon, Noel. 2010. "Penguin Family Values: The Nature of Planetary Environmental Reproductive Justice. In Queer Ecologies: Sex, Nature, Politics, Desire, ed. Catriona Mortimer-Sandilands and Bruce Ericksen, 102–33. Bloomington: Indiana University Press.

Vásquez, Elizabeth. 2009. "LGBTIQ y ciudadanías sexuales en el Ecuador: Un diálogo con Elizabeth Vásquez." Íconos: Revista de ciencias sociales 35 (2009): 100.

Walsh, Catherine. 2009. "The Plurinational and Intercultural State: Decolonization and State Re-founding in Ecuador." Kult 6 (Fall): 69.

World Bank. 2014. "Ecuador: World Development Indicators." data.worldbank.org/country/ecuador. Accessed October 17, 2014.

Yuval-Davis, Nira. 1997. Gender and Nation. London: Sage.

8

Toward a Feminist Analytic of the Post-Liberalization State

LEELA FERNANDES

The post-liberalization period of the late twentieth and twenty-first centuries represents critical terrain for feminist analysis. Women have been the object of policies and agendas of states, international institutions, and local organizations in a myriad of ways. Women from socioeconomically marginalized contexts have been the targets of entrepreneurial and market-oriented developmental policies. They have been incorporated into export-oriented and service sector industries. And they have often borne the brunt of economic restructuring and policies that have scaled back state socioeconomic support. This has especially been the case for women from the most marginalized communities who have experienced an intensified form of vulnerability produced by various forms of economic reform and market liberalization that have come to be called "neoliberalism." A feminist analysis of the political, economic, and discursive formation of neoliberalism thus provides a unique analytical lens for an understanding of the nature of inequality in the twenty-first century. However, the kind of feminist theoretical approach that is needed to grasp the complexities of contemporary inequality—and the possibilities for change—requires more than a description of women's experiences and burdens in the contemporary era. What is needed is a feminist analytic that can grasp the complex political-economic structures that shape women's lives at the local, national, and global levels. The essays in this volume craft a feminist materialist analytic that provide an avenue for a deeper understanding of the political, social, and economic effects of policies associated with neoliberalism.

Crafting a Feminist Materialist Analytic of the Post-Liberalization State

One of the distinctive features of this collection of essays is the kind of feminist analytic that they collectively develop. The essays draw on three central theoretical perspectives that have shaped feminist thought. These perspectives include (1) an analysis of intersecting and often mutually constitutive forms of socioeconomic inequality, (2) the continued salience of feminist questions that are specifically concerned with women, gender, and sexuality and (3) the emergence of transnational feminist perspectives on a range of socioeconomic, cultural, and political phenomena. These perspectives (which are of course often interconnected and overlapping) represent central intellectual trends both in the interdisciplinary field of women's studies and in cross-disciplinary feminist approaches. The essays in this volume collectively carve out a feminist materialist approach that builds on but deepens these perspectives through a sustained, comparative, and transnational analysis of the post-liberalization state.

Consider, first, how to adequately understand and analyze inequality in the twenty-first century. It has now become a long established presumption that an adequate understanding of inequality requires a relational approach—one that asks how various forms of inequality interact with one another. The paradigm of intersectionality has become one major approach within feminist scholarship and has focused in large part on the categories of race, class, gender, and sexuality (usually within the United States).[1] The essays in this volume deepen such approaches in two central ways. First, while theories of intersectionality are often associated with various intersecting inequalities, the field of feminist political economy is perhaps the least systematically theorized and researched dimension within this stream of feminist thought. Socioeconomic differences between women are often coded by race and nation—so that "women of color" in the United States or non-Western (formerly referred to as "Third World" women) serve as de facto embodiments of socioeconomically marginalized women. Race and nation, in effect, are coded by class. While historical relations of race and colonialism may in fact have meant that women of color and large segments of women in the non-Western world are in fact placed in structurally subordinated positions, assuming this class-based coding of race and nation does not provide a deep analysis of *how* class-based socioeconomic processes—or, for that matter, how conditions of poverty—interact with and are shaped by formations of race and nation. While there is a long-standing interdisciplinary field of feminist political economy within the social sciences, such approaches too often operate on the sidelines of dominant interdisciplinary feminist theoretical approaches and debates in the U.S. academy.[2]

The essays in this volume provide nuanced analyses of the ways in which specific state policies produce structured forms of socioeconomic inequality and exclusion that are constituted by relationships between class and race. For instance, Aggarwal's analysis of how African American and Latina mothers navigate stratified schools can be contextualized in an intellectual history that has addressed motherhood as a political practice that breaks with a conventional gender-centric analytical lens (Gilmore 2007). Histories of racialized segregation and ideologies of choice rooted in neoliberal economic theory join together in ways that structure and shape women's strategies of survival and ideological resistance in the context of newly formed racialized class-based forms of segregation.

What is at stake in such approaches is not a return to a unitary conception of structures of political economy that treat inequalities such as gender and sexuality as epiphenomenal or as discursive effects of socioeconomic structure. Rather, the essays in this volume develop the analytical terrain for a feminist materialist approach that can address the complexities and contradictions of the policies, ideologies, discourses, and practices that are associated with contemporary neoliberalism. The essays do not rest on a presumed binary opposition between discourse and structure or between sociocultural processes and the economy. The kind of materialist feminist approach that shapes the volume analyzes the ways in which these realms are enfolded into each other. In this vein, Naples develops a feminist theoretical approach to discourse that integrates materialist and nondiscursive practices in ways that take into account both the dynamics of gender, race, culture, sexuality, and class and the agencies of subaltern subjects whose social locations are shaped by such practices.

From such a materialist feminist perspective, the discursive regimes that shape policies of market liberalization often rest on a paradox.

If a materialist feminist analysis necessitates that we pay attention to complex dynamics of race, sexuality, class, and national context, these discursive regimes are also invested in liberal narratives of women's empowerment that invoke a homogeneous category of "woman." The category of woman, thus, has become a key component of the developmental dimensions of market liberalization. As the essays by Karim and Daftary illustrate, women are now the central targets of new entrepreneurial models of development. In the case of Bangladesh, international organizations and institutions drive such processes, while in the Indian context, state-led policies of liberalization and decentralization produce such gender- and class-based divisions of labor. Lind's analysis of the post-neoliberal state in Ecuador further underlines the complexities that surround discourses on women's rights, and she examines the contradictory ways in which gender and sexuality are resignified through political debates on normative models of the family. Lind's essay is a critical reminder that the terrain of women's rights remains a contested arena in the post-neoliberal context. These essays underline the significance of close analyses of how gender and women become central framing devices of post-liberalization discourses and how inequalities of class and sexuality fracture idealized images of women's empowerment.

Languages of women's empowerment that now routinely permeate and shape discourses, funding priorities, and policy agendas of international organizations, states, and local NGOs point to the transnational dimensions of the processes that have been analyzed in this volume. Indeed, the application of the "Washington consensus" to a range of countries and the role of aid conditionalities that international organizations have used to promote various kinds of reforms oriented toward market liberalization underline the self-evident transnational dimension of any feminist analysis of such policies and practices. As Naples and Karim illustrate, for instance, discourses associated with a neoliberal agenda have disproportionate material and political effects on the lives of women in marginalized socioeconomic contexts. This volume thus provides a contribution to feminist research on transnationalism through its analysis of the linkages between local, national, and transnational structures of inequality.

However, the kind of feminist analytic that is developed through the essays in this volume also breaks in important ways with many existing approaches to transnational feminism. Transnational feminist approaches have too often become preoccupied with border-crossing phenomena and have been methodologically driven by territorial approaches that search for visible phenomena that transcend national boundaries (Fernandes 2013). That is to say, the assumption underlying such an approach is that transnational phenomena become associated with spaces, actors, and processes that move beyond the nation-state. From such a perspective, the starting point of a feminist analysis of neoliberalism would proceed with a focus on transnational institutions that promote such policies or on the spaces where such policies have been implemented (projects funded by transnational agencies or spatialized sites of transnational capital such as export-oriented zones). This volume, through its focus on the post-liberalization *state* specifically seeks to disrupt the methodological biases and subsequent misreadings of specific national contexts that emerge from this model of transnational feminism.

The comparative analytical focus on the state in the volume provides a textured perspective on how economic policies are formulated and implemented and how we understand the economic effects and political implications of such policies. Karim's essay, for instance, provides an important example of how transnational agendas of market liberalization converge with agendas for women's empowerment and produces a quintessential model of an NGO-driven ideal of women's entrepreneurship. However, as Karim notes, the early stages of Bangladesh's move toward market liberalization were driven by a military regime prior to the emergence of the "Washington consensus" in the late 1980s. Meanwhile, in the Indian context, Daftary also analyzes state-led processes of restructuring. The complexities of domestic national politics and the interventionist role of the state in both cases do not diminish the transnational processes that interact with processes that unfold within the nation-state. However, Daftary and Karim caution against easy feminist rhetoric that casts neoliberalism as a simple imposition of Western policies in non-Western contexts—rhetoric that misses the complex role that elites (including governmental elites) in non-Western contexts play in driving such policies. Lind's essay, of course, further complicates singular narratives about the transnational travel of neoliberal ideas as she analyzes and interrogates the shift away from neoliberal policies in Latin America through her focus on the post-neoliberal state in Ecuador.

Why the State Matters: Moving beyond the Rhetoric of Neoliberalism

While a focus on the state unsettles easy border-crossing models of transnational feminism, the analytical import of this focus extends well beyond this. Such an approach disaggregates the concept of "neoliberalism" by allowing us to understand the complex political and economic processes that shape and produce inequality in the twenty-first century. Such a project does not just call attention to "varieties of neoliberalism"—that is, the idea that policies of market liberalization unfold in distinctive ways in different national contexts. Rather, grappling with feminist perspectives on the post-liberalization state provides an avenue for clearer analyses and understandings of what is distinctive about the effects of neoliberal policies; what structures of political economy and relations of power are a continuation of older models of capitalist development; and what structures and power dynamics are a product of complex interactions between past and present policies, modes of governance, and forms of inequality. Such an approach thus allows us to think about both the production *and* the reproduction of inequality.

For instance, as Aggarwal illustrates, ideologies of choice that were framed by neoliberal thinkers were central to a reworking of historical patterns and practices of racial segregation in the United States. As Heatherton further points out, urban inequality in the United States has been shaped by processes of deindustrialization that predated later decades of neoliberal economic policies. Inequalities of race and class have thus in part been intensified and in part taken on distinctive dimensions since the implementation of such policies. Similar patterns are discernible in Karim's analysis of class and gender in Bangladesh and Daftary's analysis of India. The essays throughout this volume delineate two sets of processes: (1) how some inequalities precede and are then intensified by neoliberal economic policies and (2) how other forms of inequality and relationships of power are newly created by such policies. The volume has thus sought to analyze what Naples, drawing on the work of Dorothy Smith (1999), analyzes as the "relations of ruling" that shape and produce national and transnational political economic structures. The essays analyze the role of these relations of ruling in producing, shaping, and responding to inequality in the post-liberalization period through precise specifications of such historical continuities and discontinuities.

In this endeavor, this volume has grappled with the relationship between the state, market, and civil society. Identifying what is distinctive about the nature of the state in the post-liberalization period entails an analysis of the boundaries between these three realms. As Joel Migdal's (2001) "state-in-society" approach has effectively illustrated, the distinctive nature of the modern state lies in its ability to both act as a coherent, autonomous actor even as it is shaped by often contradictory and fractured institutions that permeate and build on networks and relationships of power within the realm of "civil society." What is at stake in understanding the post-liberalization state, then, is an understanding of how the state acts in the image of a controlling actor even as the nature of its power and relations of ruling are reworked in relationship to the market and civil society. The "neoliberal state" is thus not a self-evident or autonomous actor that resides above civil society or the market. It is defined by shifting boundaries between state, market, and civil society— boundaries that shift over time and are contingent on the political, social, and economic circumstances within nations even as they are shaped by transnational processes. The essays in this volume have provided an analysis of the state as a key actor that shapes policies often by actively promoting policies of market liberalization and as a layered institutional entity whose multiple parts range from security apparatuses (such as the police) to the judiciary to local rural governance organizations. The state in this context may restructure its relations of ruling in ways that are shaped by neoliberal framings, often reproducing the kinds of segregated publics that Aggarwal analyzes.

Or, as Heatherton illustrates, the U.S. state retracts its social spending but then reassigns social welfare functions to the police in ways that transform welfare into a securitized realm. In this context, the conception of the state as a "controlling actor" remains critical. It has become commonplace now for interdisciplinary feminist scholars to invoke an image of a diffuse state—particularly through understandings of biopolitical and disciplinary power that highlight Foucaultian understandings of the state through ideas of governmentality. While dimensions of such forms of power certainly characterize the post-liberalization state as Daftary effectively illustrates, the state is not reducible to such conceptions of power. The controlling state, as Heatherton demonstrates, is central to the carceral and securitized state. Or, as Karim illustrates in her discussion of the Bangladeshi state's crackdown on the Grameen Bank, the state reasserts it role as a controlling actor when NGOs risk crossing boundaries of political power that undergird the complex relationship between state, civil society, and the market.

The post-liberalization state, then, is not reducible to the neoliberal state. In other words, although processes of liberalization have changed the state, the state is not reducible to a scaffolding of neoliberalism. Heatherton's essay is critical in providing an understanding of the ways in which state power exceeds the market logics associated with neoliberalism (and its attendant ideologies of decentralization). This excess of state power points to a deeper set of issues that are at stake in rethinking concepts such as "neoliberalism" or the "neoliberal state." Misdiagnoses of the nature of power and the causes of inequality can transform critical responses to such forms of power and inequality into ideological symptoms of the very agendas of the neoliberal political-economic order that such responses are invested in challenging.

Beyond the Entrapment of Neoliberal Rhetoric: Future Directions and the Stakes of Rethinking the Neoliberal State

The essays in this volume provide analytical and contextual specificity to our understanding of the post-liberalization state. Collectively they illustrate the impact of neoliberal policies and dismantle uniform conceptions of "neoliberalism" or the "neoliberal state." On one level, the idea of neoliberalism matters precisely because dominant conceptions associated with this ideology have shaped transnational and national political economic structures. However, on another level, the dominant model of neoliberalism cannot and does not explain the complex processes that produce inequality, exclusion, and the political responses and social movements that respond to such inequality and exclusion. I have specifically used the concept "post-liberalization state" to mark both the importance and limits of the hegemonic project of neoliberalism.

The goal of these essays is to pry open such discussions and spur more interdisciplinary feminist intellectual attention to the field of political economy. As I have noted, this volume has been driven by a set of analytical concerns rather than an area-based approach. Such analytical concerns can be enriched by work being conducted in comparative contexts that have not been covered in this volume—for instance, within Africa, Eastern Europe, and Southeast and East Asia (Emigh and Szelényi 2001; Sahle 2006; Teo 2011). What is at stake here is not the adoption of a geographical checklist of national identities but a systemic engagement with feminist materialist issues in situated contexts—issues that may not be seen as self-evident border-crossing phenomena but that play a crucial role in shaping the lives of women who are marginalized within the dominant global and national structures of political economy. This is a call for feminists to pay attention to the significance of a historically specific, *situated* feminist materialist analytic—one that understands the weight of historical continuities in the face of an onslaught of attention to the discontinuities associated with neoliberalism.

Consider what is at stake in such an approach. As I have noted and as some of the essays in this volume have illustrated, older policies and modes of state power (such as the developmental state or the racial state) continue to permeate, interact with, and on occasion supplant modes of power associated with neoliberalism. An understanding of state power and the reproduction of socioeconomic inequality thus requires a careful examination of both continuities and discontinuities in state policy and practices. The rhetoric of neoliberalism is all too often easily invoked as a shorthand signifier of socioeconomic inequality and reduced to easy narratives about privatization and the market. Such cursory invocations are not simply empirically inaccurate statements in need of correction; often they are symptoms of the very neoliberal discursive regimes that such invocations seek to challenge. To take one example, a preoccupation with the diffusion of the state that is often implicit in approaches that reduce the post-liberalization state to conceptions of governmentality (Brown 2015) misses the cross-national complexities of the developmental state and the continued salience of the controlling, centralized state. Or to take another example, an overblown focus on privatization may fully miss the role of state practices in promoting exclusionary policies that produce the kinds of segregated publics that Aggarwal and Heatherton analyze. In effect, such analytical frames become trapped within the rhetorical structures of neoliberalism as they are framed by the very preoccupation with decentralized governance and market-based processes of privatization that are central features of dominant understandings of neoliberalism.

This is not merely an academic contest over theoretical paradigms. The avenues we develop for our understanding of the nature of inequality and exclusion also shape the nature of our intellectual and political responses. Strategies of social movements and critical intellectual currents that emerge in response to inequality and exclusion can be inadvertently disciplined or misguided when they are trapped by a ubiquitous or ethereal idea of neoliberalism. Even interdisciplinary feminist perspectives can inadvertently become disciplined by the discursive regimes that underpin all fields of knowledge (as we have already seen with the integration of liberal models of feminism with policies of economic liberalization). It is often almost as difficult to disrupt the naturalized commonsense analytical frames that undergird such knowledge practices as it is to dislodge the deeper structures of political economy with which knowledge practices are grappling. In this spirit, this volume seeks to rethink how we understand the project of neoliberalism through a nuanced and contextual feminist analytic that has wrestled with the meaning, practices, and power of the post-liberalization state.

NOTES

1 For an overview of this paradigm, see Hancock 2016.

2 Nancy Fraser articulates such an argument in *Fortunes of Feminism* (2016). However, Fraser's argument tends to assume that feminist theories of identity have not been preoccupied with socioeconomic inequality. In practice, feminist-of-color thought has never created a dichotomous separation between socioeconomic claims and demands for rights, on the one hand, and demands for recognition, on the other. For an early elaboration of this terrain, see Fernandes 1997. We need a deeper analytical understanding of how socioeconomic processes intersect with various forms of inequality, continued and systematic interdisciplinary research on such questions, and a more serious feminist engagement with feminist social science research that has long been conducted on questions of inequality in specific contexts and places.

REFERENCES

Brown, Wendy. 2015. *Undoing the Demos: Neoliberalism's Stealth Revolution*. Cambridge: Zone Books.

Emigh, Rebecca, and Ivan Szelényi, eds. 2001. *Poverty, Ethnicity and Gender in Eastern Europe during the Market Transition*. Westport, CT: Greenwood Press.

Fernandes, Leela. 1997. *Producing Workers: The Politics of Gender, Class, and Culture in the Calcutta Jute Mills*. Philadelphia: University of Pennsylvania Press.

———. 2013. *Transnational Feminism in the United States: Knowledge, Power, and Ethics*. New York: New York University Press.

Fraser, Nancy. 2013. *Fortunes of Feminism: From State-Managed Capitalism to Neoliberal Crisis*. London: Verso Books.

Gilmore, Ruth Wilson. 2007. *Golden Gulag: Prisons, Surplus, Crisis, and Opposition in Globalizng California*. Berkeley: University of California Press.

Gramsci, Antonio. 1971. *Selections from the Prison Notebooks*. Translated and edited by Quinton Hoare and Geoffrey Nowell Smith. New York: International Publishers.

Hancock, Angie-Marie. 2016. *Intersectionality: An Intellectual History*. New York: Oxford University Press.

Migdal, Joel. 2001. *State in Society: Studying How States and Societies Transform and Constitute One Another*. New York: Cambridge University Press.

Sahle, Eunice. 2006. "Gender, States, and Markets in Africa." *Studies in Political Economy* 77: 9–32.

Smith, Dorothy E. 1999. *Writing the Social: Critique, Theory and Investigations*. Toronto: University of Toronto Press.

Teo, Youyenn. 2011. *Neoliberal Morality in Singapore: How Family Policies Make State and Society*. London: Routledge.

ABOUT THE CONTRIBUTORS

Ujju Aggarwal is Assistant Professor of Anthropology at the New School. Her research examines public education in the United States in relationship to racial capitalism, the state, rights, citizenship, the production of gendered political subjectivities, and processes of place-making. Her work has been published in edited volumes as well as scholarly journals, including *Transforming Anthropology, Scholar & Feminist Online*, and *Educational Policy*. She is completing her first book, *The Color of Choice: Raced Rights and Inequality in Education*.

Dolly Daftary is Assistant Professor of International Development at the School for Global Inclusion and Social Development at University of Massachusetts Boston. Her research interests include market-driven policy paradigms, the political economy of development, cultural politics, and the politics of democratic decentralization. She conducts fieldwork in India, with comparative interests spanning South Asia, Southeast Asia, Latin America, Africa, and the United States. Her research appears in *Development and Change, Journal of Development Studies*, and *Journal of Peasant Studies*, among others.

Leela Fernandes is Glenda Dickerson Collegiate Professor of Women's Studies and Professor of Political Science at the University of Michigan. She is the author of *India's New Middle Class: Democratic Politics in an Era of Economic Reform; Transnational Feminism in the United States: Knowledge, Ethics, Power; Producing Workers: The Politics of Gender, Class, and Culture in the Calcutta Jute Mills*; and *Transforming Feminist Practice*. She is currently engaged in research for a new book project, *India's Liberalizing State: Urbanization, Inequality, and the Politics of Water in India*. She has also published numerous essays and articles on questions of inequality, politics, and feminist theory and is co-editor of the journal *Critical Asian Studies*.

Christina Heatherton is Assistant Professor of American Studies at Trinity College. She is completing her first book, *The Color Line and the Class Struggle: The Mexican Revolution, Internationalism, and the American Century*. With Jordan T. Camp she recently edited *Policing the Planet: Why the Policing Crisis Led to Black Lives Matter*.

Lamia Karim is Associate Professor of Anthropology at the University of Oregon. Her work is on political anthropology, and she is the author of *Microfinance and Its Discontents: Women in Debt in Bangladesh*. She is currently working on a book manuscript entitled *Becoming Labor: Women in the Garment Industry in Bangladesh*. Her research interests are in globalization, development, gender, labor, social movements, and Islam in South Asia.

Amy Lind is Mary Ellen Heintz Professor and Head of the Department of Women's, Gender, and Sexuality Studies at the University of Cincinnati. Her areas of scholarship include critical development studies, global political economy, postcolonial studies, decolonial queer studies, transnational feminisms, and studies of neoliberal governance. She is the author of *Gendered Paradoxes: Women's Movements, State Restructuring, and Global Development in Ecuador*, and editor of four volumes, including *Development, Sexual Rights and Global Governance* and *Feminist (Im)mobilities in Fortress(ing) North America: Rights, Citizenships, and Identities in Transnational Perspective* (co-edited with Anne Sisson Runyan, Patricia McDermott, and Marianne H. Marchand). Currently she is working on a book with Christine Keating on the cultural, economic, and affective politics of Ecuador's post-neoliberal Citizen Revolution.

Nancy A. Naples is Board of Trustees Distinguished Professor of Sociology and Women's, Gender, and Sexuality Studies and Sociology at the University of Connecticut. Her research focuses on the intersection of gender, sexuality, race, political activism, and citizenship in comparative perspective. She is author of *Grassroots Warriors: Activist Mothering, Community Work, and the War on Poverty* and *Feminism and Method*. She is editor of *Community Activism and Feminist Politics* and co-editor of *Border Politics: Social Movements, Collective Identities, and Globalization* and *Women's Activism and Globalization: Linking Local Struggles and Transnational Politics*.

INDEX

Adam Clayton Powell (ACP), 72

Africa, 36–37, 39, 40

African Americans: austerity measures and, 58; education access for, 24; mass incarceration of, 18–19; public sector workforce and, 51. *See also* broken windows policing; education; low-income communities of color; women of color, U.S.

Akhter, Farida, 125

Assange, Julian, 211

austerity policies and discourse, 23; African Americans and, 58; debt and growth study and, 46–47, 48; domestic violence and, 52; economic crisis and, 32–33, 37; Europe and, 32, 39, 49, 62; gender analysis of, 61–62; in global north, 35–36; in Greece, 40, 45, 55, 61; hegemonic cultural beliefs and, 63–64; household austerity and, 45; inequality and, 33, 47, 48–50, 63; in Ireland, 52–54; in Italy, 43–44; materialist feminist analysis and, 34–35, 61; neoliberal economic logic and, 44; Occupy movement and, 58–60, 63; personal responsibility and, 41–42; precarity and, 62; recovery and, 52–56; relations of ruling and, 35; resistance and, 34, 63–64; SAPs compared to, 35–36; taxes on wealthy individuals and corporations and, 44, 58; Tea Party and, 58–59; in U.S., 32, 44–46, 48, 50, 62; women and, 50–52; women and activism for, 55–57, 63. *See also* resistance

Awami League, 110, 111, 114, 126, 127, 129

Azim, Firdaus, 126

Bangladesh, 224; aid in, 110–11, 113, 116–17, 129; Awami League government in, 110, 111, 114, 126, 127, 129; BRAC in, 108, 115; *Caught in Micro Debt* on, 126; Center for Bangladesh Studies, 130–31; Chowdhury in, 118; civil society and caretaker government in, 114; corruption in, 112; discourse in, 107, 120, 121, 131; Domestic Violence (Prevention and Protection) Act in, 124; economic growth in, 112; environmental crisis in, 114–15; Ershad in, 112, 113, 118; feminist critiques and, 107, 108, 120–21; Foreign Donations Regulation Act and, 129; GO-NGO in, 112; human rights NGOs in, 109; Khaleda Zia in, 112, 113; leftist parties in, 115–16; market liberalization in, 106, 110, 111–14, 116; microfinance standard in, 116; military coup in (2007), 114; military rule in, 12, 24, 107, 111–12; national drug policy in, 118; neoliberalism in, 106–7; NGO movement in, 114–15; Pakistani military rule in, 110; RIP in, 111; Sheikh Hasina in, 127, 128; social movements in, 122; state-NGO nexus in, 110, 115–16, 118, 122, 129; suicides and, 128; *thotkata* activists in, 130; women leading, 113; women's empowerment in, 106, 116, 122–23; Zia in, 111–12. *See also* Grameen Bank; NGOs, Bangladesh; silence; women's groups and NGOs, Bangladesh